DEEP FOREST

A Novel of the Indiana Frontier

Emsley W. Johnson, Sr.

Edited by Nancy Niblack Baxter

Hawthorne Publishing

Hawthorne Publishing
15601 Oak Road
Carmel, IN 46033
317-867-5183

www.hawthorne.pub.com

This book is an attempt to give a word picture of the lives, the habits, and customs of a few of our common ancestors who went to make up Midwest America, something like a hundred years ago. It is always interesting to learn more of the lives of a people who have developed a section of the country, especially if the reader can for a short period of time live the life of those people by sharing in their joys, their sorrows, their accomplishments, and their failures. Typical individuals are portrayed so the reader may gain a complete view of the entire community.

The pioneer period of the section of the United States, formerly known as the Northwest Territory, may roughly be defined as the first half of the nineteenth century, or, to be more exact, extending from the Battle of Tippecanoe in 1811 to the firing upon Fort Sumter in 1861. The battle with the Indians did much to bring a feeling of security to settlers lately coming into the Territory. The beginning of the Civil War brought great changes into the lives of the people who had settled in Ohio, Indiana, Illinois, Michigan, Wisconsin, and eastern Minnesota.

Our story is primarily directed to that part of the Northwest Territory which was later known as Indiana Territory and finally the state of Indiana. The pioneer homesteaders who settled in southern and central Indiana came principally from the eastern and southern parts of the United States. Much of the Hoosier dialect and customs were brought with these people. However, there were many communities, especially in northern Indiana, where the immigrants came from northern and western Europe and had only lately arrived. German settlers first settled in western Pennsylvania and then came to the new territory.

The author of this book hopes to give a true picture of the individuals who lived in the new settlements and to relate how the early settlers worked out their life stories in the wilderness. It was necessary for the pioneers to remove the giant trees, clear the undergrowth, and, after building their cabins, to battle the elements.

How these people lived, their struggles, hopes, and aspirations are set out in the following pages. You will be interested in the building of their homes, their schools, their churches; how they played their games, conducted their business, and how they carried on their family life. They were a sturdy people with a definite purpose which sometimes got them mixed up in the cobwebs of life.

The story of how these people accomplished their aims and contributed toward the building of a great nation will have sufficient variety to make your efforts worthwhile in learning more about them.

The background of this book is historically true. The narrative portrays the lives and acts of settlers in those pioneer days. The character sketches are taken from real life with only the names in some instances changed. In order to bring some of the actors into one community and to make a connected story, the author has developed a few characters from his imagination. The casual student of the pioneer period of Midwest America will have no trouble in separating facts from fiction, as facts are always stranger than fiction.

Emsley W. Johnson, Sr.

CONTEMPORARY PREFACE   APRIL 2015

My last memory of my grandfather, Emsley Wright Johnson, Sr., is of sitting on his lap reading to him from my first grade primer, "Run Dick run. See Spot run." He was excited simply because I could read a book. He loved books, collecting and actually reading hundreds of volumes: books on Lincoln, astronomy texts, biographies, children's stories, classics, world travelogues, poetry and Hoosier history books. Of course, on that day in 1950 I was unaware this was the last time I would see him alive on earth. I was equally unaware that he had finished writing a book into which he had poured his lifetime of research and direct family memories: a novel about Indiana pioneer days.

Imagine my surprise 65 years later to discover his book manuscript as I sorted old, old family papers. They apparently had been passed in bulk through five different attics at busy times when family members moved to a new house or died. The manuscript was in the form of a few hundred typed legal-size pages. Here, with expert editing and updating by historical writer Nancy Niblack Baxter and her team, is the "lost" historical novel. It seems to be a rare treasure of pioneer sentiments and many accurate details never published before. With the wish to share this story with you, we now offer my grandfather's *Deep Forest*, in celebration of the 2016 centennial of The Society of Indiana Pioneers and the bicentennial of Indiana's statehood.

Martha Susan (Johnson) Batt

ACKNOWLEDGMENTS

I am indebted to numerous persons who have helped me in the preparation of this book, and I wish to mention a few of their names.

The family of my grandfather often related to me the story of pioneer life, describing in detail some of the early characters with whom he was acquainted and who lived in the neighborhood.

My mother, Mary Wright Johnson, was born before the Civil War began, knew much of pioneer life and in later years retold these same stories, which helped to fix them in my mind.

My wife, Elizabeth Johnson, has listened patiently to me while I have read and re-read the chapters in this book. Her encouragement has helped to make the work easier.

My daughter-in-law, Bonnie Jean Johnson, has edited the manuscript, corrected my errors in spelling, punctuation, paragraphing, and has helped in the selection of words and arrangement of thought.

Miss Caroline Dunn, Librarian, William Henry Smith Memorial Library at the Indiana State Library, has supplied me with authority for many of my historical references. Finally, Honorable Curtis Shake, ex-Judge of the Supreme Court of Indiana, has helped me with the history of Vincennes.

Emsley W. Johnson, Sr.   1950

Now in 2015, additional credit should go to Nancy Niblack Baxter for her extraordinary vision and enthusiasm to bring this book to publication and her skill in editing it and to Arthur Baxter of Hawthorne Publishing for his design work. Thanks are due also to Richard Day for historical consultation and Charles Johnson Meyer for expert advice. The Indiana State Museum Fine Arts Curator Mark Ruschman gave significant help in selecting appropriate paintings for this book from the museum's valuable art collection. Finally, I wish to thank another granddaughter of the author, my sister Gracia Johnson Floyd for her recommendations about the book and Jim Fadely and Bob Everitt and the other members of The Society of Indiana Pioneers Board of Governors for the organization's sponsorship of publication. I hope this historical novel gives you, the reader, some hours of enjoyment and added appreciation for the rich heritage of Midwestern America.

Martha Susan (Johnson) Batt 2015

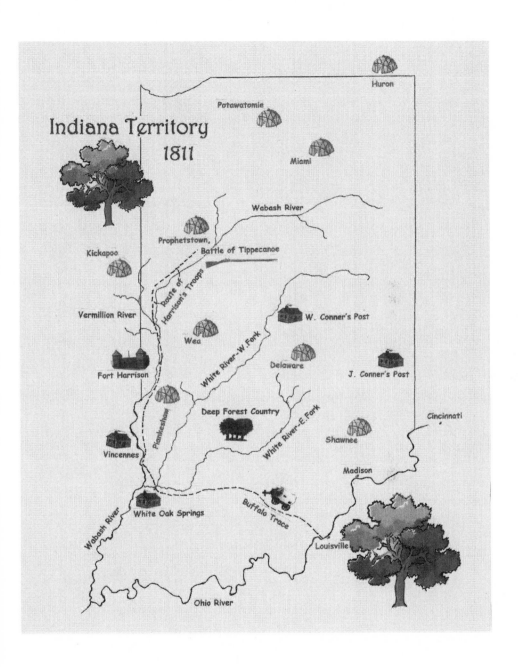

Map of Indiana in 1811

M.S. Batt

Untitled oil by Jacob Cox, collection of the Indiana State Museum

"This will be our home, and the land we shall call Canaan."

Chapter 1

Tippecanoe Battlefield
November 1811

It is always darkest just before the day dawneth.

So said our ancestors, and this cold, damp morn, November 8, 1811, the day after a desperate battle with Indians near the present-day city of Lafayette, Indiana, was no exception. Soldiers wearing wool blanket coats still felt the cold penetrating to the bone. White, ghoulish silhouettes of sycamores were beginning to be discernible on the dark horizon. Nobody wanted to sleep anyway, so the soldiers in the Corydon Yellow Jackets gradually began to mill about, scanning the horizon.

Would the avenging tribes be back? The Indians had been routed near this settlement of Shawnee known as Keth-ti-pe-can-nunk but more commonly called Tippecanoe. But wouldn't they resume the battle as soon as dawn came? The soldiers shivered and peered through misty darkness. A little food would calm the men's nerves, but that would need to wait until light.

Yesterday, it must have been about four o'clock in the morning when the attack had been made. William Henry Harrison's pickets had not been far from the main body of the army, and several of the advance guards had failed to give the alarm. They were so taken by surprise that if they had made any noise it would have meant instant death, for the Indian warriors were upon them.

The attack, they thought, could have lasted as long as two hours, though it seemed much longer. Tensquatawa, brother of the Shawnee leader Tecumseh, standing on a huge rock above the battlefield sometime before the storming of the camp, had told these Indians that they could not lose, that the Great Spirit would protect them and the bullets of the white man would have no effect. But that had not been so, thank God, and Harrison's force of 1,000 brought from Vincennes to intimidate and to defeat uniting Indian forces seemed to have prevailed. That was yesterday. After the battle, the governor had ordered stronger defenses built around the camp so the soldiers believed they were ready should an attack come this way again, and they had spent most of the day constructing those defenses and tending to the wounded and dying.

Now they were waiting, with the first hints of light seeping through the trees by these rivers. And with spirits cautious, this small frontier army in camp behind the pickets could address themselves to preparing food, company by company. The soldiers had gathered downed wood and piled it, and fires would be going in a few moments. From their wagons they brought forth venison, beef, bacon, and coffee. The sentinels were maintaining their vigil on the outer edge of the fortifications, keeping a close watch across the swampy morass and toward the Wabash.

"Look, Sergeant Hurst! I see something moving at the edge of the reeds. What is that?" Private Enos Best pointed into the dim mist. "Do you see it? In the tall grass just this side of the edge of the swamp. I've been watching it for some time."

Best was on guard as one of the advance pickets at the southeast corner of the battleground. He was all nerves. The nerves of all the pickets were on edge, and the whole camp, for that matter, was ready for any emergency. The men who were assigned to watch on the outer edge of the army flank knew that not a moment must be lost if the Indians returned. There would be no surprised sentinels. The sentinel who did not fire first would surely lose his scalp.

Best spoke again. "Whatever that is, is moving from one clump of bushes to another. It's still so dark; will daylight never come? That moving thing—man or beast—slips around quickly. Deer? The noise of last night would certainly drive away any wild animal. Do you suppose it is an Indian trying to slip up on us?" .

Sergeant Henry Hurst, who was in charge of the detail guarding the southeast corner of the camp, watched a few moments. "I can see that it moves, but I cannot make out much else in this dawn light. It is probably six o'clock now, but the coming day doesn't help much; it's still cloudy, and the sun is behind those sycamores lining the river. If it is an Indian, he must not get the drop on us, and yet I hate to shoot because the camp would be aroused in one minute. He could get one or two of us before we could even move from our tracks."

Private Best, like most of the residents of this territorial frontier, was not much of an admirer of Indians in general, and since the experience of battle the day before, he was ready to shoot on sight and investigate later. "Sergeant, let me take a crack at him. Nothing would do me half as much good as to send a ball through every one of them. I can claim but one Indian yesterday, and my old rifle cries out for just one more. Give me the word."

A group of soldiers were now upon the scene. Corporal John Taylor, who was an old Indian fighter, called out, "Hold, men. That is not an Indian; they don't fight that way. They shoot before they move. Look. He is in plain view. Whoever that is knows that we can see him and pick him off if we half try. To shoot would arouse the whole army, and I tell you he means no mischief."

"If he means no mischief," Best said, "Why don't he advance with his hands up and offer to surrender? No sir, let him just take one look down the barrel of this gun—"

"Enos, don't shoot," said the sergeant. "I think he has no weapon."

Young William Hurst, son of the sergeant, burst into the group. He had been watching. "Why haven't the sentinels given the alarm?" he said. "Too much caution on the part of the sentinels yesterday cost too many lives. Pa, you are always over-cautious. Let's all fire at once. You give the word."

"Hold, son, you don't shoot either," his father told him, putting up a restraining arm. "Those Indians may have left the neighborhood and retreated towards Prophetstown, but when they come again, they will rush through these woods in such force that we'll know of their presence. They won't be fooling around out there in the bushes. I tell you, all of you, that this is not an Indian, and if it is, it will do us little harm. Seems short, small or perhaps bent over—"

They were silent for a while, as the moving form, or animal, seemed to check itself, perhaps resting. The sounds of the camp, the smell of wood and bacon frying, told the group that the army was moving into morning. The surgeons had set up their field stations. Some of the men were suffering severely. Thirty-seven, they thought, had been killed in action, and the physicians were tending the twenty-five or so who were seriously wounded. Some were saying that the Indians had chewed their lead before firing, as every bullet made a terrible wound if it didn't dispatch a soldier.

"They played every dirty trick known to their tribes," said Private John Cline sourly. "They promised us a safe camping place. They told Harrison they would not attack until after a parley. Then they waited until the dark hours late at night, early in the morning really, and pounced upon us from every direction yesterday. They are a pack of cowards and scoundrels. And that one out there—"

"I tell you hotheads what we'll do," Sergeant Hurst said suddenly. "We'll send a detachment out and surround that gentleman out there. Corporal Taylor, you may take your six men and go to the left. Corporal Biggs, take your guard and go to the right. Surround that little Indian, for that is what he seems to be. Don't shoot unless absolutely necessary. Bring him in."

In less time than it takes to tell, the two details had surrounded the now-quiet shape and were upon him. Before they were within reach of the object through the gray dawn they could see it was not an Indian brave. It was not even an Indian woman. It was a child, a little Indian girl, and she was much smaller than they had made out through the trees and mist, which seemed to have magnified what they could see.

One of the soldiers scooped her up in his arms. She was helpless, but she fought and scratched. Frightened out of her wits, she still did not cry. She pulled back as far as she could and looked at the white man who held her. What was she thinking? She seemed angry and defiant as well as afraid. Taylor carried her to the large group of soldiers who had by now gathered with the pickets. When the soldier placed her on her feet, she started to run. Some of the men smiled as they grabbed to hold her back. She was surrounded. Backing away, bewildered, she let her glance go from one face to another. There was kindness in these faces, but she could not understand it.

At this moment Captain John Tipton appeared. The soldiers saluted their new captain, promoted only yesterday. Tipton was a native of Tennessee and had enlisted in the army eager for adventure. He had signed on for this excursion at Corydon, Indiana Territory, in the company of Captain Spier Spencer of the mounted riflemen, Indiana militia. It was said that Tipton kept a diary but was a very poor speller, and lots of fun was derived from reading his log and guessing at its meaning.

Now Spencer was dead, wounded in the head and shot in the thigh as he tried to continue fighting in that terrible conflict yesterday, when the Indians had broken through and come into the center of the camp. Governor Harrison had come upon the scene shortly after Spencer was killed and noticed John Tipton, the ensign who had followed close on Spencer, firing as fast as he could. When the governor rode up, he called out to Tipton, "Where's your captain?"

"Dead, sir."

"Your first lieutenant?"

"Dead, sir."

He asked about the second lieutenant and got the same reply, then wanted to know who the ensign was. "Here, sir," was the reply.

"You take the captain's place, Tipton. Hold the line, the Indians are fleeing."

Now Tipton was looking at the Indian child, as were others.

"Why was this girl separated from the rest? How did she get into the marsh?" asked Sergeant Pearce Chamberlin. "The scouts think they moved all their women from Prophetstown before the battle. And these are the Indians who were bragging that after the battle they were going to give an American soldier as a slave to each squaw. The Prophet and his leaders made many promises. He had said he would go up to his rock and direct them in the battle. Nobody saw him do that."

The Prophet's rock was a large, round, table-like stone, extending out from a high bluff more than one-third of a mile west of the ground where they had just fought. Often the Prophet, considered to have some sort of spiritual power, would mount his platform and harangue the braves who were gathered under him. The evil deeds of the white men were countless as stars; it was the duty of the warriors to drive out the usurpers of this land of animals to hunt and running streams. He would remain, so the Indian scouts in Harrison's army said, on that rock until the American soldiers were killed.

"I'll bet my hat," continued the sergeant, "that he never came out to the fight. Never left Prophetstown. Who could have heard him anyway, carrying across the whole Burnett Creek Valley? That morning hour was pitch black; he could not have seen how the battle was going. I've heard that one of the wounded Indians said scornfully that the Prophet stayed where it was safe with the old women and children, ready to flee if the battle went against him."

Sergeant Hurst called to Tipton. "Captain, come closer. Take a look at this little girl," he said. "Why do you suppose the Indians left her as they went back, and how did she get through that swamp?"

"Well, I surely don't know," Tipton said, stroking his chin, staring at the little girl, who with many soldiers nearby was cowering now, sitting on a log someone had brought and set near Sergeant Hurst's feet. "Every act of the old Prophet has been a mystery to me. Mebbe he is sending this little girl to us so he can go among the tribes and tell that the American army kidnapped one of their children. The Prophet may be a coward and a fool, but he knows how to influence the Indian mind."

"You think he's smart?" one of the picket group asked, looking back at the camp, where breakfast noises continued. The smell of coffee drifted in on the slight breeze.

"Seems to me he took a long chance," Tipton continued. "He staked his reputation on the surprise attack yesterday morning. He may be trying some kind of trick. What in tucket is this old owl going to report to Tecumseh? Before Tecumseh left Indiana for the South, getting converts to his cause of uniting the tribes against us, he warned his brother not to strike us."

William Fowler, who was a scout with this company but not duly mustered into it, spoke up. "The Prophet has been a fraud for many years, 'tis God's truth. He has a certain power over the Indians because of his strange demeanor and past events and visions. Standing up there promising, telling his men that the white man would flee without firing a shot, that his visions, the spirits told him so. We took few prisoners, but those we took are talking. They feel angry towards Tensquatawa, acting against Tecumseh's exact orders not to attack while he was gone." He turned toward the camp. "I hope they are right, that these tribes are gone, beaten. We may now be able to find some security for homes and families."

Back in the camp smoke was rising. Army skillets were over the blazing wood fires, and everybody was hungry. The little Indian maid must be hungry too, and the sentinels needed to find out her part in the drama they were living. Captain Tipton and the men from the Yellow Jackets company, together with the pickets and stragglers from other companies who had gathered at the gloomy edge of the camp, now headed back for breakfast. They carried the little Indian girl, still squirming and glowering, in the hopes that some food might calm her down and some of the scouts might discover more about her. As they entered camp, they found that Governor Harrison was selecting a detail of experienced scouts to find out what had happened at Prophetstown. The troops needed to tend to the sick and bury the dead and must plan for what was to come. It appeared they would not be in danger of immediate attack, but they needed to be sure of that. Some of the men, accompanied by the scouts, would go out immediately.

Chapter 2

Koo-wa
November 1811

What about these scouts? Who were they? Some, like Jim Simpson, a cooper from Vincennes, were local militiamen whose duty was to canvass alternate routes and good campgrounds on horseback. Some were professional army scouts who could assess the enemy's strength. Then there were the Indian scouts, full blooded or half breeds, whose job was to advise on Indian ways and sometimes act as interpreters. Were these "metis" mixed-blood Indians themselves completely trustworthy? The incidents of two days before, when Harrison had finally brought his men from Vincennes into the vicinity of Tecumseh and the Prophet's camps, had not reassured the general about the reliability of the promises the Shawnee and others at Prophetstown had made: no battle until a conference. Harrison had to trust the Indian scouts who had joined themselves to the cause of the army, most of whom had come with him and proven loyal. They were willing to denounce their fellow Indians. They themselves had warned Harrison that he could not take the word of White Loon, Stone-eater, or Winamac, the messengers who had come from the Prophet and offered to show a campsite to the arriving troops.

The governor believed he understood the treacherous nature of the Indians surrounding Tecumseh and his brother. He had already had experience with them, so he took every precaution to protect his small force in case the Indians broke their word. Why should the Prophet care about promises as he sent his people to meet the soldiers? If the American army could be defeated, it would not be necessary to worry about broken promises.

The events of the day before were on everyone's minds as the Corydon Yellow Jackets ate breakfast on this morning after the battle, watching their little Indian captive. There could be no boisterousness or rejoicing after so many were dead or wounded, even if the battle had gone their way. Still, they talked in quiet tones about the night before the battle and yesterday's brutal fight.

Most of the soldiers in this army had literally slept on their arms, and they certainly had kept their powder dry. A wet powder pan on a flintlock musket was not a very reliable friend in need, so these muskets were tucked under their coats and hugged tightly all night.

It was obvious why the Prophet had his messengers so carefully explain the virtues of the campsite he was proposing. It wasn't difficult to see that it could only be because it would be to the Indians' advantage. Still, the site the representatives of the Prophet pointed out, a certain oak grove ahead of the troops who had just arrived, could be a good place for the night encampment. A small stream of clear, cold water hastened over the boulders on its way to join the Wabash, which it entered about one mile farther on. Prophetstown was about one and a half miles to the northeast. A dense forest lay to the north, and the stream upon the west flowed through a thickly wooded tract. The campsite, on high ground, was shaped like a flatiron, with the small point to the south. The stream therefore formed the boundary upon two sides of the campgrounds. To the east all was willows, underbrush, and weeds to the very banks of the Wabash. Along the entire north side was that high wooded ground.

Well, Harrison reasoned, it would lend itself easily to a surprise attack, but there was no other campsite suitable for miles around. Major Joseph Daveiss of the Kentucky volunteers, who had come along, had urged Harrison to attack Prophetstown immediately after the army arrived. The Indians fought best under cover of darkness, and they should not be given that opportunity. Still, the general had orders from the President of the United States that every method of persuasion should be used to settle the dispute with the Indians over land before going into battle if there was a chance, the promise of a meeting. Now Daveiss was himself dead, killed in the middle of intense fire as his men fought dismounted.

On that day before battle they had taken necessary precautions and set up a military camp that made sense. The dragoons had tied their horses to saplings in the center of the army formation. The militia had staked the cattle next to the horses, surrounded by army wagons with the army around the outer edge.

In that bitter dawn the Indians fought differently from the way they customarily did, rushing the American lines in groups under leaders with pre-arranged signals instead of moving from ambush and in single file. Black-painted faces were everywhere, hard to see, but the militia with their deer rifles and the regular troops with their muskets loaded with twelve buckshot to the charge eventually did effective work, though it had been touch and go. The tribal warriors had made it all the way into the center of camp, but Harrison's troops' resistance was relentless with counterattacks. Just as daylight dawned, the Indians, worn out and out of ammunition, left the field.

Now, there could be no celebration; the price had been too high. Many commissioned officers had been killed. Captain Spencer's fourteen-year-old boy James, who had come with his father, was wandering around lost without his father, and the soldiers were giving him many attentions.

As the little Indian girl sat in their midst with the arms of Sergeant Hurst clasped strongly about her, she warily accepted a piece of hardtack. Drinking coffee from tin cups, the men began to talk about what might be found at Prophetstown, where the Indians must have gone. Would they yet come storming back from this camp? It was an Indian village made up of two hundred bark-covered cabins, wigwams, lean-tos and the council house and guest houses. The village had recently had tribes from all the northwest intent on joining the "Twin Chiefs." It was protected by horizontal log breastwork laid in a zig-zag fashion, and behind it was dug a trench where warriors could stand and shoot between the logs.

All eyes went to the small Indian girl. There she sat with the sergeant, among the Yellow Jackets, wrapped in a blanket. She had been thoroughly chilled and was shaking like a leaf. The men murmured, watching her. She was cold and frightened, away from her people. Still, she was a prisoner, wasn't she?

Word had spread throughout the camp that the Yellow Jackets had captured this little waif, and as men went off and returned from details, they came curiously forward, maintaining a respectful distance because she was so obviously afraid. The circle of soldiers surrounding the little one grew larger as the danger from surprise attack grew less.

She stood up, still holding one of the crackers the men had given her, hardly even nibbling. It occurred to some that she was the only remaining person from the battle of the day before; all the rest of her nation had departed. She was silent; it was evident she did not understand a word of what was being said to her as the Yellow Jackets and others tried to ask her questions, quiet her fears. Every attempt to question her brought only stares and further withdrawal.

Sergeant Hurst put her down onto her own two feet. As she stood in the light of day, the soldiers observed that her hair was dark and long. It had not been cared for and hung in tangles over her shoulders. Her eyes were large and dark with long, drooping lashes, her hands small and almost blue from the cold. Cold wind, hot sun, and much exposure had made her hands and face rough and chapped. Her legs were bare from her ankles to above her knees, and they, too, were suffering from exposure. The brambles and the thorns of the marshland had scratched her arms and legs; they were still bleeding. The moccasins she wore, tied to her ankles and offering but little protection for her feet, had almost disintegrated.

She wore but one garment, the tattered remains of a deer skin. It had been laced around her neck and a short distance down the front. The soldiers guessed this outfit had been put on her to stay; she had worn these things since cold weather set in. No wonder she was shaking like a leaf.

Something needed to be done. Private Enos Best made a run for the army wagons, which were only a short distance away, as they had been placed in the center of the army formation. Yesterday during all the shooting the oxen and other cattle had broken their tie ropes and were scattered. The horses had been claimed by their owners early in the battle and had become warhorses. Enos knew where to look, and with one hand he grabbed a blanket overcoat and a shirt and with the other a pair of wool socks. He returned to the child and pulled on the yellow hunting shirt that gave the Yellow Jackets their name. Then he added a blanket coat for warmth. Even though this small-sized point blanket made into a coat was much too large, he seized the unwilling child and had her soon wrapped in it. He made the coat fast with the belt cord. He then proceeded to pull on the big socks. The child was a bundle, but at least she would be warm. The uniform of a Yellow Jacket looked strange on her, Private Best thought.

Captain Spencer's Yellow Jackets wore a uniform peculiarly their own. The singing of the rifles and muskets of this group yesterday had left a number of tribal fighters lying upon the battlefield. The tradition of these uniforms added to their pride as they recalled their own losses. Each cavalryman, before enlisting, was required to provide himself with a horse, saddle, bridle, saddlebags, boots, and spurs—and pistols and ammunition and a uniform. The army tailor had to see that all officers' blue uniform facings, such as collars, lapels, cuffs, and vest fronts, were yellow. Other units present in the battle also had their own distinctive uniforms. Major Daveiss's squadron of two troops of dragoons, for instance, wore blue coatees and pantaloons and bearskin caps.

The little Indian girl could not, of course, appreciate the fine tailoring of the Yellow Jacket uniform. Still, she did not attempt to remove the blanket coat but eyed the brass buttons and then began to stroke the yellow satin facings. The bright colors were calming her, and the flush had begun gradually to go out of her face. Captain Tipton now joined the group watching the little girl and asked if she seemed to understand any words. "I'm sorry," he said to the nearby men, "that we don't have William Conner here and about. He is some interpreter—not only with Delaware. He's got himself a few words in the language of 'most any tribe." Many of them recalled that Conner had delivered the news to Harrison that the Lenape, the Delaware, would not be joining the Prophet at Tippecanoe. This he had done as the army stopped at Fort Harrison, built on the high ground, the Terre Haute, as the army advanced towards Prophetstown. Then he had returned to his own home on White River south of Anderson's camp.

The child was looking at the unusual uniforms of the regular army soldiers, the federals, as some of them passed by. These men had tails to their dark blue coats, skin-tight trousers trimmed with white cords, and impractical tall stovepipe hats, each one bedecked with a cockade. She paid little attention, though, to the militia foot soldiers accompanying the unit. They were clad in deerskin frocks and black slouch hats and carried knives and hatchets in their belts. The rough dress of these uniforms was much like that of the Indians among whom she had lived. There was nothing new there.

Knives, trinkets, and gimcracks were fished from the soldiers' pockets and handed to the little maid. Watches were held before her and bright handkerchiefs waved at her, causing her even more alarm than she already felt. She had only picked at the crackers offered her, but now it was time to see if she would eat real food. One of the soldiers offered her a sizzling piece of venison steak just out of the skillet, on a stick so it would not burn her fingers. She grabbed it and snapped it into her mouth. She was very hungry, it seemed. Her face was soon smeared with grease and burnt meat, and she appeared as if she had just emerged from an ash heap.

Young James Spencer, that son of Captain Spencer, was the only boy in the camp, and the little girl seemed to enjoy his antics, jumping and singing, as he tried to please her. Perhaps it took his mind off the death of his father. This boy, although too young for enlistment, nevertheless wore the uniform of a Yellow Jacket. After his father was killed, he had used his musket so effectively that the soldiers declared he downed at least one Indian.

Some of the soldiers were seated upon an old fallen log. "I hear scratching," somebody said, and this led to an investigation, which showed something inside the opening of the log. That same soldier seized a pole and began to poke in the log, when out of the small hole came William Tulley's little tan-colored dog. Tulley was a chubby, short, and swarthy young man who as a scout was not required to observe strict regulations. He had been allowed to keep this dog with him. Only a few minutes before, Tulley had said, "I'm pretty sure some Indian has grabbed my dog," and now here the little beast had appeared from hiding and stood shaking and afraid before the men. Three cheers were given for the bravery of Billy's dog Tan.

In a few moments Tan was himself again. Seeing a newcomer in camp who was attracting considerable attention and being accustomed to being the pet of the men, he half crawled over to the group and up to the Indian girl. As the dog approached, the child reached down and began to pat it, and she bestowed on it her first smile since coming into camp.

"Is there no one in this whole company who can speak a word of Shawnee?" asked Corporal Taylor. Some who were in the group mumbled that they might speak a few words of Delaware, but not one would venture to try Shawnee, Kickapoo, Potawatomie, or even Miami.

"What shall we call this little miss?" the corporal continued, looking towards his new captain. For Tipton's part, he looked at James Spencer, feeling responsibility for this boy who had lost a father only a few hours before. "Jim," said Tipton, "you should know a few words of Indian talk, don't you? Your mother was captured by the Wyandot and taken to Detroit." The boy shook his head sadly. His mother had lived among the savages for several years until she and her sisters were ransomed. Out in the wilds, Indian child-snatching was every parent's bad dream.

Jim was thoughtful. "When Mother was kidnapped, she said, the Indians treated her with kindness. They thought her a beautiful child and dressed her in pretty dresses. They called her 'Yeksa Koowa,' which meant "beautiful little maiden." Her playmates called her Koo-wa."

"Did that stick to her?" Tulley, now stroking the head of his dog, wanted to know.

"When the ransom money was paid, and Mother was given to the white men who came to get her, the Indians asked them to call her Koo-wa. Grandpa and Grandma hated the name and would not use it, but Mother liked it and sometimes signed her name 'Koo-wa' when she was writing love letters to Pa." He smiled sadly.

Captain Tipton was not slow to act, and calling the company around him in a very solemn manner announced, "As one of my first official acts as captain of the Yellow Jackets, let me 'nounce that from this time on the name of this little Indian girl shall be Koo-wa." He stopped to look at her grim, grease-smeared face. "But as of this moment, she 'ant very beautiful."

Chapter 3

Prophetstown
November 1811

That same day, November 8, Governor Harrison sent out his scouts to see what had become of the Indians. The tribal people had come like a flash and had disappeared almost as quickly. He supposed, and the rumors were, that they had retreated to Prophetstown and intended to await the follow-up, the retribution, of the American army. The governor knew that some of the houses in the village were of heavy logs and his army would be at a disadvantage if they attempted to attack with the Indians in their fortresses.

When the scouts returned, they reported the village appeared to be entirely deserted. They found only one old man and one old Indian woman. The man appeared to have a broken thigh. The domestic animals were gone, also.

It was hard for the general to believe that the Indians would flee and leave nothing behind. More scouts and dragoons were sent with instructions to draw fire from these sturdy blockhouses. When the dragoons approached, it seemed no one was defending this town. Finally, signals were given to the soldiers to advance into the town. It was apparent the Indians had departed in a hurry; large quantities of corn and other provisions were left behind.

Harrison received the news thoughtfully. If the redskins had retreated behind the thick walls of their stockade, they could have kept his army at bay indefinitely. He wanted victory, a clear victory. The Prophet's braves were armed with new British-made firearms, but they did not stay to use them again. They could have had the advantage in that village, and they had wasted it on a stand-and-fight battle.

The men heard with some grumbling the news that the Indians had fled. Some wondered why Governor Harrison had not followed Daveiss's advice to proceed at once against Prophetstown, although the soldiers would have had little taste for marching against an Indian village with log houses where the foe might hide. There was plenty of ammunition and food supply, according to Zacharie Cicott, a fur trader long experienced with the Indians, who hated the Prophet and was one of the general's scouts and guides.

Cicott said the village had become the principal Indian village in this area. British agents kept the kettle of hatred boiling. No war had been declared by Congress, but word had it that could be on the way over maritime rights and struggles on the northern frontier. Tecumseh had threatened to join the British if recent treaties were not put aside and the Indians given back their lands. He and his brother had selected this site at the junction of the Tippecanoe and the Wabash Rivers as a good central meeting point for many tribes.

Floods often covered the land where the Tippecanoe joins its parent stream. When not in flood, the cold, clear water of the Tippecanoe made a beautiful sight as it spread out into that of the darker shade of the Wabash. The village was more than a mile from the Wabash where the banks were high, the trees were giant, and cold springs poured freely through the nearby land into the stream. Tecumseh could see the obvious advantages of the site, and had the Indians waited, the outcome of their planning might have been different.

But then Tecumseh was not here, had not been all the time Harrison was making his march up the river. And this Indian girl, Koo-wa, was a problem for the governor now that the tribes had left. She would have to be returned to her parents. It must not be said that Harrison's army had kidnapped an Indian child. The soldiers felt sure the parents of the child would be hunting for her and would return to the village to see if they could claim her. Part of the scouts' mission was to see if they could get information on how to return this young captive.

The advance guards had reported seeing the two old and infirm Indians. Perhaps they could give directions as to where the parents of the little girl were. If nothing else, the soldiers could take the girl to Prophetstown and leave her with the two old Indians.

Jim Simpson, the cooper from Vincennes and one of the scouts, was delegated to go back to the village as the march advanced tomorrow, taking charge of the child. Jim had two little girls at home, and it was known that he was a good father, often talking in a homesick way about wanting to see his family.

The cold rain continued all that day, and when they were not on detail, the soldiers formed in little groups around the campfire, trying to keep warm and also keep up their spirits. So the Indians had indeed left Prophetstown. Many were the guesses about where they had gone. They had just given up the fight without at least one more battle? It seemed too good to be true.

The bodies of the soldiers killed were in one central tent where they were being prepared for burial. Many of the men had been killed with arrows. Why had not the Indians used their new and superior British Brown Bess muskets? The wounded, accompanied by soldiers, had already begun their trip back to Fort Harrison on the high ground above the Wabash, Terre Haute. Christian burial services would be conducted at vesper time that evening for the fallen, and the soldiers would be buried with military honors. Still, the soldiers did not forget they must be on the lookout for a surprise attack from the Indians camped somewhere in the woods.

The order of the day was that they would move out tomorrow. There was much to be done in camp yet this afternoon and evening. Some companies had lost their officers, and the volunteers now had to elect new leaders. Most of the oxen and cattle, having pulled up stakes during the battle, were still out in the marshes along the Wabash. Some horses had escaped when their riders were killed; they had to be found. Everything in the camp needed cleanup, military discipline, and adjustment. And due caution had to be exercised at every moment.

Jim Simpson was taking care of his little charge. She was about the same age as his younger child, Mary. He had left home to do his duty as a member of the militia assuring himself that he wanted to confirm his family would be safe from Indian attacks in this bright new and promising territory where they were making a home. He had no taste for war and no use for Indians, but then this little girl didn't fit his picture of an Indian, universal in his neck of the woods, men all greased up with paint, dirty and slipping around to steal or take advantage of the white man. Some people who had lived among them or gotten to know them said these people were human beings, too, but the Indians Jim had met near Vincennes were a motley group and in his opinion deserved little confidence or respect. He and his family had lived for years in fear of them. God's truth was everyone in Vincennes was afraid for their lives and those of their families.

Jim lived at the end of a road in the outskirts of Vincennes. Stories of Indians were common in Vincennes. Although the Piankeshaw, who had lived on the site of the town, had sold out and gone to Terre Haute twenty-five years ago, a small remnant band remained just out of town. This small group was usually friendly to the whites, but Jim had come to think of them in terms of what he saw: they got drunk too often and they stole. His generation had come out of stockades and Kentucky forts where to live was to fight with hostile Indians. He had little truck with the argument that their livelihoods had been taken from them, that they were stranded in a new age where they couldn't, or wouldn't, cope. What he saw was the Piankashaw wouldn't work, trespassed into the townspeople's gardens and helped themselves to corn, beans, and potatoes. He actually did know some of them as men, true; he had learned to hunt and trap with them and was good at that, better than most. Still, he considered them an irritation to the citizens of the town. And they traded with hostile tribes up north, the menacing ones. There were stories of killings and child abductions, and that time was not long ago. Despite this, Jim found himself drawn to this little Indian girl, as were the other men, who brought her food and trinkets. He saw to her needs as the day progressed just as he would to his own children's, and she was coming to accept, to trust, him.

The next day the main body of the army, as well as all extra wagons with the wounded and supplies, would go on towards home. The men of the militia would be released. So the orders went. The child would be taken in one of the wagons to Prophetstown and left with any available Indian, as the governor had directed, since it would be impractical to track her parents. Jim was beginning to resent this order; he did not want to give this child over to any Indian. He did not want her to perish from starvation or cold. The soldiers' questions were endless; Koo-wa gave them something to talk about and broke the monotony of camp life, the tending to the wounded and saying goodbye to the dead, and the rounding up of livestock and loading up. How did she get into that terrible morass? Had she come all that way from the village through the brush and weeds? Seems impossible! Where was she during the battle? Where was her mother? It was well known that Indian women would brave any danger to rescue one of their own children. The Indians were accustomed to coming and going into camp when battle was not on; even if the child's father was killed, her mother could have come to claim her child.

Beyond that, the soldiers spoke of her neglected condition. It seemed as if this child had never received much care or attention. Her clothing was unfit for human use. Why had she been wandering around in the early dawn in this condition and this weather? Jim tried to understand it and couldn't. All he knew to do was to place her in the wagon, fed and with her coat on and an additional blanket over her. He was doing his best to make friends with her. Jim catnapped near her and listened for her slightest movement. He was determined she should not get out and run away.

At Prophetstown many kegs of gunpowder and guns had been found and taken by the scouts. They were packed in their original wrappings, stored in a central storehouse with ammunition. The Indians had not used these complicated rifles, though they should know how, as they had been doing so for years. Several dead Indians had been found in the wigwams, and only a few newly made graves could be identified. Some soldiers dug up the corpses and scalped them as warnings to the Indians. Orders were given to burn the town and seize the stores, and that was done.

The morrow came. Now, for Jim Simpson, leaving the body of the troops moving towards the Wabash, the job was to go with a few other of the Yellow Jackets to the deserted and destroyed town to locate the old squaw the scouts had mentioned and, in this camp where everything seemed to show haste to leave, and where embers smoldered, to leave Koo-wa with the woman, as much as he did not want to do that.

The old, crippled man who the scouts said had formerly been a chief and the elderly woman were the only people he could locate, and he approached them. All evidence indicated that the whole Indian tribe had fled northeastward towards the lakes, perhaps to find refuge with the Wyandot. Or perhaps they had just dispersed, returning to their home territory after the failed uprising.

Koo-wa had been in the army wagon Simpson had been given for the purpose of returning the child. Now Jim lifted her down and let her walk around, in the hopes she would return to her home, if it still existed, and perhaps find some traces of who she belonged to. But she clung to his side. She was either afraid to move about, or she did not know what to do. Neither the old man or the woman would give any information concerning her. When Jim brought her before them, they grunted and turned away. She certainly seemed afraid of them. Was this child somehow trouble for the village?

A scout began to question them. How many Indians had lived in this village? How many braves were in the battle? When did the women and children flee? And, most importantly, why did they leave this child? The soldiers got no reply to their questions except that the old reprobates were angry at the Prophet. They believed these white men could not force them to give up information, so they would give the soldiers no satisfaction. The men and Jim talked among themselves. How about some persuasion? Some suggested a hickory club, others a rawhide whip, and others merely began raising their voices using their choicest vocabulary of profanity. It was obvious that the little girl was afraid of the old couple, and that they had no use for her.

Jim wondered what to do next. His kindness was winning over the little miss. From the moment she had seen the old woman, the child crowded nearer to Jim. He was her protector. Jim viewed the surroundings carefully. What if they left this little child in such a place? With that old squaw? Jim thought of his own little Mary at home and imagined what might happen if she were left in such a place and with such people. The old woman was dirty, and her skin hung in deep black wrinkles. Her eyes seemed wicked; she looked like a witch, and her attitude was hateful.

The men, eager to be away but still in the mood to do something to "thank" this pair, remembered a large horse scrub brush in the wagon. Private John Taylor placed a long handle in the brush opening and suggested that if he had a bucket of water, he might improve the looks of the old hag. He asked one of the boys to hold her while he applied cold water. "I can soften that outer coat of dirt if I scrub long enough," he told them. The old chief seemed to come to life and take considerable interest in the process of giving the old woman a good ducking. He shouted with glee and tried to encourage the soldiers to scrub hard and to use plenty of cold water.

After the washing procedure, and giving up all hope of obtaining information, the small group of soldiers let them wander off, leaving the burnt village. The last the soldiers saw of the couple, the old man was trying to keep up with the woman, and she was giving the soldiers a good tongue-lashing in choice Shawnee.

They immediately took off with their small charge to rejoin the main company of regulars and some of the Yellow Jackets who were already starting on the road. Jim sighed as he recalled what they were leaving behind in their camp. The dead had been buried in a large grave and a bonfire built over them in the hope the Indians would not dig under the ashes for the scalps. The wounded were riding southward on beds of hay in the wagons, which would have to serve as both springs and cushion. The livestock were being herded along. At their slow pace, it was not difficult to catch up.

The Yellow Jackets pondered over what should be done with the little girl now that the attempt to leave her at the remains of the Indian camp had failed. Private Best wondered if she could be left with a friendly tribe; if not, Governor Harrison had given permission for her to come south with the returning army to Vincennes. By this time Jim was much attached to the little girl, and he resolved that he was not going to give her up unless he was convinced that she was going into hands which would take good care of her.

Koo-wa spent the rest of that morning playing in the wagon with Tan. The girl was losing much of her fear of the soldiers, who were still showing her much attention and kindness. The camp tailor had been busy altering one of the big army blanket coats, and it seemed to have some semblance of a fit for a child. He had ripped the seams and used an improvised pattern, and all the parts had been cut up and sewed together again. Care had to be taken to reset the big, bright buttons. The altered coat was warm and comfortable, and it helped to win the little girl over to her new traveling family. She was no longer afraid.

Chapter 4

Toward the River and Home
November 1811

They were heading toward the Vermillion River, where they would board boats held there for them and pass down that stream until it entered the Wabash. Then they would move by boat and horses with wagons to the fort on the high ground, part of the Terre Haute, as the trappers called it. Every wagon was put into line as they camped on the first night of the trip home. A bed of straw was made in one corner of "Koo-wa's wagon," as the men were calling it. Here she would be reasonably comfortable and she could be watched. Jim Simpson had lost his horse in the battle, and he was glad for the opportunity of spending at least a part of this trip in the wagon. Jim didn't fancy walking home, and the Vermillion was a few days' walk from these northern forestlands. Captured British guns and equipment filled several of the wagons. Corn and provisions were riding in others, and the wounded were yet in others, groaning and agonizing over the bumps in the springless wagons and trying to live long enough to get to their homes. There had been one wagon left, and in it rode the little Indian girl and her protector.

Fourteen-year-old James Spencer had refused a seat in the wagon. He would ride his own pony. He had come as a soldier with his now-dead father, and he would go back as a soldier. He considered it beneath his dignity to take care of the little girl; he was not a nursemaid but a militiaman. He wanted it understood that he would stand guard when it came his turn, and he would go on any detail. Jim Simpson, who was not required for other duty, was the proper person to take charge of this Indian girl, James decided, and the captain of the company concurred.

Before daylight the next morning, their second on the road home, the campfires were burning, the bugle sounded its wakeup for late sleepers, and the drums were rolling to give notice that the army must be ready to move in a short time, breakfast gobbled on the run.

Jim had been startled by the noises outside. He had jumped up and wiped his eyes, trying to adjust. He had overslept himself, having slept like a dog. He looked nearby. The girl and the dog were both gone. He jumped from the wagon and began a search. He was not only exasperated at himself, he was also embarrassed. She was his charge and she was gone.

The child was not in the neighborhood of the wagons and neither was the dog. Jim tightened his coat around him; the wind was chilly. The watch had been unusually good and had taken every precaution to prevent anyone slipping into camp—or out. She could not get beyond the picket line. Having started late the day before, they were not far from the original camp near the Tippecanoe.

Jim must first find Billy Tulley. The dog no doubt would search for its master, and the child would be led by the dog. But when he found Tulley, the man inquired after the girl right away. The dog had returned to Tulley before midnight, not seeming to be concerned about the loss of its playmate companion. Tan would be no good at tracking his small friend, anyway.

By this time it seemed to Jim that every member of the company knew that Koo-wa had disappeared. The soldiers were too shocked to find fault with him. They wanted to help search and insisted the movement of the army must be delayed until she could be found.

Jim checked the watch and was assured that the pickets had been changed every two hours, with the guard in close formation, and nobody had seen anything. The soldiers in the wagon formation had heard no noises in the night. The only thing that was certain was that the little girl was gone, taking her new coat and that was all, having thrown her blanket to one side of the wagon. She had fallen asleep with the dog by her side and had covered it and herself with the blanket. He reprimanded himself: he had intended to keep one eye open on the little charge, but the cold air and activity of the day before had transformed his catnaps to the deep sleep of the exhausted.

Trumpets were blowing and orders were being passed along to hurry. The army must be on its way. Jim wanted no food; he was sick at heart. All around him felt some guilt. Jim made an appeal to Captain Tipton to delay the start of the movement just an hour or two until a careful search could be made. Soon soldiers were scattered and searching in many directions. Jim thought the child might go back to Prophetstown, even to that morass. She could not have gotten far, though. Scores of men from the Yellow Jackets were now trooping towards the east. Billy Tulley was asked to take his dog. A considerable tract had to be searched. As the soldiers neared the banks of the Wabash, the dog began to run towards a large sycamore, then run in circles around it, all the while jumping and barking. A large narrow opening was in the trunk of the tree, and the dog bounded inside.

The soldiers could not get their heads in the opening, nor could they reach far up the trunk inside. A soldier was dispatched to the wagons for axes. After a few moments these strong, expert woodsmen were making the big soft chips fly in every direction. The hole was now enlarged. Jim entered the trunk, and reaching up with one hand, he was able to pull the little lost lady from her perch. She fell into the soft rotted wood that filled the base of the tree.

It took Jim a long time to remove the stains and particles of decayed wood from the hair and the huge blanket coat of the little Indian maiden. He was astonished as well as irritated at her, in spite of his relief. She had managed to evade the sentries of the army that had just won a major victory for the United States of America and find a hidey-hole to suit herself with a good portion of that army looking for her.

Chapter 5

Down the River
November 1811

The army would follow the same general course going down the Wabash as it had used coming up. The banks of the river were always to be near them, but better traveling paths lay a little distance from the Wabash. The army wished to stay away from wooded tracts and the deep cuts and gullies made by streams as they entered the larger river. They would head west to the Vermillion River, a tributary of the Wabash, and enter the Wabash in this better way, and the mounted scouts would ride ahead to be sure the paths were the best ones, level country for foot soldiers, who would find it difficult to proceed through the brush. Even the men on horseback were willing to follow any trail which had the fewest fallen trees or deep gullies.

Provisions had been left with the flatboats as the army came up the river. The men had constructed a blockhouse, and a small company of men had been assigned to guard these valuables. The men marched towards provisions, food. They did not want to live on corn alone, especially as they had no way of making meal. This part of the country had been scoured by the Indians in their search for food, and there had been so much commotion along the upper Wabash that game would be scarce.

Soon, on the march, the soldiers felt that they were out of danger from Indians. They began to relax and insist there was no longer need of restraint and strict military discipline. Now that their mission had been accomplished, army regulations could pretty much go by the wayside. Harrison was a regular army man; he had been trained to believe in order and military routine. The governor seemed to have much sympathy for the militia, but he could not welcome disregard of duty.

The second day on the march the army covered fifteen miles, which encouraged the men, for they had marched only eight miles the first day. Most of the second day had been spent upon the open prairie. They had crossed Little Pine Creek and Big Pine Creek that second day. The banks of these two streams were high, and that slowed the army to some extent. Still, they were leaving Indian territory. All of their lives they had heard of the threatening Indians of the Upper Wabash. The stories had conditioned their responses, imprinted their views, and haunted their dreams. While they rejoiced in their victory upon the Indians' home ground, they wanted to be out of the territory they had come to hate even before they knew or experienced what it was.

In the evening as the men smoked their pipes around the campfire, they began to talk to each other about how and why their officers had been wrong the night of the battle. Major Daveiss was a brilliant man, they contended, and he should have been listened to. Attack as soon as they had arrived would have been the best plan. Some defended the governor: Harrison had been in the dark. He didn't know the Indians' strength, the number of weapons and blockhouses, the extent of fortifications. How could he go into battle immediately? The arguing got hot and heavy, and the men went to bed with unchanged minds. Most were willing to give Harrison the benefit of the doubt: his cool conduct under fire, his wisdom as a commander, his fairness to all the men did more than anything else to keep him generally popular among the men. And, after, the Indians had fled and had not given pursuit. Nobody knew where either the Prophet or Tecumseh was.

Harrison had been firm in his belief that Indians must accept the treaty which granted Americans huge tracts of land in east and west central Indiana. That they were planning an uprising to reverse the treaty was intolerable; he had told Tecumseh that at a meeting at his house Grouseland in Vincennes the year before. Both Harrison's soldiers and Tecumseh's braves had stayed nearby, near the scene, where Tecumseh promised retaliation for the loss of the lands of many tribes and Harrison stood firm. It was Tecumseh's view, strongly given, that no chief and no group of Indians had the right to sell the Indians' land. It belonged to all the Indians in common, and the land must be preserved forever as a forest for the use of the Indians.

James Simpson had been walking from group to group as the soldiers refought the battle they had just endured. He was holding the hand of the little Indian girl. All the men seemed glad to see the child. The heat of the argument about Indians, despised as they were by these frontiersmen, always seemed to cool when they saw Koo-wa, this child without a home, without relatives and with only a bunch of rough men to help her survive in the deep woods. All of these opinions about Harrison, the Indians, and Indiana Territory were only that, opinions. Time would settle more than they could. They could extinguish their campfires and go to bed without feeling they had to solve anything for the United States of America.

The third day found the army singing and whistling and hurrying toward the Vermillion. Koo-wa's trip in the bouncing wagon was a new experience for her, but she seemed to enjoy it and clapped her hands as the men sang their songs, whistled, and provided themselves and the little girl with entertainment. Jim was generally by her side; he did not want her out of his sight. Tan the dog was in the wagon with her most of the time, but sometimes he would run beside it. On this third day Koo-wa learned to say "Tan" and "Jim."

Late in the afternoon of the third day, the soldiers caught sight of a certain oak grove. This grove seemed to stand out at first like a cloud low in the southern horizon, growing bigger until as the army came nearer, the beautiful virgin oaks could be seen as an oasis in the prairie landscape. Eagerly they headed towards it; it had meant a lot to them as they had headed north. The grove was on a slight elevation. They called it "Black Rock," and at the foot of a small knoll they remembered the fine large spring from which flowed cold, clear water. Here would be real rest. Two of the desperately wounded men in the wagons were saying that if they had to part from their comrades, they hoped they might be buried in this beautiful grove.

On November 13, before leaving the grove, the chaplain offered prayer over the graves of these two brave men.

After leaving Black Rock the army veered further away from the Wabash, which they were now following on its west side, and by the time they halted for supper, they had covered twenty-five miles. Large, blazing fires were soon supporting pots over their coals, and the smell of cooking turkeys and prairie chickens made the men still hungrier than they had been on the march. Broth and chicken would taste good.

Although the men were desperately tired and some of their number were very sick, these big, rough men were ready for jokes and fun. Wrestling matches started up as the men pushed each other off the sitting logs. Then they jumped up for footraces, amidst shouting and laughter. Playing cards flew from pockets, and a little ready cash changed hands. The little maid was supplied with plenty to eat, because Jim saw to it that his charge had some of the best morsels. Before the sun was long gone, Koo-wa was sound asleep in her corner of the wagon, Tan cuddled close to her. Jim, in still another corner, slept soundly.

The soldiers all slept the sleep of those who have made a long march, but the roll of the drum saw the blankets fly the next morning. Koo-wa looked for Jim to wash her face and hands; she had gotten to like the feel of the warm water he used. The menu for breakfast was pretty much the same as for supper: fried steak and hominy. The foragers were finding wild honey and this, spread over corn cakes, was not bad eating, and the food was shared with Koo-wa. Jim taught her to say "thank you," or something which sounded like it, to the men who brought things to her.

Captain Tipton was writing in his diary, and the men continued to joke about it: was it written in Egyptian word pictures or a dialect of the Iroquois Indians? He was praising the men: "If you keep up the present pace," he said, "you'll be to home in half the time it took to get to Tippecanoe." Forty-four days it had taken only a month or so ago. It was true that they built a fort and blockhouse during the trip up the river, and that was included in the reckoning of the time, also. Now, with nothing to build and no Indians to fear, they could skip every other campsite. Of course the speed had to be regulated by the pace of the oxen. "Don't let your guard down," Tipton warned them. "There are wanderin' redskins around here, and who knows when the Shawnee may find us again."

The weather had cleared. The hopes of the men were high as they pushed on, realizing that with good moving they could reach the boats before sundown. Koo-wa and little Tan by this time were inseparable friends. The dog paid little attention to his owner now. Billy Tulley could not coax the dog to leave the child, even for a short time. For her part, Koo-wa clung to the little dog, and none of her admirers could convince her to leave him. "And," Billy said as the men laughed at his dog's cowardice, hiding as he did in the log, "if he waren't wanting to get shot, and wanted to take himself out of sight, that's no more than some of the men would want to do."

The men gazed across the prairie. Not a living animal could be seen. No settlers had yet claimed this county, not a cabin, no barn, no cultivated fields were in sight. It had not been safe for settlers to live here in these river valleys; soon it would be. Only the Indians had roamed here. How long had they been in the Wabash Country? Their chiefs had said they had been there for countless ages, but some of their stories seemed to say they had come from the east—or the north. They were wanderers, nomads.

Scouts were busy selecting the best route. Coming up they had made many mistakes, which had slowed the wagon trains. The army's formation on the march was always the same: mounted regulars followed the scouts, who in turn were followed by the wagons. The mounted militia men and dragoons followed the wagons, while in the rear marched the foot soldiers. The mounted men were expected to do some foraging, while the expert riflemen brought in game to the camp. Governor Harrison and his staff, who had rejoined the group, rode among the men and set an example of good cheer.

The army wagons were mostly open box wagons, with no springs and generally used for conveying freight. As these wagons rolled over the rough country, no one clamored for a seat in the wagon unless he was too badly crippled to walk.

A few ox carts, with their crude construction, were in the train. Spoke wheels, no springs, the axle extending from wheel to wheel, and for a tongue a long pole which connected with the ox yoke. The oxen served a dual purpose: when the army was well provisioned, there was no need for the oxen under the yoke, but when the loads became lighter and the food more scarce, the ox relinquished his post so that his steaks might supply hungry men with food.

Just before dusk, the country became rough, and it was evident that the army was approaching the river lands. Additional food awaited the men at the blockhouse, and the wounded would be transferred to boats, which would afford transportation without ruts and jolting.

The men were glad to see that all was well at the fort—the boats, the blockhouse, and the men guarding the post to keep it from being occupied by Indians. They had spent the two days before the arrival of the army searching the surrounding country for game. Venison steaks, wild turkey, grouse, and prairie chickens that night made a feast that was rated as best on the whole campaign. After supper the men found sleeping spots, and the army was soon fast asleep. In the wagon home, Koo-wa, her pup, and her adoptive father slept the sleep of the good-hearted and peaceful.

By sunrise the next morning the boats were loaded, the wounded being transferred to flatboats or ordinary rowboats. The wagons had been greatly

lightened of freight; everything that could be carried by boat had been loaded to travel that way. Koo-wa, Tan, Jim, and four oarsmen were assigned to
one of the flat-bottomed rowboats. As the fleet pulled out of the Vermillion River into the broad Wabash, there was a loud cheer. The troopers and
wagons now crossed the Wabash and proceeded to follow the east bank. As
many as possible of the foot soldiers were given places in the flatboats, for
the men were footsore from marching.

As the fleet of boats gained midstream and started south, the men began to sing. Rousing boat songs like "What Shall We Do with a Drunken
Sailor?" and ballads like "Barbry Allen," but also "We'll Never Be Royals,"
which made the men think and talk about the conflicts with England on the
high seas and in Canada. Murder ballads like "The Two Sisters" and "The
Cruel Brother" had more verses than anybody wished to sing—or listen to.
Koo-wa listened, eyes wide, and more than one man murmured, "What will
become of her? Her kind are not readily welcome in our towns." She did not
seem anxious about herself; from what they had seen at Prophetstown, she
had not been happy there.

Jim was thinking seriously about the same subject. He wanted Sarah,
his Sarah, to see this child. Her clothing was in tatters and dirty; he would
try to improve her appearance a bit. He was washing her hands and feet,
although when he dipped her hands in soap suds she put them to her face,
and the taste caused considerable sputtering, and if the suds got into her
eyes, she grabbed for a dry rag.

When the boats stopped for an evening meal or in the evening near
the fire, the child would follow Jim and pull the dog behind. The soldiers
tried to teach her English words. She never spoke the Indian language unless excited. Then she would utter words wholly unknown to the men. Jim
spent a good deal of time repeating the names of common objects, and she
seemed willing to learn and bright enough. She learned the English words
for "wagon," "boat," "oar," "coat," and "button." Some of the soldiers had
spent much time with the Delaware and Piankeshaw, but not a word from
those tribes registered with the child. She must have spent much of her life
with the Shawnee or Wyandot, and none of the men knew those languages.

One day when Governor Harrison visited the men in the camp, he
said, "How I wish again for our friend William Conner. He can speak so
many tongues; he could speak to this lost little one."

The men nodded. They well remembered the former meeting with this most famous of Indiana pioneers; he was a legend.

Chapter 6

William Conner
November 1811

They sat around the campfires at Fort Harrison at Terre Haute, to which they had finally come, soon to be released and split up to go their various ways. Now these seasoned veterans of Tippecanoe had one last time to be together, and William Conner, whose reputation was told in song and story, was the subject. He had been at this fort not long ago. They had seen him and heard his own story as they traveled to Tippecanoe, and now they were remembering it.

On the way to Prophetstown, Harrison had sent for his old and trusted friend William Conner: William from the country of the Delaware on the West Fork of White River in Indiana Territory. Here William Conner had a home and maintained a trading station. Harrison knew that Conner had negotiated treaties with the Indians and was known as a competent interpreter. He knew many tribes and was regarded as a trusted man among them because he had treated them fairly at his station, a rarity among the white traders' ways.

Conner had influence with the Shawnee chiefs and had on numerous occasions tempered their war-like intentions. He had accompanied the army north from Vincennes and was tarrying while the soldiers built the stockade with blockhouses to be called Fort Harrison. Harrison had Conner tell him of his impressions of the coming conflict over the land treaties the Shawnee were to be part of—or not. The Delaware and Miami were not hostile and would carry out the treaty obligations, Conner said. "The northern tribes, though, intend to resist any movement of the whites to settle land north of Vincennes. The Wea village near the high ground is not safe." Conner had stayed through the building of the new blockhouse and fort. He said he was glad to see Zacharie Cicott, a friendly French fur trader from the north, with Harrison. Cicott could be useful and knew the ways of the Prophet better than anyone else.

Lieutenant Colonel Miller, officer in charge of the fort at Terre Haute, asked Conner to come to a campfire and tell the men about his life among the Indians. He was a friend of Tecumseh and knew Indian history, and his own personal history was interesting in itself. At this time Conner had an Indian wife and several metis children.

The men's faces were illuminated by the bright logs of a fire that was leaping and sparking as Conner had begun his tale. He said that he was of Irish-German descent, but had been among the Indians so long that his ancestral tongue "played but little part in my conversation." He spoke the language of the Shawnee and Delaware tribes easily and could carry on a conversation in almost any dialect common to Indians of the central part of the territory. It was not until he was a big boy that he learned to speak good English, which he absorbed at the knee of the Reverend David Zeisberger, a Moravian missionary, who worked among both whites and Indians. "This good pastor," Conner told them, "spent years trying to teach the Indians, but in the end all his work was destroyed by the hostile Indians urged on by the scheming British." Always the enemy from across the sea. An old story it was to the group looking up into the eyes of this frontiersman.

"Father engaged in the fur trading business in Pennsylvania and was of course impelled to go further west. He kept moving until finally he reached the Ohio country, where furs were plentiful. Pontiac ruled this western country, and he was opposed to the white man coming west of the Alleghenies. While trading among the Indians, my father met a white girl, Margaret Boyer, who had been held as a captive by the Shawnee Indians from the time she was six years old. She had been taken in the Lehigh Valley in Pennsylvania in 1757.

"My grandfather Boyer, while working in a field, had been attacked by the Indians. He tried to hide his children and then go for help. He swam the river nearby, and as he was climbing the opposite bank, he was shot by the Indians, then scalped in the presence of his children. At that time my mother was six years of age, her little sister was four, and her brother thirteen. All of the children were reared by the Indians. The little sister lived among the Indians, married an Indian chief, and brought forth a large family of children. The brother lived for five years with the Shawnee until released by an Indian treaty, and he now is a farmer near Lehigh Gap, in Pennsylvania.

"Mother lived with the Indians until she had almost forgotten the white men's ways, although she said she prayed every night that she might sometime be delivered. Father and Mother fell in love but were not permitted to marry until they had agreed to pay her captors two hundred dollars and had further promised that their first-born son James would be given over to the Indians. The treaty of 1774 freed my father and mother, but it did not restore their little James. Father lived the winter of 1774 and 1775 near Pittsburgh, where he carried on his fur trading business. On one of his trips to the Shawnee, he found his boy and ransomed him by paying forty dollars."

An occasional man arose from the fire to answer a call of nature or to seek more firewood, but most were in rapt attention. Sergeant Hurst and his son sat together, and the young man's eyes glowed to hear the story, perhaps imagining how it would be to grow up among the savages. Conner cleared his throat and went on. Life around the time of the recent War of Independence was dangerous, he said, because the Indians induced renegades such as Simon Girty to join them. He was brutal and depraved. "The Delaware joined with the Shawnee and made it difficult to live on the edge of the wilderness in Ohio. My family went to Schoenbrunn so as to be under the teaching of Reverend Zeisberger, but they were soon driven away from their homes into the wilderness, and the reverend's church and school destroyed. We were marched from one place to another until we reached the Huron River near a little village named Detroit, much frequented by the Indians. This was a miserable place, and we longed to get into the Indiana territory.

"I was reared as an Indian. I dressed as one and I learned their language. I came to admire some of their ways, as they seemed one with the forest and its inhabitants, treating them reverently and cautiously. I could track animals as well as any Indian, and every movement of the trees meant something to me. In 1800 my brother John and I came to Indiana, which was complete wilderness.

"I will not deny that I am a man of enterprise. I look for opportunities, for building of my fortune. But then who of us on this new frontier is not looking to build his fortune? I have gone where I can trade and sell land. And I have brought some prosperity to the Indians." He was silent a moment. "And we have all brought sure disaster for them, that is the truth. The closing of their age."

He leaned back, and was thoughtful for a moment. "I wed Mekinges, Chief Anderson's (Buckongahelas's) daughter. My children are now at home with their mother. We lived happily. We were surrounded on all sides for many miles by a deep, impenetrable forest, which seems always to speak to me. Wea, Piankeshaw, Miami, and Delaware had land in the White River Valley, and these people have done fairly well in living up to their treaty obligations.

"In 1802 I left Andersontown, called by most of us Wapeminskink, and established my own trading station about twenty miles down White River. I wish you men could visit my home." There were grunts of affirmation from around the fire. "I would show you a beautiful prairie, lying between the bluff where my station stands and the silvery stream called White River, Wapahani. My land is fertile, and many come to my post to trade. I am also able to help the new land in negotiating treaties with the Indians and am considered a friend among most of them. This makes me happy, as I admire my friends there also for many reasons and long associations. I live a happy life.

"My brother John went to the Whitewater Valley and there established his post. When I go to Cincinnati with my furs, I aim to make his home by the end of the first day. I wish you could see my packhorses loaded with the pelts from beaver, otter, raccoon, fox, mink, muskrat, wildcat, marten, panther, deer, bear, wolf, weasel, groundhog, opossum, and sometimes I take furs from squirrels and rabbits." Heads nodded. Most of them easily could and did shoot these animals, but the variety of this man's means of living impressed them.

Enos Best said, "But you will not be going with us, now as we go to Prophetstown." Conner cleared his throat. "No, I do not wish to do that. You have your own axe to grind; I will not grind it with you. My companions and I will take the Indian trail extending from this fort you have built to a point on White River. It is about seventy-five miles from here. Then we will be at my Prairie Station home."

He spoke briefly of his friendship with Tecumseh. "I see his viewpoint. He and his brother (they were twins), dedicated themselves to opposing the white man's coming into the grounds of deep forests and animals. My brother John has been active in the treaty negotiations, and I am also helping. I hope we can come to the day when the white man and Indian can live together. We are all brothers under the God, as they say the Great Spirit, who made us. This fighting—" He threw up his hands and reached over to pat the shoulder of a rough-looking man near him.

"You can place your reliance on this man, Zacharie Cicott. He will act as a guide for the general. Cicott is dependable and particularly hates Tecumseh and the Prophet. Of course the Indians know the governor is going up the river, and they will try to check him, but old Cicott will know of their intentions. He is the son of Canadian parents in Detroit and is much admired by Governor Harrison." Conner smiled briefly at Cicott, who held up his hands above his head and nodded, giving his friend permission to continue with the tale.

"His French father brought him up to favor the Americans and hate the British, whom he knew only cultivated the Indians to beat down the Americans who were occupying territory the British wanted.

"You, sir," he said, gesturing towards the scout Cicott, "—I will tell it for you—fell in love with a beautiful Potawatomi maiden whom everybody now knows as Marie. This girl has many suitors but prefers this trader white man Cicott. It was known by Marie's people that she was meeting this white lover, and although they followed her, she was smart enough to outwit them, and her meetings were held in secret. Marie's own brother Perig was her most persistent persecutor, for he knew that Marie relayed Tecumseh's schemes to her lover. Cicott accused Tecumseh of being a tool in the hands of the British, and Tecumseh ordered him—my friend there—killed.

"And for her part, Marie was an outcast, too, as Tecumseh suspected she was telling his plans to the Americans." He went on to tell the group that the Shawnee burnt traitors at the stake, but since Tecumseh opposed burning at the stake, having watched this cruel death as a child and vowing never to do it, if Marie were caught, she would be executed in another way, perhaps holding her head under water. "Let us hope this couple can be united and in peace." Heads nodded.

Someone asked, "And what of the Potawatomi? We are entering their country, aren't we?"

Conner thought for a moment. "I do not believe that Chief Winamac of the Potawatomi will join with the Prophet in any attack upon General Harrison's army. Winamac is very hostile towards the white man, but his hunting grounds are much further north, and he probably will not know of Harrison's trip to the north Wabash country."

"How does he feel about us?" the senior Spencer wanted to know.

Conner prepared to light a pipe. "I remember upon one occasion

Winamac said, 'The whites are as numerous as motes in the sunshine, and it will be useless for us to try to head them off. First come their soldiers, then their trappers, traders, and finally the settlers. It will not be long until they take charge of our hunting grounds.'"

"Hmph, true," Spencer said. Who would know that a little more than a week from this campfire, Spencer would be killed on the Tippecanoe battlefield?

Sergeant Hurst's son asked Conner about the Prophet.

"This man isn't the clown you have heard about," Conner said, filling the bowl of his pipe. "Several years ago he stopped drinking and preached a doctrine of abstinence and purity of the Indian race. He believes there should be no individual ownership of land, no intermarriage, that clothing should be animal skins, and bows and arrows are better than guns."

"Didn't he perform a miracle of some sort?" Spencer's son Jim wanted to know.

"You could call it that—the Indians did. He told his people that the Great Spirit was opposed to transferring land to the whites and that he had been given special powers to heal sickness of every sort. To prove his point, he directed his people to gather with him on the sixteenth day of June, five years ago, and he would have the sun hide its face and all would be darkness, the sign from the Great Spirit that He was sorrowful because the Indians had given up their land."

Jim's eyes were large, wondering. "And didn't that happen as he said?"

"Yes. He had learned of the solar eclipse from white surveyors."

Nobody spoke for a while. The fire was beginning to die. "What about the third brother, the third of the triplets?" Jim Simpson wanted to know. He had stayed at the back of the group, almost within the trees. He was a member of the militia only because it was required and because he wished Indian troubles to cease. He did not see himself as a military man.

"Some say there was a third, a triplet. But I know nothing of that. I doubt that he ever existed."

That had been the scene on the way upriver, on the way to the battle they had just won. Now, as they planned to disband after the comradeship and shared danger of the battle, Jim Simpson in his bed near Koo-wa and her little dog wondered if the battle would relieve the fear and anxiety his town had lived under. Clashes of the two cultures had been irritating and sometimes dangerous, brutal. The Shawnee had burnt early pioneers, relatives of the pioneers at Vincennes, at the stake. The Sieur de Vincennes had himself been burnt after he founded the town, going south and affronting the Chickasaws, who killed him. But the terror and destruction went both ways. During the revolution, in the last years, some of the leading citizens of Vincennes had been part of George Rogers Clark's band, which had come from the fort at Harrodstown to retaliate against a kidnapping party that had taken settlers from the fort to Detroit. The Clark regiment caught up with the Shawnee and fought a battle with them at Piqua in Ohio, killing all Indians who advanced in a line in front of their wives and children and destroying their winter stores.

Vincennes people knew this and also that their own town could not really rest in peace. Homes had been burned, fields plundered. Housewives did not leave their doors unlocked when they went out; stealing was a pastime of the Piankeshaw. Would they know that the Indians had been defeated and seemed to have scattered? The town's newspaper had not been published for several months, perhaps at someone's orders, but letters had been sent downriver from Fort Harrison by express messengers, and these messengers themselves would have filled in the story. Certainly a jollification would be held in the public square: bonfires would blaze, bells would ring; cannons would be fired and oratory would flow. All his friends and neighbors and all the rest of the town would be on hand to shout for joy.

And now, several days after the evening campfire at Fort Harrison and miles down the Wabash River, and having just passed Fort Knox, Vincennes was at last in sight. The high ground upon which the town had been built stood out in relief; the homes were visible through the bare tree limbs. The belfry upon the church was discernible and the big bell could be heard. "And see," Jim said to Koo-wa, who seemed to sense something was afoot, "the whole town is astir." How had this happened, that there is such a welcome? Scouts from Fort Harrison, riding hard, had announced the time when the boats were expected to arrive. The dragoons and mounted militiamen were timed to arrive at the same time. The horsemen were now coming down the river road. The wagons, though, would be a little late. The strong oarsmen rowing the boats were pushing with might and main, and the people on shore were waving handkerchiefs and flags. Jim could see their arms out, fingers pointing out their dear ones and neighbors among the soldiers. Some were pointing at the mounted men, too.

There, there, are Sarah and Mary and Virginia, at the water's edge. They know who they are looking for, and they have had word that he is bringing a little Indian girl and many stories to share, though some already have been told. The family is running to Jim's boat. For a moment he forgets the little girl as he seizes his wife and the little ones and rains kisses on them. He then steps back and reaches for Koo-wa. In a moment the two little sisters have the Indian child by the hand. They lead her up the bank followed by the father and mother. The crowd steps back, and all watch the Simpson family with their new charge. This unusual family group cannot help but be the full center of attention.

Uniformed militia, Kentucky guards, and citizens joining from the neighborhood, marched through the streets of Vincennes in the fall of 1811. They were preparing to follow Willam Henry Harrison to confront the Prophet at Prophetstown as depicted by the author at the Battle of Tippecanoe, and they returned to this town for celebration after the battle. Shown along the sides of the streets are two-story clapboard houses and the territorial capitol building. Illustration by Richard Day

Chapter 7

Home to the Simpsons
November 1811

James Simpson's education had been neglected. He could read and write, but he was not at home with books. Sarah read to the family, and Jim was proud of his wife's accomplishment; not many people in Vincennes could read or write. The parents were determined that their little girls should have an education in keeping with the best on the western frontier. Some of their neighbors sniffed at this. Many parents considered it a waste of time and money to educate a girl. Girls must cook and spin and raise a family, and it was quite sufficient if that could be well done.

But their family would do as it was inclined. Virginia, who was only seven years old, could read and print. Mary, aged five, had started to school just a few days before her father left for Tippecanoe. The girls' school in Vincennes was supported by tuition paid by the parents. Jim and Sarah planned to lay aside a small part of their earnings each year to help insure instruction for their children. Jim's earnings were meager, but they were regular, and he worked hard, provided well for his family, and saved some for the "rainy day." The girls' teacher was present now as the family headed to their home from the river, and she was thinking of the new child for her school.

Miss Marie Thoreau, the school's headmistress and teacher, had heard of Koo-wa, even before the child alighted from the boat. Miss Thoreau had been at the landing spot, curious to see the little Indian child. From the moment she saw Koo-wa there on shore, the teacher had plans of her own. She knew something of the Simpson family's finances; it was an effort to keep two little girls in school. She determined to follow the family home on this evening, then take a good look at the Indian child. What beautiful features and grace she seemed to have. She had never been close, or even attracted to, an Indian child before, but she was ready to be of assistance to Sarah Simpson if she could.

All around the family and Miss Thoreau the victory celebration continued. Flags were waving and banners flying as one by one the other men disembarked from the rowboats or got down from their horses. There was sadness, for some of the fathers and brothers had not come home and their graves were far away, under lonely trees in the northlands. These last resting places would be hard to find. Some of the men had to be helped and others carried, but the wounded carried brave faces and felt some of their pain eased as they met their loved ones. All carriages in the town had been offered to convey the wounded to their homes. Several companies recruited from southeastern Indiana territory and the Kentucky militia had been mustered out at Busseron Creek further north, but those from Vincennes and southern Indiana would be paid and discharged at Fort Knox.

The chairman of the town's borough had appointed a reception committee for the arrival of the troops, but the committee members were lost in the general hubbub. All the formalities had been forgotten in the desire to see the men, and the crowd made way for relatives. After the hugging and kissing and exclaiming, everybody wanted to see Koo-wa. The messengers sent to the town from Fort Harrison had not failed to tell the story, and so there was some gentle pushing and maneuvering to see the little Indian girl.

Tan was by Koo-wa's side, with Billy Tulley watching him from nearby. Tan nervously wagged his tail, not understanding all the fuss and noise. There was no hollow log, Billy wryly observed, where he could hide. Koo-wa looked earnestly up; soon the child and the dog sensed the faces around them were friendly. Liberal portions of soap and water had been applied to Koo-wa that morning, and Jim had made her as presentable as possible for the reception he knew she would receive. Even her hair had been trimmed and combed. The scratches and bruises on her arms and legs were gone, her skin was now smooth, and much of the exposure color had disappeared from her cheeks. She had developed into a beautiful child during the days coming down the river, and the men felt proud of her—and the fact that they had rescued her.

So home they went, waving goodbye to the crowd. Tan trotted along beside the three little girls. Sarah Simpson was happy that her husband was home but also that he had been entrusted with the care of this Indian child. She was ready with several questions, however. Everybody took it for granted that Jim and Sarah would take this child and care for her. Her first thought was for the relationship among the three children who would now be in her home. Wouldn't Mary be jealous of this odd child who was her own age? Wouldn't both of them be afraid since she was an Indian? That would be natural; still, she trusted her unusually kind children to do their best, as they were being asked. They had been wanting another sister, and it did not seem she would be able to have another baby. Now this child had come, perhaps as a gift, perhaps as a puzzling responsibility.

As they walked, she got a few words in about some of her other concerns. "Jim, do you suppose the Indians will come and claim her? She's so little and pretty, and the children seem to have taken possession of her. They all seem to be so happy. But what would we do if the parents come after her? Hostile? And what if the friendly Indians around here complain that we are keeping an Indian child? Do you suppose they will believe that story of the soldiers as to how she came into the camp? What if they say we stole this child?" Sarah kept up such a barrage of questions that Jim didn't even attempt an answer.

Mary had appropriated the Indian child. Virginia could do nothing more than simply look on. Koo-wa seemed content, looking happy to be with children her own age after all the grown soldiers. Neighbors were waiting at the Simpson home with their questions. Finally, the questions came down to one: what would Billy Tulley do about his dog? If that was all the trouble they had to solve, Sarah told herself, they would do well with this child.

Inside they went, the family and their teacher, shooing neighbors on their way. The family took off their coats. Koo-wa had not changed her one garment since she was first discovered by the soldiers, and inside there she was, standing in that cut-down army blanket coat, which was buttoned tightly around her. It was warm inside the Simpson home; that coat should come off. Sarah offered to help the child, but Koo-wa would not allow anyone to touch her prized coat. "That's a miserable garment underneath," Jim said. "It needs to be taken off her and burnt. We can't let the neighbors in until that thing is disposed of and she is dressed properly."

Sarah tried all forms of persuasion then, but without success. She knew it would be a mistake to remove the coat by force. She thought her husband might have better luck with Koo-wa, but he told his wife that since the coat had been placed upon her back, no one had been able to remove it. In the wagon, around the evening campfires, and on the boat she had clung to the coat.

Miss Thoreau, who had been glad to accompany the family from the boat to the house and who was an adviser as well as a friend of the Simpsons, was appealed to. She suggested that the three children be placed in a room with a bathtub and that Virginia and Mary remove their clothes, go through the act of taking a bath, and then put on their prettiest dresses. If this process was followed a few times and one of Mary's pretty red dresses held before Koo-wa, the child might try to imitate her new sisters.

They tried it. The child faltered, looked frightened, and tried to grab the coat without going through the earlier movements. Finally Mary succeeded in getting Koo-wa to lay aside the coat. The mother and teacher then saw with horror the miserable garment clinging to the child. With a few deft movements, Sarah poured a little water on the dress, and with her scissors she soon had the deerskin off the child. It was quickly thrown into the fireplace. The truly dirty Koo-wa was then bathed head to foot. Both the mother and the teacher stood in wide-eyed astonishment, for as the soap was succeeded with rinse water, the skin of the child showed white with only a pinkish glow. Both women exclaimed together, "This child is white!" Her hair was examined carefully, and they found it fine, soft, dark and wavy. Her eyes were large and brown and she did not have high cheekbones. Sarah rushed to the door and exclaimed, "Jim, this child is white!"

In a few moments and in the midst of the surprise, the supper table was spread, and Miss Thoreau was asked to remain. The new family sat down together. The children took their places at the table. Miss Thoreau knew her place, for she often ate with the family. A place had been set for the little newcomer, but she eyed the supper table and walked around the chair, evidently afraid to get up on it. The Simpsons decided to let her take her own time. The soldiers had taught her something of the white man's way of eating as they were in camp and coming down the river, but they had left her much to her own devices. Knives, forks, and plates did not interest her. Mush and milk was placed in front of each chair. She finally climbed upon the one vacant chair. The children attempted to show her how they ate their mush and milk with a spoon, but the whole process seemed to confound her. She finally lifted the bowl to her mouth, which was hard on the clean dress, but it was her first lesson in table manners. Biscuits covered with jam were passed to her. She crammed the food into her mouth, leaving a good deal of jam on her face. Then she began to watch her little sisters and tried to imitate them. The family was encouraged that she would soon learn to eat at the table. Miss Thoreau watched every movement with avid interest.

A celebration was planned for that evening in Old Vincennes. The road in front of the church would be decorated, and a military band was going to play. The city fathers wished to tell of the glorious deeds of the returning heroes. Every citizen of the town would attend the celebration, some bringing piles of brush and wood to light a huge bonfire in the commons on the edge of town. The group would move to Grouseland to visit the general and so he could make a speech from his balcony. The public reception was to start at seven.

Word had been passed around, though, that the little Indian girl might be seen at Jim Simpson's house. Only a few had been able to see her when the boats came; she was small, in the midst of the Simpson family, and had been whisked away. The crowd decided with one accord that they were more interested in seeing the child than hearing the oratory. If they hurried to Jim's house they might see the child before the orating began. The crowd began to gather soon after dark, and first the house and then the yard filled up with the curiosity seekers. Soon many began to yell, "Bring her out. . .we want to see the Indian child."

No one had been told the incident of the coat, the bath, and the fact that this Indian child was white. Many who despised the Indians were smirking, ready to condemn the Simpsons for taking in "a savage." Why didn't they just dump her out onto the Piankeshaw camp near Terre Haute? they asked. Others were supporting the Simpsons' Christian charity. Now they wanted to see this child "captured" at Tippecanoe for themselves. Jim's home at the edge of town was a one-story log cottage with a loft. The street leading out that way was not much used by wagons or carts and there were no stones. Grass grew in the street, and the yards around the houses were large. In the roof of this cottage a sort of dormer window had been constructed, used to ventilate the attic, not to let in light. In front of this dormer was a small platform, and this was surrounded by a miniature railing or fence. Jim decided to take the child up to this miniature balcony so that all might have a look at her. Candles were placed on the balcony.

As the small form stepped out, three cheers went up. Jim knew he must tell them the story of the bath and the discovery that Koo-wa was not Indian after all. He did this in his simple, direct way and held Koo-wa up for them to see. Then he acknowledged the cheers and took Koo-wa back inside.

James Simpson loved his home and family and he loved his work. He enjoyed the music of his hammer as, with rhythmic strokes, he turned out a high grade of barrels, the smell of the seasoning wood, and the fitting of the staves in the form he controlled with his small handmade furnace. He knew how to fit the staves in the form and then apply the tightening rope as it brought the staves into their proper places. He could regulate exactly the winch with his foot and with his hands guide the staves as they went together to make a barrel. He knew where the reeds grew that could be used to seal the staves. The children of the neighborhood gathered to watch the shavings fly as he made the hickory hoops to hold the barrels firmly in place and add to their life. The boys and girls would then take the shavings home to help start fires. Simpson barrels did not leak and lasted many years, even with rough treatment.

He spent only part of his time in the cooper shop because he loved the out-of-doors. He planted his large garden with care in the early spring, end of February. He knew how to select the best seed and grew enough to supply the town with vegetables. His watermelons and muskmelons were large and sweet; the rich, sandy loam of the Wabash valley was ideal for vine fruit.

When Indians or town loafers or roving fourteen-year-old boys stole his watermelons, Jim swore vengeance. He was generally a man of peace, but he feared the Indians of the north, who were threatening and had killed scores of citizens in recent years in the territory. When the president of the U.S. finally ordered that a campaign be organized against the Indian tribes, with settling issues as a primary goal but the prospect of battle real, Jim had responded to the call-up of the militia to go to the area of the Tippecanoe. He had taken down his flintlock musket, in which he took great pride, and readied it for action. Then he had said goodbye to his wife and children to join the troops as a scout.

Now he could put the musket aside and hope his town and all of Indiana could live their lives without threat. He and Sarah had a new child to care for as a result of Jim's campaign trip. In the day or two after the soldiers had returned, Koo-wa had begun gradually adjusting to life in the home with new friends, who seemed to be fast becoming sisters and only occasionally were impatient with her. Mary, particularly, loved the spirit of adventure this new friend showed all day long. The two romped through the house, built rock villages outside in the dirt, climbed trees, and made little men's faces with apples. Tan Dog was at their side still and constantly, and that was an issue, Jim realized. Billy Tulley was still in town ready to leave for his own home farther east and was increasingly coming to watch Koo-wa and Tan romp outside the cabin home. Sometimes Billy went up to the children in the yard and whistled. Tan, though, seemed to have forsaken his old-time pal.

Billy decided he would make no more calls. He would go out to the Simpson home and bodily take the dog, perhaps early in the morning before the child was up and about. Billy was a charitable fellow, but he could see no good reason why he should lend his dog any longer to the young girl and this family. When his Kentucky company was ordered to start on the morrow for their home across the Ohio, Billy called early in the morning to claim his dog, but Tan was not outside the cabin. A knock on the door showed he was not inside, and so he scoured the neighborhood—with no results. Every cabin cellar in the vicinity was investigated, every barn and haystack carefully searched. Calling produced no dog. Billy was obliged to leave with his comrades, but he was sad and altogether out of sorts. He was afraid to complain that these people had kept his dog, because he knew that his comrades would accuse him of being a poor sport. They had been won over to Koo-wa coming down the river, and he knew that if he had that dog the others would insist he return it to the little girl.

The next day after the Kentucky troops left camp, Tan appeared, ready for play. He was hungry but seemed glad to be back among friends. A few days later, as Jim was looking for a backlog for the fireplace, he found one with a large hole in it. Upon inspection he found the hole worn smooth and almost lined with brown hairs. Someone, or ones, had driven a wide board into the ground to cover the entrance. Tan had clawed his way out of a rotten spot back in the log. Sarah looked at it with Jim and decided that a hollow backlog had been put to good purpose other than holding fire in a fireplace. Bygones should be bygones, and no more should be said about it.

Chapter 8

Ohio-Wabash
September 1803

Sarah Simpson was a motherly soul whose whole life was centered in her home, her two children, and her husband. She and her husband Jim had come to Vincennes in the year 1803. Sarah had an elementary education, although she had not had time or opportunity to go beyond that in recent years. Life in a small town on the western frontier kept her extremely busy with things other than reading; however, whenever she could she borrowed books, which she read aloud to the family. She read national newspapers that came to neighbors. Some of her well-to-do fellow Vincennes citizens subscribed to eastern papers and were willing to loan them out after thorough reading. Thus, from that first year of her marriage she could keep up on the affairs in Washington and the world: the naming of Napoleon as emperor in France, the commissioning of Messrs. Lewis and Clark to go west to survey the new territory of the Louisiana Purchase, the uprisings in the newly free nation of Saint Dominique, soon to be known as Haiti.

After July 1804 Sarah could read a local newspaper, which would soon be called *The Indiana Gazette*. It always looked the same. The first page was a reprint of some act of Congress; the second page gave the notices of sales and local advertisements; the third page had items of local news and reprints from eastern papers; and the fourth page usually carried an essay, some poetry, wise sayings, an anecdote or two. Reports from London, Paris, or Moscow were usually copied from New York or Philadelphia papers.

Sarah was also called upon to write letters for her neighbors and friends. Most of the neighbors spoke French, and Sarah's education in her own home had included study in French conversation, which helped her now. She had brought with her to her new home on the frontier valuable books from her own father's library. These had been collected over a long period of time, and as the family was growing up, her father had brought in children's books such as *Little Goody Two Shoes*, *Cobwebs to Catch Flies*, or *Pilgrim's Progress*, which would amuse them or advance them in knowledge of science, art, or history. Among Sarah's prized books were *History of the Decline and Fall of the Roman Empire* by Sir Edward Gibbon, Buffon's *Natural History*, and the children's books. For her family she read a few verses from the family Bible and insisted that the children commit choice verses to memory.

Sarah's family had come to Cincinnati after the Revolutionary War, when the town was small and only a stopping place upon the broad Ohio, and they had lived in the town long enough to be considered substantial citizens. Her parents had been reared among the hills of western Pennsylvania, and hearing of the splendid opportunities downriver, they had decided to follow the Allegheny to Pittsburgh, where they would take a larger boat and float with the stream to the young town just established near the mouth of the Licking River. Reports spread of the wonders of this new country along the Ohio and of the other families migrating towards Cincinnati. Some families, a little more venturesome than others, were not content to stop at Cincinnati but had continued down the river even as far as the Falls, and some of the boatman could even brag of having seen the Father of Waters.

Sarah's family had prospered in the new and growing town: they had eventually built a substantial farm home and accumulated some property, and her father owned a furniture factory. They were ambitious for their children to succeed, and they decided the best way to achieve that was to be sure both boys and girls had a liberal education. Sarah, their youngest, attended private tuition school and after finishing the elementary course was well along in the boarding school for girls when the malignant fever epidemic of 1800 struck the town. The contagious fever took the lives of many citizens during the hot, sultry summer months. Sarah's father and mother volunteered to tend the sick, and both were stricken and died within a month of each other.

The boys took over the shop, and Sarah did not want to be supported by them. Neither did she want to be a charge upon her married sisters, so she organized a beginners' school for small children. While teaching at the school, she met Jim Simpson. Jim was a big, brawny fellow who carried himself with an easy grace and did not appear to be one who would allow the cares of the world to weigh too heavily upon his shoulders. He had just finished his apprenticeship to a Cincinnati cooper and was ready to make barrels on his own.

The courtship of Sarah and Jim didn't last long. Though they had known each other for a time, Jim never thought that Sarah would want to marry a mechanic. She was a teacher, after all. Then, too, he had been dreaming of the western frontier, and Sarah would surely not want to leave her brothers and sisters. Would she? Still, they found themselves together a lot, in church and beyond. Jim found more courage as his admiration of the lovely and independent young lady grew. He wanted to get started with his trade and own a shop of his own. The cooperage business in Cincinnati was in the hands of a few, and it was either work in one of the established shops or try to build up a trade by underselling. Jim wanted to make better barrels, and this could not be done if he had to succeed by lowering price and quality.

This determined young man persuaded Sarah that they should join hands and go into the new Indiana Territory, and so they decided to marry, with definite plans in mind. It sounded big, this Northwest, and Jim was ready to do his part in conquering at least some part of it. The name "Vincennes" sounded musical to the ears of the young couple, and that capital of the vast empire enticed them to pull up stakes and go. Jim had heard that there was a big demand for barrels in this small but growing town on the Wabash. He questioned every traveler returning from the Wabash country and learned that there was a distillery and a flour mill run by a man named Cooper at Vincennes. The country around would surely soon be open to settlement, to farming. Making barrels that would carry grain and pickled hogs and produce down the rivers to New Orleans would soon develop into a splendid business. Jim drew a beautiful picture for Sarah of a cozy home amidst giant forest trees in a pretty town along the Wabash. He did not know, or left out, the history of the town as a former French outpost, a crude trading post for obtaining Indian furs, slovenly households with uneducated traders, and drunkenness with all its associated problems. He apparently did not know Vincennes was on a stretch of prairie, not lying beneath forest trees, though there were plenty of them nearby. Sarah, thinking of an idyllic paradise, was not hard to convince, and before long, each was contributing plans for a river trip. Together they visited the wharfs and examined boats; they talked to the river men, and they inquired as to the fare. They could travel on the broad Ohio in one kind of flatboat and take a smaller boat up the Wabash.

Their plans were announced at the wedding frolic, following their nuptials. Then their friends and many relatives, old and young, came to the river wharf to bid them goodbye. This bride and groom were going so far downriver to make their home in the wilderness; it gave those who loved and cared about them anxiety. These townspeople had often looked down the river and wondered what lay beyond their shores. In their minds' eyes they could visualize jungle-like forests, wildcats, howling wolves, and Indians. Stories of scalpings and fortified homes around the town had filtered over to Cincinnati. Some who had had more experience pictured what was developing beyond the isolated, earlier French village: a little town with pretty homes nestling on a treeless prairie upon the high bank of a grand river. Without considering many details, all these folks probably already knew there were pigs in the streets, smelly disposal of chamber pots, mud when the streets flooded, flies, ticks, vermin, rats, and disease (in the summertime particularly). They did not need to visualize these realities because they were what they had in their own town of Cincinnati to a large degree.

Jim had procured passage on a large keelboat that was to take them down the Ohio to the mouth of the Wabash. There they would change to a rowboat, which plied the waters between Vincennes and the Ohio River. The couple had considered taking the trip in a cabin flatboat, but they had also been advised that it would be more comfortable to take a light and swifter boat manned with oars, a keelboat. They had made their choice; they were in no particular hurry, and they hesitated to take the barge or raft and simply depend on the current.

Each of the newlyweds carried a large carpetbag that was filled with personal belongings for a month, until they were settled in their new town. The huge family trunk was packed full of articles needed in their new home. Strong men had stored it quickly in the hold of the keelboat; they knew exactly how they wished to stow the craft. It would take this boat about two weeks to reach the mouth of the Wabash, when it would then go on to New Orleans, had they wished to go there.

The young home-seekers stepped lightly onto the boat with their hopes high and a firm courage about the future. As the boat was loosed from its moorings, they turned to take a last look at their friends on shore, wishing them well. There were no cheers, no holiday calls, and no bantering voices, for all their Cincinnati friends and relatives felt this couple was leaving for an unknown venture in perilous country with an unknown promise. The stories coming back from the river told of brigands and Indians. The two had lately heard some of these, too; still, they turned their backs on the past and launched their thoughts into the future.

The boatmen were busy; it was a trying task to get this big boat straight into the river current. As the keelboat floated down the river, the steeples and trees of Cincinnati grew smaller until finally the boat rounded a sharp curve and the view of the town was lost to them. Hand in hand Jim and Sarah walked to the center and sat upon the bench provided for passengers. For a long time they sat there holding hands and thinking of their unknown course in an unpredictable, but promising future.

Sarah and Jim's boat was a long, graceful craft, about eighty feet in length and sixteen feet wide. It glided over the water like a swan even when heavily loaded. Oars propelled it, since it was going downstream. Sarah asked about trips against the current. Had it been going upstream, a steersman told her, poles would have been used. Each of the ten boatmen would be provided with a long iron-tipped pole about twenty feet in length. Five men were stationed on either side of the boat; they would set their poles against the bottom of the river, then the captain would shout "Ready!" and then, holding the pole against their shoulders, the boatmen would brace themselves by placing their feet against the cleats nailed to the catwalk and while pushing the pole, walk toward the stern of the boat, straining every muscle, while the boat would glide forward. When a boatman reached the stern of the boat, he pulled his pole from the water and rushed forward to the front of the boat, head of the line. Some would be pushing, the man at the stern told her, while some would be running forward all the time, thus maintaining momentum. Jim and Sarah's boat did glide surprisingly swiftly on this downstream journey without all that effort. Watching the men helped Sarah and Jim pass the idle hours on the river.

When the boat was in the current, two men guided it and kept it in the center of the stream. This boat, if well managed, would be returning in the way the man described from New Orleans in a shorter time than might be imagined.

It was indeed a luxury keelboat that had been operating on the river for a few years. Jim and Sarah had but little money to spend on the trip to their new home, but as this trip was to be their honeymoon as well as a relocation voyage, they decided that they would spend their ready cash and enjoy their vacation as much as possible. They said to each other that they could have gone by flatboat, but traveling on a raft with a house built on it would not have been very comfortable.

Many did choose, or had to choose, this option, however. Their vessel passed flatboats with pens loaded with cattle and horses. They saw barges with whole families quartered in rude huts on top of the barge. They saw homesteaders with farm equipment and livestock, including clucking chickens and quacking ducks. The flatboats or barges would be hard to pull against the current when they would return from New Orleans, so many were disassembled and their timbers used for lumber. Cotton, molasses, and tropical fruit were brought back upon returning boats, but only the better grade of boats could be used to return upstream. The freight business appeared to be almost a one-way traffic.

The young couple had talked of their new home and planned what they would do when they reached Vincennes. They were anxious to get to the new town and begin their married life, but they made no complaint about the slowness of the current.

In summer, or early fall when this trip was undertaken, when the river was low and the current looked lazy, boats moved leisurely. Berths were provided in the center of the boat, but not much space could be allotted to passengers. The two were loathe to miss any of the scenery and sat in the center of the boat much of the time watching the panorama of shore and stream. Some of this area was still unclaimed, and deer and bear and smaller wild animals came to the shore for a drink or bath. Water and game birds winged their way above them, often close to the water's surface. Late in the evening they would hear the cry of strange waterfowl, seeming to laugh or lament, and it was all so interesting. Jim often remarked that he wished they were going all the way down the Mississippi, because what could be more pleasant than sitting beside the girl he loved and floating over this river. "The Wabash must be wonderful, but what can be more beautiful than the Indians' beautiful Ohio," he said.

As they floated along, it seemed to them that the Ohio had just been left to wander its own way, and at times it had lost its way. They knew they were bound for the west, but most of the time the stream swung from one side of the foothills to the other, hardly knowing in which direction it wanted to go. They often needed to look at the sun to guess at the direction. The stream moved eastwardly, it seemed, part of the time. Perhaps it was trying to take them back home, they joked to each other.

In the sunshine the river appeared white, but in the moonlight the water looked dark and deep and the shores seemed far away. As the couple watched the hills fade into the darkness of night, the stream surely grew narrower and the current swifter. The glimmer of the moon's rays in the soft ripples of water shone like diamonds trying to out-sparkle the fireflies that twinkled in every direction. Every day a new scene opened before their eyes, as if they were in an audience with a curtain going up. The green hills suddenly appearing around a bend, the open valleys, the streams tumbling into the Ohio kept the couple exclaiming in wonderment and pleasure.

Soon they would "shoot the falls," something the other passengers had been talking about for miles and days. They watched as large boulders appeared in their path; the stream seemed to rush around these giant rocks as the current became swift and shot spray up on all sides. The boat was hard to guide, and Sarah felt apprehensive. All the boatmen flew to their places, and immediately ten poles were in action. "Stay in the center of the boat," the captain shouted at the passengers. The boat glided to the south side of the river where the current was swift and the water deeper. A channel had been cut around the big boulders, and the boat was soon past the rapids and in deep water again. The passengers, a few families and assorted bachelors, heaved a sigh of relief, and the boatmen soon resumed lying in their bunks or sitting on their lounging stools. They had shot the falls successfully.

The river grew wider and the vegetation on the banks greener and more lush. Queer formations appeared upon the high banks. Tall trees stood out in relief. Boats were increasingly coming from the west. Several days they advanced before the boatmen told the couple to go to rest early, because by the time the sun would rise, they would spy the river of their dreams. And so it was: before dawn the next morning the shouts of the boat captain announced the Wabash. The young couple rushed to the front of the boat and there before them they saw a broad delta and a beautiful stream flowing into the Ohio. Upon the banks of the stream, some distance northward, would be their Indiana home.

Just above the mouth of the Wabash and away from the low delta land was a crude boat landing made entirely of logs. The big boat edged up to this wharf, and a few feet behind they saw a large rowboat, which appeared very small compared to their keelboat. Four sturdy men were going to row this boat up the Wabash. Freight was soon transferred to the bottom of the rowboat as the morning came in full. Two men who lived in Vincennes and were returning from a trip to New Orleans would accompany Jim and Sarah to the territorial capital.

The Wabash was also winding, and its lower course seemed to have a hard time finding a way to the Ohio. For one hundred miles the oarsmen would have to fight the current; the way would be slow. Their new companions advised them it would take three days of hard pulling to get the boat to Vincennes. The beauties of the shoreline captivated the travelers, with birds of color and song filling the towering trees on shore and views of deer with heads down drinking at the shoreline. It was like paradise, Sarah said—until the rain began to pour down that evening and they huddled beneath a blanket made of oilcloth, a heavy thing but practical.

The next day they came to a spot lying along the river where White River flows into the Wabash: the water was shallow but very rapid, making much noise as it dashed among the rocks. Just before reaching this ford they saw a few buffalo crossing the stream; these fellows were going south. "Not many left, only a few now. You should have seen them fifty years ago, they say," one of the men told them.

In the evening of the next day, a fire was built on shore and a stew that had been brought was warmed up as hot biscuits toasted in the spider pot over the coals. The crew pitched a tent for the young couple, and the two other people on the boat slept under the stars.

It was the afternoon of day three when the boat pulled around a bend in the river and there in the distance the lovers saw upon the east bank of the river what appeared to be a vast tableland covered with fields of corn, wheat, and tobacco. Behind the town was the commons—where the town's cows grazed.

Further on could be seen glistening white cottages among fruit trees—along with some ruder-looking log cabins. The short belfry of the Catholic church and some boathouses along the river came into view. The sun was low in the western sky. The south bank gradually grew in their sight, and soon they could see men, women, and children. The boat was past due and they were curious, and as the boat moved towards the landing, some people came to the water's edge. The couple stood on the prow of the boat, holding hands and straining their eyes. Was this their future home? The pier was low and at the water's edge; steps led up the high bank. Men stood ready to grab the rope and tie it to a post.

Jim and Sarah stepped from the boat. Willing hands came to help them. Weariness was forgotten in their eagerness to see their new home. They climbed the rude stairway. Villagers helped them with their luggage; the old family trunk was seized by a couple of hearty young men. They looked up at the scene at the top of the hill—strange faces all, but friendly smiles. Some were speaking French, some English. There were a couple of Indian faces, they thought, and that of a Negro woman. "Free woman of color?" Sarah whispered to Jim. "Could be a slave," he answered. "It's against the law, but it is happening here."

Sarah had a little sinking feeling. Not one soul knew them, not an aunt, a cousin, an associate in this crowd. No one was expecting them, and they had no place to go. The villagers withdrew, wishing to allow them space to collect themselves. The smells of the river, the privies, the stink of mud plains, the hog ordure, the perfume of summer roses blended together in a potpourri not much different from that of Cincinnati. Somewhere, nearby, here in the late day, one of the town drunks was yelling, was it from a jail? "I want out right now! Now!"

Their boating companions were walking toward a Catholic priest. They saw beyond him a sign "Traveler's Inn, Welcome," and with it a painted face of Thomas Jefferson. A tavern could shelter them for the night, but would the rate be too high? They were already worried that their cash might run out. Perhaps they had been a little too hasty. Sarah sighed, and Jim tightened his hand on her arm. The sun was getting low behind a red western haze. It would soon be dark, but it could be no darker than their immediate future.

Father Jean Francois Rivet, of the church of Saint Francis Xavier, had been watching the couple. He was standing on the bank when the boat came in, hoping for a delivery of some books he had ordered from Cincinnati. He noticed Sarah and Jim were there on the front holding hands, and he had guessed their mission. The boat companions had approached him to tell him that this couple would be settling in Vincennes. He waited to see if they had relatives or friends. He guessed they had meager funds. They were sitting looking a little bewildered there on the bench.

He approached with his arms out, asking in English with a slight French accent if he might be of assistance. Jim looked up, interested. "You can stay at the parsonage for a few days. After all," he said with a smile, looking at Sarah, "I am in need of a cook." Sarah and Jim nodded and smiled. The father questioned them and they were not long in telling their story. At that moment a friendship was made that would last until, sadly, the good priest would pass on in February of the next year.

Chapter 9

Vincennes
September 1803

Sarah at once made herself useful in the rectory's kitchen. In a cooler chest she found recently killed quail. Embers were in the fireplace, so she put on more wood and secured the little birds onto the skewer and began to turn them. Bread had been recently baked, no doubt by some parishioner; dried apples would make up the rest of the meal, with cinnamon and maple sugar sprinkled on them. The strangers had met a kindly man. She began to hum a song. Supper was soon on the table.

The couple had forgotten to eat since morning. The three were enjoying themselves and a lively conversation was underway. On their way down the river, Sarah and Jim had learned that President Jefferson was completing negotiations for the purchase of the Louisiana Territory. They wondered if they should have purchased passage to St. Louis instead. If their cash had been more abundant, their wedding trip might have been extended.

Over the next few days the Father would tell them of the early history of the town, of French settlement, English possession after the French and Indian War, and the harrowing days of the revolution, which through the staunch fighting of George Rogers Clark brought the town into the fold of the new United States. With Indian difficulties around them, they must always look to the protection of Fort Knox beyond the edge of town.

The priest would have some time to give them brief tours, and they could walk out on their own to see the commons land south of the town. Jim would visit the commons trustees and obtain an allotment of land where they might cultivate their own garden. A few acres were allotted to each inhabitant for grazing animals. In some instances, a villager might have a garden, provided he would agree to care for the land in a proper manner.

It was too late in the season to plant a proper garden, but Jim would be ready in the early spring. He would have to fence his little plot. Crude instruments of cultivation were available, but the strong arm and a hoe were dependable after the ground had been turned over. This area was high enough to be out of the water's flood area and was a prairie rich with loam.

The French had used it for grazing purposes for years, no doubt, but when the sod was turned up, it was found vegetables would grow very well and in abundance. During gardening season the citizens worked in the evenings in their gardens, and there was a race to produce the best cabbages and beans from spring until harvest time.

But on this first evening, Sarah and Jim were interested in all things connected with the town, and Father Rivet told them the story from the time it was founded by the Sieur de Vincennes to the present moment. They learned it had been founded with a Piankeshaw village nearby and that the Indians had moved farther back from the village. The early settlers complained the Indians had no interest in taking land and farming it and that they were lazy, while the Indians complained that the settlers had spoiled their grazing grounds and now there was no place for their ponies. The Indians wanted to keep the forests and grasslands and small streams where they might fish. Father Rivet had in his library a volume published by a Count Volney, a French nobleman, who visited Vincennes in 1796 and wrote, "The men and women roamed around the town all day merely to get rum, for which they eagerly exchanged their peltry, their toys, their clothes and at length when they had parted with their all, they offered their prayers and entreaties, never ceasing to drink till they lost their senses. . .they display all the freaks of vulgar drunkenness. . . they become mad or stupid. . .it is rare for a day to pass without a deadly quarrel."

Sarah was thoughtful. Her parents had grown up in the Pennsylvania woods during the times of the French, English, and Indian troubles. "Still," she said, "the white man gives them the rum. They seem to have little resistance to it."

Father Rivet nodded. "And we cannot in this town forget the Piankeshaw Son of Tabac. During the revolution he aided Clark by supplying Piankeshaw to help capture the fort. The Potawatomi—the British enlisted them—came in and fought the Piankeshaw allies, and Son of Tabac was killed. Clark ordered him buried with the honors of war. I have come to admire many of them when they come in for their treaty talks and to trade. And of course there are a few left as remnants beyond the town."

He went on, trying to put his thoughts into the best English. Occasionally he coughed. Sarah noticed that he appeared pale, not well, but the presence of visitors seemed to be enlivening him. "I say that splendid folk generally live in this little town, some well educated, most of the high character, caring about the future of the territory and their own small ones. Many, I have to say, are French." He smiled. "Names like Dubois, Lasselle, Brouillet, and now a Badollet, Swiss, we hear, coming soon to open the land office—these I can speak for. But there are others, traveling in now from Kentucky and the east and also of my own nationality, descendants of the traders, who know nothing at all of civil or domestic affairs. Their women neither sew nor spin nor make butter. No, they pass their time in gossiping and tattle-tale-ing, while all in their home is in dirt and disorder. The men take to hunting, fishing, roaming the woods, and loitering in the sun. When Saturday night comes, these new Kentuckians particularly, they go to the taverns and confront each other, spoiling for a fight. They may block the roads out of town, and when men come by, they offer to fight."

"These are the Scotch Irish?" Jim wanted to know. "They have been in Pennsylvania and now have come into Kentucky and through the mountains."

"Yes. They are coming now across the Buffalo Trace." Jim seemed to have a question in his eyes. Were none of these newcomers good men? The Father raised his hand. "Wait—I assure you many are fine landowners and have fought for the nation, but others—they have far to go." He waved his hand dismissively. "The few Indians we have left hate these shiftless men, and if one of them affronts an Indian, or steals from or provokes him, the entire race comes after the white dirt, as they call these folk." He hastened to add, "But these shiftless are few in our town. They count for little in our life, and for the most part nobody pays attention to them."

Father Rivet never tired of telling the story of Vincennes; he was proud of his assignment as the pastor of Saint Francis Xavier Church, and he loved the people of the town. Not only did he act as parish priest, but he assumed the duties of village schoolmaster. He had come to act as a missionary among the Piankeshaw, but found when he arrived that most had already moved to Terre Haute. At this time he was enjoying a salary of two hundred dollars a year in his educational work; this had been voted him, he told them proudly, by the Congress on the recommendation of George Washington. He said he was born on the isle of Martinique and educated in France, and he particularly liked living and serving in Vincennes because it was a French town and French people lived here. "I am hoping to get better from my illness, but God's will be done." Sarah did not ask; she thought he must be suffering from consumption.

Jim and Sarah were attentive listeners in the pretty little parlor of the parsonage as Father Rivet told how Father Gibault, one of his predecessors in the parish, had encouraged George Rogers Clark to attempt the recapture of Fort Sackville at Vincennes from the English, during the revolution, and how the priest had persuaded the French citizenry to help the young red-headed Virginian and his men, sending the women out of the town with food they had prepared to feed the hungry soldiers in Clark's army. These men had been wading through the forests and swamps for days, coming from Kaskaskia in the Illinois territory under the auspices and orders of Patrick Henry, governor of Virginia, preparing to make a surprise attack on the post, which the British had taken over after the French and Indian War.

"My father fought in the revolution," Jim told him.

"Yes, and the fighting was hard here, small as we were. These Virginians and other settlers took the post from the English Hamilton after he, with British troops and Indians, had taken it from a couple of American soldiers left to hold it. These Indians—they had been corrupted, turned into murderers and scalpers by this Hamilton. The people around here have a name for Hamilton—'the hair buyer.'" Sarah and Jim listened solemnly. They did know this story in general, but to hear it on the very site where it had occurred—that was something to think about. "Hamilton surrendered and was marched out and the flag of Virginia went up. And ever since?" He smiled and shrugged his pleasure at Vincennes's being a part of the United States of America.

A few evenings later the priest was in a reminiscent mood and offered his own historic theory of the famous explorer LaSalle. "I maintain that LaSalle crossed the portage from the Maumee to the Wabash, that he then floated down the Wabash to the 'Beautiful River Oyo.' I say—I think it is true, my friends—that he spent much time around the Great Lakes, especially Lake Erie, and that he wanted to reach the Ohio and it would be only natural to take this convenient route, no? If he spent time in Illinois, he would have to go down the Illinois, then the Mississippi to the mouth of the Ohio, but he wanted to see the Ohio far above its mouth, and the Indians would certainly have told him this easiest route. Is this not true?"

He looked at Sarah, and she, wanting to shrug her shoulders, instead smiled to encourage him.

"You know, perhaps, that LaSalle believed that the Ohio flowed into the Gulf of California"—here Jim opened his mouth to laugh but thought better of it—"and that the gulf was only a short distance from China. I am of the opinion that LaSalle did stop at our little village here, then occupied by the Piankeshaw, and as he was friendly with the Indians, he may have stayed a few days in Vincennes. I believe that LaSalle found the Mississippi River even before Joliet or Marquette. I know that Colonel Vigo insists that LaSalle was a good letter writer and he had a priest with him who kept a voluminous diary, and that neither of them ever claimed to have seen the Wabash, but upon one of his trips south when he was deserted by his men"—here he raised his hands in bafflement—"and left to his own knowledge of woodcraft, he must have found his way to Canada by way of this river. He speaks of traveling with a companion through the unbroken wilderness for more than one thousand miles. You know under the law of discovery if LaSalle discovered the mouth of the Wabash in the name of France, then all the land the river drained belonged to France, and the British had no right to lay claim to any part of it." Sarah moved a little uncomfortably in her chair. It was too late to think of this sort of thing, and she had been brought up to think of the French as enemies. But not this kind priest. "And France had other claims to this area, my friends. Think of the many coureurs-de-bois, and French fur traders who in the name of the king laid claim to the territory drained by this Wabash." He was silent then and finally said, "I cannot help but recall with admiration the Sieur Vincennes, the junior one, of the earlier age. He brought gaiety and joy to this post, balls, carnivals, celebrations, with his young, bright-eyed wife. Then…" All were silent as they recalled the fate of this young man at the hands of the Chickasaw.

But the good Father was not done with this subject. "In a town where the citizens were accustomed to those wearing the skins of wild animals, and where they wore the hunting shirts and skin of buck pants, the dashing young officer and pretty wife Marie Dulongpre made quite an impression." Sarah noted how many words emphasized the last syllable—"impressION." Sarah spoke some French, and she had been practicing with this priest. But for these complicated history lessons, she was glad he was speaking passable English. "Marie's father is said to have paid the largest dowry ever given in the western country. Marie's mother was a Kaskaskia Indian, and this accounted for her black hair and flashing black eyes."

Rivet's eyes were far away. "He died a gallant soldier without ever knowing that the town would be named after him."

After Jim and Sarah had been there a week and were ready to take up their new life, Jim had a question for Father Rivet. "This is called the buffalo country, and you have said the Kentucky people are coming across the Buffalo Trace. We saw some of those animals. Many we have been told, were here in herds?"

Father Rivet sighed, and he discretely turned and picked up a handkerchief to cough. "Until recently you could have seen great numbers. But with the settlement, the wagons coming over, changing times, there are fewer. They have gone west, I suppose. Within memory you could see them at the salt licks down the trace east and south of town and on the open prairies, where there was excellent pasture. They came in herds, both in the spring as they were returning from their southern pastures and in the fall, when they left the prairies of central Illinois and went to winter grounds south of here in Kain-tuck." Sarah noted he had picked up the jargon of some of the local Scotch Irish newcomers. "At places along the road you could see big hollows, where they rolled in the mud." In answer to Jim's raised eyebrows, he said, "The mud keeps off the flies which torment the beasts.

"And now you will be going out to land of your own, to build your own place. Let me give you some fatherly advice." He smiled and told them to respect the creoles for their French heritage and put away any hostile attitudes from the past. "If you are industrious and treat your neighbors with consideration here in Vincennes, you will prosper. James, have you set up your business contacts?" Jim had told him that as a cooper he wanted to start his own shop, and he wanted to develop a reputation for making the best barrels. He thought the miller and the distillery would be regular customers, and there could be many others as this new land was opened to settlers.

"In truth," Jim said, "both the miller and the distiller have encouraged me by saying they will help me build and equip my shop." Not many tools were required to make barrels, and Jim had brought some with him in the old chest. A drawing knife, an edger, a hammer, and saws would be sufficient to start his work.

As Sarah and Jim bade goodbye to Father Rivet, he clasped Sarah's hands and said to her, "We would be glad to have you in the church. You have said nothing of your faith."

"We are Presbyterians, Father, and have been for several generations."

"Presbyterians are meeting in this town," the Father said with a smile and added, "They have traveling ministers, but will soon build a church, I know. You will be welcome among them, and in this town, also."

And so after several days, Jim and Sarah went to the land they had been able to secure with a loan from some citizens. The next year, so the news went, there would be a land office, but there was land available under the old territorial system, and they chose their lot. Jim began to build a furnace on the back of the stand in which to season his staves, a winch with which to draw the staves together, and a center heater to keep the staves hot while he was shaping a barrel. He returned the land he held on the commons and made his own garden and there began to happily spend many of his mornings until frost came.

Jim soon learned to know the "straggler" Piankeshaw, for they liked to visit his shop. They watched him form the barrels but never offered to help; it was out of their sphere, and they did not do this kind of work. He did not enjoy their company particularly but did not know what to do with them. These Indians were not dangerous except when they had too much to drink. The northern Indians who came down the Wabash were the dangerous ones. A week seldom passed without a report of some crime committed by some Shawnee. They would slip into a settlement, steal horses, and kidnap until the settlers feared and hated them.

Jim was everything else before he was a soldier. He had little use for the pomp, strut, uniforms, and discipline of the regular army men stationed out on the edge of town at Fort Knox, but he knew they were a necessary evil. The Shawnee and other hostile Indians must be reckoned with sooner or later. During the building years he and Sarah had in Vincennes, eight of them, they joined petitions to send an army north to subdue the Indians. And when the time came, he too had gone.

Chapter 10

The Little White Cottage at the End of the Street
1811

The Vincennes home to which Koo-wa had come and to which Jim returned after the Battle of Tippecanoe was seven years old and not a mansion. Still, it would be adequate to take on a new family member now, as the tide of Tippecanoe subsided and normalcy returned. There were not many other houses nearby; people had until very recently had the fear of Indian attacks on the edges of town. All houses near the commons seemed constructed after the same pattern, as both home and if necessary fortress. Portholes were placed at convenient places to command a view of the outside from any direction. Cellars were dug and walled with wood logs to protect the family members who were vulnerable, women and children without guns. Father and mother if necessary would rush to the portholes, where muskets and rifles were at the ready. Perhaps that would not be necessary now; one could hope, anyway.

Jim and Sarah's home had been built of heavy logs which had been hewn upon two sides, morticed at the ends and placed one upon the other to stay tight and allow no bullets or arrows, should such things come their way. The logs were daubed or cemented with clay that became hard and kept out cold. The large fireplace, which covered the whole of one end of the house, was built of flat stones carefully cemented together. The fireplace chimney grew smaller as it approached the top of the house, until it terminated in an ordinary small chimney.

Jim, being the good hand with staves that he was, had covered his entire house with well-dressed clapboards. Instead of weighing them down with log poles, as was so often done, he pegged each board. Lime made from the burning of mussel shells, whitewash, furnished a good substitute for white paint, and Jim's home was often referred to as "the little white cottage at the end of the street."

Two good-sized rooms downstairs furnished plenty of space for a family of four. The great room served as a family sitting room, kitchen, and

dining area. In summer a little lean-to room backed up to the fireplace afforded a good place in which to cook and eat, but during cold weather all
was moved into the living room. The bedroom on the other side of the house
was ample because only two beds must be in it, and now, with the new addition, three children would be in one bed. Later on, a trundle bed would be
slipped under the girls' bed. The ceiling also furnished a floor for the upstairs
room. The attic was reached by means of pegs in a corner post, and no other fixtures were necessary in the upstairs room. The attic floor was covered
with furs and heavy comforters. When overnight company came, the men
were bustled up the ladder while the women and children appropriated the
downstairs beds.

The attic, or loft, also had some other uses: for dried apples upon
strings, popcorn tied in rows, nuts in baskets, and in one corner of the room
a barrel (made by Jim, of course) filled with apples. It didn't matter much if
a few flakes of snow crept in on the sleepers, for they were well covered with
the furs and blankets.

Cane-bottom chairs were made neat and strong by Jim, for he took
pride in the crafting of his furniture. There were no half-log seats or tables in
the Simpson home. In some of the homes you would find a log split in two
in the middle for the table with pegs driven; here both the upper and lower
sides of the table were flat. Jim knew how to bend hickory saplings, and
from small trees he made artistic chairs and benches. As Sarah could not afford to have furniture manufactured by the local master cabinetmaker Pierre
Roux, or an expert furniture maker in one of the big cities, she contented
herself with the thought that her house was furnished better than most with
comfortable and sturdy-looking furniture, and with some artistic feeling.

Industry of a good housewife was in evidence from the beautiful needle
work upon chair and table covers. Her quilts and comforters and tablecloths
were worked with careful stitches. The candlesticks and iron pieces in the
house were polished to shine, and her spotless linens showed the frequent
use of soap and water. Well-sanded floors and tabletops gave evidence of the
time she had spent scrubbing with white sand. Dishes were placed in order
on the hutch, pans were hung on their pegs, cooking utensils were scoured.
Meals were on time, and Sarah was a good cook. It was into this orderly
home that the little girl from Tippecanoe had been brought.

Jim looked after the outside appearances of the home almost as well as

Sarah did the inside. He kept the grass carefully sickled. Marigolds, holly-hocks, foxglove, and sweet William grew plentifully around the cottage. Jim allowed no sagging doors or squeaking hinges.

In one corner of the living room was a well-carved and highly polished stand. This little table was covered with a velvet coverlet, and upon it was the family Bible. There were family Bible readings most evenings before bed, and the little girls liked to look at the writing of family names and dates. In this large Bible, between the last pages of Malachi and the first pages of Matthew, were the carefully recorded births. Jim and Sarah's names, dates of birth and their marriage had a proper place in this Bible. What was to be done concerning the date of birth of their new little girl? No one knew the date of her birth or the name of her parents.

Miss Thoreau came to call and solved the problem by suggesting that the mother write these words: "Joan Simpson born Jan. 6, 1806." She told them that Joan of Arc, the Maid of Orleans, heroine of all Frenchmen, was born in Domremy in the province of Lorraine, January 6, 1412, and died at the stake a saint May 30, 1431. She was heroic and helped change the Catholic church and lived and died for the independence of thought which pointed towards the Protestant Reformation. It seemed proper to use the birthday of this saint, and so this entry was made in the Bible, even though Jim, raised a strict Protestant, mumbled about naming his new daughter after a Papist saint.

Chapter 11

Marie Thoreau
1815

The teacher of the Simpson girls had been present the evening the neighbors gathered to see little Koo-wa and had come every day for a while. Miss Marie Thoreau loved the Simpson children. They were intelligent, obedient, and mannerly, and most of all they wanted to learn. Their parents were ambitious for them and tried to improve their minds, so it was a pleasure to teach them. From the beginning she had been considering what the new pupil would bring to the school—and the town.

Koo-wa's—Joan's—sisters were fine young girls. Virginia and Mary were clothed in dresses of the same pattern: the calico had the same figures and the dresses differed in size only. Their hair ribbons were of identical color and tied in similar bows. The dresses were trimmed with bright sashes, which no doubt came from the same bolt. Their hats came from the same box at the store.

In spite of this, these two girls were quite different in temperament. Mary, the younger, was full of life and fun and always asking questions, while Virginia, the quiet one, was reserved and not likely to romp around. Miss Thoreau took a special interest in these little girls and was frequently a visitor, like a loved aunt. Sarah's gentle, learned manner and Jim's kindly, considerate way made the schoolteacher feel a part of the family.

After Koo-wa came into the family the day of the troops' return, Miss Thoreau took even more interest in the family. The teacher found herself fascinated by the mystery of the child. How did she become separated from her real parents? She felt truly in her heart that this child had been kidnapped while she was a mere babe. Miss Thoreau told herself, "This little girl is the child of refined and splendid people. She must have come from the north. Many French people of noble descent live in Quebec. I have read stories of the Wyandot, the Huron, Indians—they have taken white children to obtain a ransom."

She lay awake many nights trying to picture in her mind just how this child could have been stolen. She searched the Canadian newspapers to see if she could find who had been stolen. To this day this mother and father did not know if their daughter were still alive. What anguish! She figured the child must be about five; evidently she had been taken before she had learned to talk or had learned the white man's ways. She must have been with the Indians three years or more before the Battle of Tippecanoe.

The schoolteacher told Sarah and Jim that Joan must be educated so that if she had to be returned to her parents, against all they hoped for, she would be an accomplished little lady. Training Joan offered the French teacher a challenge that she accepted with interest. She imagined she could see many characteristics of the French in Joan. "I see the clear, creamy skin of Normandy, the dark brown eyes and the soft dark wavy hair of southern France," she proudly affirmed. She said that the grace and dignity of the child showed that the child was from the "highest type" of French parents. Sarah sent Joan to school right away, and Miss Thoreau observed her to begin cultivating her better qualities, to develop her natural graces.

The name of Joan d'Arc would be one that the child's parents up in Canada (where they must indeed be, the teacher was sure) would approve of. French, heart and soul, she knew they would be. Miss Thoreau was proud of her own connection to France. She was a creole from New Orleans, reared there as a child. Her grandparents had come from Lorraine many years ago, and every one of her relatives spoke the French language, now along with fluent English in Miss Thoreau's case. Her father had decided to come to the early wilderness town on the Wabash, where he became a successful merchant, putting up his merchandise shop among those of the fur traders like Hyacinth Lasselle and Francis Vigo. After the death of her mother, Marie assumed full charge of the big house, but as she was well educated, she wanted to be useful and so started a school for girls and young ladies. French would be spoken at times, but since the area was now part of the United States of America, parents wished her to conduct the school in English. Her father was proud of her and the high esteem in which she was held by the citizens of Vincennes.

Miss Thoreau was French through and through, even though she understood the reality of the situation in Vincennes as it grew increasingly non-French. For a while earlier, she had believed England might come into possession of the Louisiana Territory, and that was a cause for dismay; she despised the English. When she heard that Thomas Jefferson had purchased the vast territory west of the Mississippi, she was delighted, for it would become a part of the United States and would not come under British rule.

To be clear, Miss Thoreau loved everything about dear old France, and she admired the art, literature, and history of her parents' original home, but she had no divided allegiance. She was loyal to the United States of America. She was well aware that her own parents had recounted the best of the deeds connected with their former homeland and, like so many others, had forgotten the misrule, suffering, and poverty which had driven them to America. The excesses of the French Revolution, the Reign of Terror, and Napoleon's arrogance and mistakes were not to be forgotten. Still, she could not bear that Canada would be in British hands. She was firmly of the opinion that both Canada and Louisiana should be part of the United States.

She rejoiced that so many settlers were coming west to establish homes. Now that the treaties had been signed it would be safer; Governor Harrison had quieted the Indians at Tippecanoe, and the British could no longer help the Indians, now that the war with Britain was over. She was disturbed that some battles had been fought in the Indiana Territory, but Vincennes was safe, and the Indians would no doubt be driven or moved beyond the Mississippi.

The part of American history which dwelt upon American victories over the British was especially pleasing to her. In her mind, Oliver Hazard Perry was a hero and, as the War of 1812 progressed, she taught her pupils to recite in unison, "We have met the enemy and they are ours: two ships, two brigs, one schooner, and one sloop." It wasn't enough to say just the first part; they must number and name the ships. A street was being named after him in Vincennes.

Grammar was also a strong point of her teaching. She noticed that many of the settlers coming from Kentucky, Virginia, and the south spoke a dialect which was soft and slurry. This way of speaking was hard upon the king's English.

The lack of regard for grammar coupled with the use of unpronounced words or syllables grated upon Miss Thoreau's refined ears. Sometimes one of the men said something like this: "If ya wanta see the horse it an't herabouts; it's down yonder a fur piece." The fact that any pupil attending her school was sure to speak a better grade of English than her neighbors gave rise to some snide criticism that her pupils were "uppity."

Miss Thoreau also taught manners, which, she said, were merely consideration of the rights of others and an attempt to be helpful. Hanging on the wall was a motto worked with yarn and framed which said, "Consideration of the other fellow is the ironclad rule of this school." Parents of the girls in Miss Thoreau's school took a pride in their children's improving speech and considered the neighbors' criticisms as a compliment.

The progress of Joan in school was rapid once she was enrolled. She was an intelligent child, and Miss Thoreau gave her many opportunities. The new student was obedient and bright and soon was helping her teacher. The three little Simpson girls were happy together. Mary and Virginia were not quite as quick as their sister, yet to keep any possible jealousy from arising among them, Miss Thoreau would see to it that Mary was kept abreast of Joan, and Virginia a little ahead.

From her earliest days in school, Joan was reminded of her past, for the children often heard the story at home of how little Joan had come into the Simpson family. Joan asked her father to repeat the story to her and questioned the parents often as to how and where the soldiers found her. She could remember some of the wandering in the mist, camp life, and the trip down the Wabash, but not the days in the Indian camp. They had vanished, blotted out, and it was probably just as well.

Miss Thoreau would have preferred not to have the child think about her lost parents, but as it was impossible to keep such an interesting secret in such a small town, she decided to do the best she could under the circumstances. The teacher told Joan the important thing was her duty to love and honor Jim and Sarah, for they dearly loved her.

Joan learned about the birds, the flowers, and the trees. She would spend hours looking at the river, watching the dragonflies and butterflies as they played over the smooth water. She learned to write stories about bird nests, multicolored birds, and their eggs. Miss Thoreau loaned the Simpson children books telling the stories of nature and adventures of children in other lands.

At first Jim and Sarah had an unexplainable feeling in their own souls that some day some stranger would come and claim their little girl. They hoped for the best for Joan, but would they be willing to give her up? They wanted to keep her as their very own. Deep in their hearts they hoped the real parents had enough children of their own that they would not miss this one too much.

As time went on, though, the Simpsons lost their fear that the child might be taken away by the real parents. These people had not searched; surely they would not come. Secretly the parents found themselves thinking that she had changed so much since babyhood that the real parents would never be able to identify her, and they formed convincing arguments to resist the proofs of any claimant. The child had no marks of identification, but Jim and Sarah realized that children often looked so much like their parents that one could immediately identify the child as "theirs." Miss Thoreau often spoke of the child's intelligent big brown eyes, graceful feet, and long, dark wavy hair as typical of the French in some areas up in Canada. What if a man and woman who looked like that appeared? She and others in the town continued to scan the newspapers from up north but found nothing to indicate the parents of a stolen child were looking for her.

Miss Thoreau's school was composed of children from the homes of people who could in this town be considered well-to-do. The mothers of the girls in the school took pride in doing something fine for their daughters and kept a close watch on what went on at school each day. Most of the girls in the school wore better clothes and had greater opportunities than the Simpson children, and yet these three little girls were well treated. Some of the mothers seemed to notice special treatment. One mother complained to the teacher. She was neglecting her daughter and giving too much attention to "those little Simpson girls," this woman asserted. This mother told Miss Thoreau that she believed Joan truly was an Indian in spite of all that had been said, and she saw no good reason why special treatment should be given to an Indian. The mother went on. "The best families send their daughters to this school, and I have heard many of the parents say they do not like the favoritism. One mother I know has said that you have given too much attention to a savage child. I am only wanting to be kind and am saying this so you will know and for your own benefit."

Miss Thoreau stood with her eyebrows raised, saying nothing as the woman went on. "Indian children have no need of an education. Spending time with them is a positively wrong thing to do. When she grows up, no young man from a prominent family will marry her. She'll go back, you know, to a wigwam and marry an ugly Indian buck." Miss Thoreau could hardly hold her tongue, but managed to do so as the woman finished what she had to say. "If you are wise you will accept kindly advice and drop Joan from the school."

The teacher had listened politely to this harangue. She knew how to control her temper. In a calm voice she replied that she would give the matter her careful attention. Later she was grateful for the incident, for it made her realize that Joan would have many hurdles to jump, with prejudice and misunderstanding to overcome. She resolved that if possible she would be on hand at such times, and as the obstacles presented themselves, would be there to help Joan with all her might and main. As the meddlesome parent left, she stated she hoped the teacher would act promptly, and Miss Thoreau repeated in a stronger voice that she would give the situation her careful consideration. She did not mention the conversation to anyone, and there was no change in the pupil enrollment in Miss Thoreau's Classical School for Girls, Vincennes, Indiana Territory.

Chapter 12

Peter Morningstar Cooper
1801

The Simpson family were not the only ones to experience change of a major sort in their family. The home of Hiram Cooper, the miller who lived on a street in town, who would eventually buy Jim Simpson's barrels, had experienced an unusual night that changed his life and that of his wife, some years before the Simpsons had their startling addition to the family.

Hiram Cooper had been a miller all his adult life. His home was a comfortable two-story frame structure in the small residential area of Vincennes. The Coopers had been millers for many generations; Hiram's father had built a mill in Pennsylvania, and Hiram had grown up there, then come west.

Hiram's Vincennes mill had been built ten years ago. Of course improvements had been made, and the grindstones had often been changed. The young miller prided himself on the excellent grade of meal and flour which came out of the mill. It was no easy task to produce good grist when the miller was entirely dependent on the local farmers' grade of corn and wheat. The Indians and some rough Scotch Irish brought their corn to mill, and it was generally of an inferior grade. It should have been better; the rich soil of the bottoms and uplands around Vincennes produced good crops of most grains, fruits, and vegetables, but the Indians were not dedicated to learning agriculture. The miller took his pay in grist and, of course, the Indian-Scotch Irish meal was not exactly in demand. Everybody in Vincennes understood the situation and was willing to buy some meal and flour at a reduced price and of inferior quality.

Houses in the neighborhood of the Cooper home were two-story frame dwellings. The framework was hewn timbers, and the finishing parts were done by Vincennes's new class of skilled joiners and carpenters. The houses were built after the old French pattern and were usually painted often enough to look neat. Green shutters at windows and doors and broad verandas upstairs and down gave a dignified appearance to these homes. Apple, cherry, and peach trees were planted around the house, giving it some bowers of shade.

Mrs. Cooper was fond of all kinds of garden flowers, but the scarlet runners and golden tea roses which almost surrounded the house in summer framed the house in bright color. Honeysuckle climbed the porches. The sweet scent of flowers on a summer evening added to the restful atmosphere of the entire neighborhood. A grape arbor enclosed the rear path. The Coopers spent many of their evenings working in their garden and discussing the growth of each flower bed—and the pests which might be bothering it. Many of these "starts" had come from New Orleans and points south.

The Coopers kept a driving horse and family carriage. This carriage was a work of art and had been turned out many years before in one of the best shops in Cincinnati. They took good care of this vehicle, for it would be hard to replace. Some evenings the Coopers, together with their neighbors, would drive out along the river road. This road might not have been noted for its smooth construction, but it could hardly have been surpassed for its scenic views of the countryside surrounding it. A carriage would pass through a mile or two of prairie, then pass into marvelous virgin trees. Many of the oaks were eighty feet tall, and three grown men could try to hold hands around them and still not touch. Elms, poplars, hickory, ash, and other giants clung together at their tops and seemed to reach the sky.

The front porch of the Cooper home was surrounded with an ornamental railing, or fence, with the entranceway in the center. At the edge of the porch was placed a large, round millstone that had been worn smooth by long use at the mill. Several large stones, which had needed to be replaced, had been retired to the Coopers' yard. Passersby came to know these stones. The Coopers had many visitors, and strollers were common along that street. The walkers would watch the advance of the Virginia creeper and English ivy in the attempt of these plants to cover the millstones. In the springtime the little green leaves would begin to appear among the brown stems, and gradually the stems would appear greener and begin the race for the center of the big stone. The shaft opening in the stone was filled with fine white gravel.

The large millstone in the Cooper yard was an object of interest to those in the town. Hiram Cooper and his father before him knew how to dress these stones so they would grind, and they knew the stones became harder and harder the longer they were exposed to the rain and cold weather. With a horse, large fieldstones could be pried from the ground. Once he secured such a relatively flat and large stone, Hiram would pounce upon it with the tools that had been in his family for years. After a while the stone would take on the shape of a solid cart wheel.

Next the openings for the shaft would be chiseled in the center. Two stones were prepared in this way; one would revolve in one direction, and the other stone would be driven by a shaft in the other direction. In some mills, though not the Coopers', one stone was anchored fast while the other stone revolved upon it. The grain was fed between the two stones and ground to the proper consistency. All milling grindstones weighed several hundred pounds and were hard to handle, to say the least. When a new stone was needed and had been located, they must wait for a snow. These old stones were loaded upon sleds and with several teams of oxen were dragged across the country to the mill of Hiram Cooper. The mill was upon the creek and was expected to meet the need for grist for several years to come.

Hiram and Minerva were in their late thirties and had been married ten years. Although they had no children of their own, the children of the neighborhood were welcome at the Cooper home. Prizes of doughnuts and candy were given out to children who had been respectful of the Coopers' garden. Minerva wanted the children to enjoy her garden, but the blooms were not to be disturbed. At Christmastime the young people congregated at the kitchen door to receive the treats which they knew would be waiting for them.

The mill out on the race was a couple of miles from the town on Mill Creek. This creek entered the Wabash at Yellow Bank and furnished the water power to keep the mill wheel going, and a dam had been constructed of heavy timbers about one mile up the creek where the boys fished in summer and skated in winter. Water spread out over the lowland and furnished a pond, which was amply filled.

As the water left the pond and entered the race, with speed and force it rushed under the big wheel, which, in turn, moved all the machinery in the mill. The grinders received the grain and produced meal or flour. Farmers for miles around brought their corn and wheat to this mill. In season a long line of waiting wagons told that the harvest was over and the grain was ready to provide food for the winter for families. Some farmers brought their grain in sacks on the backs of horses. In every instance the farmer had to wait his turn and be ready to help with his grain. The farmer left a certain part of the ground grain as pay for the grinding. The miller held his part and supplied the neighborhood or sent flour and meal down the river.

Sometimes whole families came in the big wagons, and while father waited his turn, the wife and children took the horse and wagon into town. If ready cash was available, the women would visit the stores for bolts of cloth, sugar, salt, and perhaps some pretty china which had come to Thoreau's store all the way from Cincinnati or Baltimore. The distillery was not far away, and while the family was in town, the father might slip over to add to his whiskey supply. Drinking to excess was common everywhere on the frontier, and Vincennes was no exception. Many a grumbling mother would have to drive the wagon home with "the old man" sound asleep in the wagon bed. The distiller never seemed to suffer from a lack of grain, even if the flour or meal for bread seemed to run a little short.

The Cooper mill was known up and down the river for miles and was the favorite for many folk among the several mills built in this area. People knew that the honesty of the miller counted as much in the minds of the farmer as the excellent results of his burrs. No thumbs on the scales in Cooper's mill. Boatloads of grain traveled up and down the river and up the creek to the mill. Hiram and his wife lived modestly but well. Their table was well spread, their clothing comfortable. Minerva was happy to put her white linen tablecloth on the large maple table, set it with pewter ware, and set out her fine china. Then she served up chicken fried crisp, green beans cooked for three hours with a ham hock, and biscuits made from the very grain her husband had milled. Strawberries in season would end the meal, heaped high in pie shells that were stacked on top of each other and topped with mounds of whipped cream. A hired girl did the dishes after these feasts.

The Coopers occasionally took trips down the river or over the Cincinnati trace, Captain Kibbey's road, and enjoyed a short vacation time in Cincinnati. A boat was by far the best. Though it was dangerous to travel over the trace, the Coopers and some of their friends decided to risk it for an adventure one year and went by land to Cincinnati. It was a rough and dangerous trip. Sleeping under the stars or in caves is not pleasant, and the women complained they did not know it was going to be like this. They also did not respond well to traveling on horseback all day long, climbing hills and fording streams and sometimes finding their way through acres of brambles and huge dense forests. Who knew what was lurking? The men laughed, but they too vowed not to repeat this venture.

But the Coopers, with money in their sock and some time at the end of the milling season, sat talking the year after the disastrous trace trip. They had long promised themselves a trip to New Orleans, and it might be that this year, 1801, was the time to take it. The grain crops had been good. "Perhaps a boat powered by steam will eventually come to our rivers," Minerva said, "but not nearly quick enough for our trip."

That evening they sat by the candle, finally talking little but dreaming and dozing a bit. The candle burned low, and the tired couple fell completely asleep in their chairs. It was after midnight when they awakened with cricks in their necks, finding that they had forgotten to go to bed and that these parlor chairs were uncomfortable. They were soon ready for bed, and in a short time they were fast asleep.

As Minerva lay dreaming of the trip down the great river, she could hear the song of the boatmen as they stroked in unison and the luxury boat went skimming over the water. Suddenly, she was aroused by what sounded like a cry, an unusually plaintive sound coming from outside the house. She awakened her husband. "Listen," she said, and they did. This time it was like an injured animal. They sprang from bed as the wail became more prolonged. Hurrying downstairs with their lighted candle, they started for the door. Flinging it open, they saw the bright moonlight lighting up the front yard, almost as light as day. There was a bundle upon the millstone. The cry came from a basket, filled with wraps, and in it they saw a tiny babe.

They looked about. Not an object was moving in the shrouded darkness beyond the house. Hiram seized the basket, and soon all were in the house. Minerva lit more candles. The basket was made of reeds, such as grew along the river and were woven by Indian women; warm blankets enveloped this child, dressed in a white flannel nightgown. The moment the child was clasped in Hiram's strong arms, it stopped crying. The baby blinked its eyes in the candlelight. Hiram handed the babe to Minerva and again rushed around the yard trying to see the messenger who had presented the gift to the millstone. No one was there in the deep quiet of the night. The morning star arose, full of promise and light.

As they closed the door and held the child tightly, they spoke quietly to each other. A gift seemed to be given to them. It was a little boy, and it had come to them, childless up to this time, to love. Minerva, smiling broadly, could hardly bear to give up the child for a moment. His eyes were big and blue, even in the candlelight she could see that. His rosy cheeks and chubby fists were soft as down. First one, and then another, held him. A pewter bubby pot filled with milk had been lying by the baby. He seemed hungry, so they put the tip of the bubby pot in his mouth and he began to suck. In the arms of Minerva the child was soon asleep. They laid him quietly in their warm bed.

They began to pepper each other with questions. Where did he come from? To whom does he belong? Will we get to keep him? Will someone come in the morning to collect him? Let's pray and think he is to be ours, and if he is, what shall we name him? He can't be more than a few weeks old. Will we be able to take care of a baby? His skin is white and pink. His hair is light. He is a beautiful and sweet child. He is asleep and seems perfectly content with us.

Minerva said firmly, "Let us think he is for us. What shall we name him?" Hiram answered, "We found him on a rock, and so he shall be Peter."

"Yes," Minerva said. "As he came to us, the morning star was shining on us all. He shall be Peter Morningstar Cooper."

Vincennes at this time had no newspaper, but the news flew from mouth to mouth and home to home. Before noon of that day in October 1801 every soul in Vincennes knew that Hiram and Minerva Cooper, heretofore childless, had a little son, and they also knew his name. No serious attempt was ever made by the Coopers to find the child's parents. So far as they knew, no serious attempt was ever made by the natural parents to find if the little one was welcome, and then happy, in his new home.

The Coopers, though, could hardly put him down to sleep without feeling he might disappear. Being childless had been an unspoken sadness for them for many years. This child seemed particularly beautiful and good-natured. Rumors abounded, the most prevalent that some outlying woman had a child "without benefit of clergy" and, unable to face her shame, had left him with someone who would love and care for him beyond others.

Established in their own routine, it took Hiram and Minerva a while to adjust to having a child, and they would sometimes wake themselves up in the night to see if he were really there. The town physician pronounced him a perfect babe of not more than one month old. Minerva was not long in learning how to care for her new baby; in fact, she had lived in a world of nieces' and nephews' and neighbors' babies. She was a good mother from the first. Hiram purchased a healthy milk cow immediately and milked it himself, and he took it upon himself to see that the milk was kept clean and cool. Each evening he went to the commons and drove the cow home. Many acres had been fenced upon the commons, and neighbors kept cows, calves, and goats in the enclosed part. As the child grew, he became much attached to his foster parents and grew up knowing no others.

Aunts, cousins, and neighbors made baby clothes for Peter or shared outgrown ones. The mystery of his arrival was eventually forgotten, and the neighbors ceased talking about it. It was often remarked by some newcomer to the town that the child resembled his father or his mother.

Still, Hiram and Minerva worried that the real mother might have some claim on him. Would she be jealous of them? Where did she live? Did she derive any comfort from the fact that they took good care of the child? They consulted a lawyer, Edward Hempstead, who was on an extended visit to Vincennes, to determine the best way to make the child legally their own. The laws of the Indiana Territory were not well developed, and no statute was in force on the subject of adoption. The lawyer suggested that common law would apply. It would suggest that if adoption documents were drawn up and notarized and submitted to the public record, the child would be declared theirs. He seemed genuinely interested in the child and reassured the parents that all should be well. He told them he hoped to settle in their village if opportunity came.

Peter slept in a little trundle bed, but Minerva never put it under the larger bed. She dressed the little bed as a little girl might decorate her doll bed. It had its feather mattress, its pads, comforters, blankets, sheets, and its own little pillows. He grew and began to play as children do. He learned to talk, and the mother and father borrowed and found children's books to read to him. Minerva related the boy's antics to Hiram each night. She believed too much attention never spoiled a child. Interest should be placed on his Christian upbringing; he could and should be taught to regard the plight of others. Hiram believed a well-mannered child was one who helped others and divided treats with his playmates. Peter grew and became a sturdy youngster.

He was quite normal: he had his fights, he pulled hair, and he was soundly trounced by larger boys and went home to cry about it, as all children have. Hiram and Minerva held their own church services at home and did their part to bring up their boy as a good Christian, but Hiram had the habit of venting his feelings from time to time with a good deal of profanity. Peter was taught Bible lessons, most of which he did not care about. Samson was an exception. Hiram never interested himself in complicated theological questions, but not so Minerva. She was well versed in the latest theories of "the soul sleeping until the Resurrection morn," and she had definite theories about infant baptism and damnation. She had no patience with those who did not keep the Sabbath holy. She was a staunch Baptist in a town which had many Catholics but was rapidly growing more Protestant. She condemned the citizens who attended dances and gambled with cards, and she was not altogether in sympathy with dramatic performances. The masquerading that still went on in the town was to her a crime.

Minerva's family came from Virginia originally, and she spoke only English with a soft southern drawl, but she took a little interest in picking up some French. Hiram could make himself understood in French but spoke it only when forced to. He was, however, one of the long-time residents among many newer ones who were crossing the Buffalo Trace to come to a place they considered a city of their futures.

Chapter 13

A Frightening Time
August 1804

Peter was no more than three years old, a child who was spending much time building little mills and millraces. He would rather be over at the mill than with the other boys most of the time. He loved to see the old wheel as it journeyed around, squealing and spilling water from its broad paddles. If a small fish was lifted by the broad board and flopped its way into the race, the boy shouted with glee. Of course it was not safe to have a child of his age around machinery so powerful and with so many open spaces, but it was worth much to Hiram to watch the boy in turn watching the wheel. He did not leave his son's side when Minerva brought him over to visit.

It was only on lax days, out of the milling season, that Peter could come to visit the mill. Minerva usually kept the boy busy in the yard, where he had plenty of room to play. In summer the yard was shady; there were fruit trees that offered interest to the boy, but he was likely to sample too many apples or peaches. The children of the neighborhood shared with little Peter his sand pile, teeter totter, and two-child merry-go-round. The swing under the big apple tree was an attraction to the older children. The yard was enclosed, and in summer Mrs. Cooper was content to be there, knitting in a chair, as Peter played. In winter she dressed up and stood watch while he and other children used a winter sled made by the village cabinetmaker.

Minerva believed the boy was safe in this little town, in her own yard, but since he had come to them the way he had, and would always be their only child and delight, she kept an eagle eye on him. One day, as Hiram hurried back to the mill after his noon dinner, she noticed a man, surly and shadowy, down the street. Was he an Indian? He dressed as many other townspeople did. Perhaps he was a member of the rough group of both whites and Indians who drank too much in the taverns and were suspected and sometimes brought in by the constable for disturbing the peace—or worse. She watched him round the corner and disappear.

"Mama, can I have a cup of water?" Peter was asking. She went out of the gate, shut it, and went into the house to the water she cooled for drinking. She poured a cup and went out; she did not see her son. When she did not see him and there was no answer to her call, she searched the premises. Becoming frightened, she called her neighbors, and they all began the search. Minerva sent word to the mill, and when Hiram came, he called the men of the neighborhood, and they all began to scour the town.

The sheriff and constable were notified. Soon shopkeepers and apprentices appeared, then all who could joined in the search. Several of the neighbors had seen the lone Indian, but no one had recognized him or knew where he had gone. The Piankeshaw were in full force in town for treaty talks and had been staying at the small remnant village on Mill Creek, not far from the Cooper mill. Men mounted their ponies and made for the village. The church bell rang, and the populace of the town assembled. Young men and old undertook to extend the search. Every store, shop, and mill in the town closed, and every person who could hobble joined in. This Indian did not look like a Piankashaw. Even the local reprobate tavern gang began to look; he was obviously not one of them. Who was this dangerous stranger? The women who saw him said he was a vagabond, ranging in age from twenty-one to sixty. His weight varied in the reports from 120 to 200. He was anywhere from 5 ½ feet to 6 ½ feet tall. None of this was any help. Upon two things they did agree: he was alone, and was a stranger.

But perhaps he did not make off with the child; all other options must be pursued. Maybe the child had fallen into a well or had hidden himself in a corner. All wells, cisterns, cellars, haylofts, and dark corners were searched carefully. Finally, they had to face the situation: the Indian had taken the child. Some people thought that for the brief moment in which the mother had gone inside, a confederate of the lone Indian had slipped in the back way, pulled the child onto his pony, and hurried away, but no one had seen a second Indian or heard a pony trotting. Then Hiram asked the crowd what business this stranger might have had in town. Had he gone into any stores? He was not seen carrying anything in his hands. The local Indians could peddle fish, but the catfish they enjoyed were not favorites in the town. Anyway, it wouldn't take long for a freshly caught catfish to spoil on a hot summer day like this one. His actions were very strange indeed.

Someone from the crowd asked Hiram if he had any quarrels with the Indians. Sometimes Indians came in to sell furs, but this was the wrong time of year, and they had no business at the mill usually anyway.

Perhaps there was something the Indians didn't like about Hiram. He made them pay in money for what they bought, not keeping his share of the grist. They weren't good at growing grains for grinding in a mill. But these few Indians who knew the people in town wouldn't steal a child. Would they? Some people mumbled that a demand for ransom might be involved.

As evening came on, Francis Vigo, the Revolutionary War hero, now commander of the Vincennes militia, spoke to the crowd which had assembled, milling about in the center of town. "Don't go after the Piankeshaw. They have friends here." There was mumbling. "And they have to live nearby with us. If someone among them tried to steal a child, others there would know it and report back to the whites. The tribe up north, the Wea, are also friendly to us and have never in their known history done any kidnapping. Yes, ponies when they are drunk, but not children. It's not their way."

"But what of the mill, the money those Indians must pay when the whites get off with part of the grist?" a local shopkeeper asked. "Not only these around here but further up the river."

The colonel looked at him. "The Wea take their grain to a mill nearer to them and have no grievance against Hiram Cooper. It is the Kickapoo, the Shawnee, the Delaware, and some Miamis that I found could be difficult in my fur trading days. Roving Indians to the east of us in the hunting grounds and those gathered this summer for the treaty talks…that's who you should be looking at. Leave no clue unnoticed."

"We must venture north and east and seek beyond our town," said the young lawyer Edward Hempstead, who had settled in town this very year and was assisting in the treaty negotiations. On his earlier visit, he had helped the Coopers adopt the boy.

"I offer you my large boat," Vigo went on. "And I will finance a search party." The colonel was then in the prime of his life and knew something of fighting. Though he was a native of Italy, he had chosen to make his home in the town he had helped to save during the war. It was decided that the sheriff of the county, William Prince, would assume second in command if Colonel Vigo would lead the posse comitatus.

Miranda stood at the edge of the gathering, which was composed mostly of men. She had a handkerchief clutched in her hands, but her chin was out and her eyes defiant. Miss Thoreau and some of her relatives were at Miranda's side. But the men were heading out; no time must be lost. Whoever it was, and it seemed to be Indians gathered at the forks of the river to the east, would travel night and day because they knew what was waiting for them if they were caught. The search party would shoot and then investigate. Horses and ponies were brought to the Coopers' home, and men of the town, young and old, volunteered to ride them. Colonel Vigo said the posse should divide and groups go in different directions to various Indian camps and villages. If the Indian got too much of a head start, the child could be taken north and traded to the Wyandot or others on the Great Lakes who had in the past a reputation for trading for kidnapped people, both whites and of their own kind. In this case the ransom idea seemed foremost; although abductions for ransom were quite rare in this country, all kinds of Indians were gathered now in southern Indiana and it was known the Coopers were people of some means.

In spite of the need for haste, the searchers thought it best to await the daylight. At daybreak a determined body of men gathered at the Cooper home. Each man brought his own horse or had borrowed one. Colonel Vigo divided the men into three posses. The first pursuing group of three men would go to the Piankeshaw again. Although they had denied any knowledge on the first quick visit, there needed to be further inquiry. The second group, of twelve men, was to use Colonel Vigo's large boat and go north to the Wea village, or further if they thought it advisable. The third posse of forty men, under the direction of Colonel Vigo himself, assisted by not one but two sheriffs from the town, was to go east to the hunting grounds on White River where Indians of various tribes assembled during this late summer time. They were particularly in attendance this year because a treaty was to be signed late in this very month. The men were all well armed, and the neighbors took pride in seeing the men were supplied with food. A Catholic priest blessed the group and prayed for the safe return of the child—and the men.

Not a clue had been left; their work was ahead of them. No one had seen a pony or a rider. Only the old Indian stranger had been about, and Minerva herself had seen him heading around the corner and out of town. The child had disappeared as completely as though he had been swallowed by the earth. Whoever had taken him had known the child's habits, something of the Cooper household, and that the mother might take five minutes to go into the house now and then.

Peter had been dressed in his small child's knee-length shirt and little else. He had no shoes or stockings; it was summertime. The weather was warm, and the child would not suffer without a coat or hat—unless he was left out at night.

The Delaware had a village at the Blue Bluffs, but some of the derelicts of this tribe as well as rovers both Indian and white would gather there and go further into southern Indiana at times. This year there were hundreds more come to talk about the lands they would cede, the rewards they would receive. The caves and the licks were frequented by whole tribes on summer hunts at times. The land east of Vincennes was still an unbroken wilderness, and the posse would have to cross many streams, climb high knobs or hills, and wade swamps. There were no roads and only a few paths.

They struck out upon the Buffalo Trace, aiming for the forks of the two White Rivers, and from there would follow the east branch. Traveling twenty miles or more from there along Lost River would take them to the hill and cave country where many strange springs were to be found. Animals would not drink the water, and the Indians were afraid of it. It had been recommended for certain ailments, but nobody knew just what ailments it would help, and nobody wanted to test it. This water smelled bad and had tasted worse; it was a cathartic.

As the morning sunlight filtered through maple trees, they rode, with the rivers and forests presenting views of great beauty before them, but these determined men were not interested in the loveliness of nature. They were in a hurry and were looking for means of covering ground rapidly. The posse took with them not only their blankets to use as beds and their guns for protection and to shoot game for food, but they had whiskey both for themselves to drink and for Indian bribery.

They traveled single file with the best guides in front. Some of these men had spent their lives in the forest. They would travel only during the day, and the sun was their guide. Colonel Vigo carried a compass, but it would not be needed, as the sky at this season was unusually clear. They planned that breakfast would be over by sunrise, the noon meal eaten while the horses rested for a few minutes, supper to be after dark. The horses needed to graze at night, while they were tethered to saplings with long ropes. Some ground corn that could be eaten easily by the horses was carried in the saddlebags.

From sunup to sunset the men would be in their saddles. They hardly hoped to catch up with the Indians who took the child, if they were able to catch up at all, until they reached the main village or some good hiding cave, and yet they must. If the Indians reached their village, they might trade Peter to northern Indians who would be among them now and perhaps on the watch for children to hold for ransom. No time was lost through these difficult paths and forests. Speed, speed—that was what was needed, imperatively.

They depended on game. The forest abounded in turkey, grouse, and deer. The advance mounts were to take shots and bring down game; it would be thrown over the pommel of the saddle for stewing over the fire during the night. The men thought they would be gone a week. The licks were about sixty miles from Vincennes. As the posse hurried forward, solitary Indians could be seen traveling through the forest, but when they were stopped and questioned, they did not seem honestly to know anything.

During most summers, the Delaware who had many villages along the west branch of the White River gathered at the forks. The Shawnee were hostile because they believed their lands were being stolen from them, and they could be in this area, too. The Miami, who also lived in northern Indiana, would come to hunt here during the summer months. Indians from both Indiana and Michigan met at the caves and river lands and sent out their foraging parties. There was sometimes friction with the few people in the blockhouses out here, confrontation and killing.

After the posse had been at White Oak Springs and picked up the Buffalo Trace, they followed in some measure the course of the east fork of White River. Towards evening of the second day, the group reached the banks of Patoka Creek. Not an Indian had been seen all day. Tired, hot, and hungry, the men prepared a young fawn and wild turkeys the marksmen had secured. Feathers flew, skin was jerked, and soon turkey and venison pieces were stewing in the same pot. They planned for an early turn-in so they could get started at dawn. Plans were laid for the next day when the licks would be reached and the Indian village would be nearby.

At that spot on Patoka Creek was an abandoned cabin, and some of the men thought it would be better to spread out their blankets inside that cabin than out by the fire. They did not enter until after dark and then had hardly lain down when they heard a scratching and a growl. Striking a flint in some straw, they saw two bright spots at the other end of the cabin. A wildcat was prepared to leap and strike. Hempstead aimed at the cat, and that was that. In telling of this incident afterwards, he said that he was so exhausted, he fell immediately asleep and spent the rest of the night fighting imaginary wildcats in his dreams.

The posse started a little late the third day out. Two long days of travel, a heavy supper, and a wildcat serenade had interfered with the sleep of every man in the detail, including the colonel. This day's travel, when it took up, seemed without end: over high hills, deep gullies, along dried creek beds, around big boulders, through undergrowth and tangled briars. Towards evening they saw a high hill, almost a mountain, and beside this hill an open space or prairie. The men of the posse stood and looked with wonder.

The high hill appeared as the backdrop of a huge stage on which was an Indian village in motion. The posse could see men, women, children, ponies, dogs. They seemed to be gathered in groups with slightly different dress and appearances: varying tribes. The residents of the camp were preparing their evening meal; fires were burning, groups were forming around campfires, and steam was rising from kettles. Not too different from the scenes they had just experienced themselves on the trail. Could this peaceful-looking body of people, women and children occupied with the same homey tasks as in their own villages, be the Indians they were tracking? Some of the men had lived with Indians; some had fought in the Indian wars. And yet, it seemed to some that these were also families. Fate, history had driven them apart, and now they must enter and confer, even accuse, and that before dark. Vigo knew he must be careful in his words; the treaty was all important to the future of the area. Yet, they must find this child. In mass formation, mounted on their horses and with guns in readiness, they advanced upon the village.

Colonel Vigo rode in front, while Sheriff Prince and the former sheriff, John Small, the gunsmith, were close behind. The Indians looked up, their eyes turned to Delaware chief The Owl, who gestured for the three men to draw near, to come to their campfires, where seats opened up for them. The other tribes gathered would look to The Owl to speak for them. Colonel Vigo spoke diplomatically, saying that the group was searching for a lost child. The Indians appeared not to understand. As the conversation went on, it became apparent that the group believed the Indians could be involved. The Delaware began to turn to each with angry faces, growing increasingly hostile. They denied all knowledge of a white child. Vigo looked at his companions. If these Indians were not ignorant of the whereabouts of Peter Cooper, they were certainly good actors. The posse briefly convened; most did not want to accept the word of these Indian leaders. Vigo and Small requested, rather than demanded, that they be allowed to make a search.

The Indians indignantly refused. Colonel Vigo told them, solemnly, "You have your own families here. Consider the pain of this mother and father. More than that, consider that you are to meet with our leaders shortly to sign a treaty which will benefit all parties. You need not cast a shadow on these negotiations. Let us just search the camp." Frowning, the Indians held a parley and agreed to the search. The village was searched one end to the other. No child was found. Colonel Vigo then took leave of them, with a face that showed he might still have suspicions.

The posse withdrew to camp in sight of the village. Not a man slept that night. At sunrise The Owl appeared again. He was greatly offended. "My people have been insulted," he said. "It is like your people to make false accusations, to cheat us, to make false promises. We want to have nothing more to do with you or this matter. If you harm any of my people, you will face retaliation. And when we come to agree on these lands, let us assume this did not occur."

It was a sorry lot of troopers who made the return trip to Vincennes. They knew they would have just as much trouble returning as they had going out. Still, the men began to find they were very tired, as were their horses. Their spirits were down; they had exerted themselves to the utmost when they thought they were on the track of kidnappers, and now they knew that was not so and they had no results to show to the poor parents. In the afternoon of the first day of their return, they realized they needed some rest and relaxation. Then a young bear was spotted, pursued, and killed.

Among the posse members was Peter Jones, the keeper of the tavern in Vincennes, and he offered to grill some excellent bear steaks once they made camp—early. Jones was glad to be useful and began to prepare the dressed meat over a fire with a spit, which he carefully turned. It was certainly ruder than the cooking apparatus at his tavern, a two-story building with a long veranda in front that stood at the head of St. Jerome Street. None of his excellent madeira wine would be available for these men on the trail, but the men who had shot the bear acted as hosts with Jones and brought out the whiskey that had come along with them to induce the Indians to give up Peter. That night's banquet around the campfire in the deep forest would long be remembered.

But Edward Hempstead, who had taken such a sincere interest in Peter and his parents, could not forget the scene at the Indian camp. These people were preparing their dinners and taking care of everyday tasks. Their own children were playing around the village, pushing each other on sledges and throwing deerskin balls to each other. Their fathers and mothers seemed to be caring for them just as deeply as anyone in Vincennes. What forces in the land of promise had done this to all of them, whites and Indian peoples, to make them bitter enemies of each other?

Three days later, the posse comitatus came to the familiar Sugar Loaf Mound, on the edge of the highlands. Here was a prospect view of their hometown, two miles distant along the prairie. They would have to bring the sad news into Vincennes. As the men rode through the town with serious faces, they were followed by the populace. Colonel Vigo made his report: the child had been so completely spirited away that not a single sign could be found of him. Every man, woman, and child signed a petition for Governor Harrison that troops be sent against the Indians and that they be driven from the country.

The other two groups of searchers had had no better luck. The members of Vigo's posse spoke of the probable fate of Peter at the Cooper house, and half the town crowded around them. He had surely been taken up north, perhaps taken to the central Indiana Territory tribes and on up to the Wyandot. Perhaps he was among the Shawnee at Prophetstown; no white men entered there. With such reports circulating, all was sadness in the Cooper home. After the men from the eastern trail had made their report and departed, the house grew quiet.

Minerva and Hiram sat for a long time in silence. Finally Minerva said, "Many have lost their children to fevers and the ague on this western frontier. And there have been killings all these years as we struggle with the Indians. I wonder if we ever will have peace and security." Hiram was silent, and Minerva went on. "If I only knew that he was not hungry, that he was not cold if he has been taken to the cold north."

Hiram finally spoke in the darkness. "Where can Peter possibly be?"

They did not go to bed. Somehow that would signify acceptance, defeat. Exhaustion overcame them in their chairs. Then a slight noise awakened them, something around the front door. They flew to open it. There, in a large basket on the millstone, was little Peter. He was asleep and awoke to look up at them. He was wearing the same child's shirt he had worn the afternoon he disappeared. It was clean and pressed. When he threw his arms around his astonished parents, it seemed to them as if he were returning from a visit to a neighbor across the street. They carried him into his own bed.

Early the next morning, he was ready for breakfast and for play. Where had he been? He seemed unable to give much information. When his mother asked him where he had been and who had taken him away, he replied, "She took care of me. She gave me big red apples and candy. I played with a big dog. There were lots of trees. I rode in a nice wagon. I want to see her again. She kissed me and her face was wet."

Edward Hempstead heard the wonderful news the next morning as he sat in his office working on a will and thought about the child's comments, which were being repeated throughout the town. He said out loud to no one in particular, "Sounds like we had been barking up the wrong tree."

Chapter 14

Life in the Town
1816

Indiana Territory was on the brink of statehood, and Vincennes could be proud of its part in the history that had led to this monumental event, a time for celebration. In Washington James Madison was president, and he supported the western frontier. The voters of Vincennes supported him in return, approving also of his strong history of animosity towards Britain. There was still a strain of discontent, though: the territorial capital had been taken from Vincennes "and hidden in a little village in the west called Corydon." There was also rancor directed at Jonathan Jennings, a lawyer who had resided in Vincennes for a while and who had despised William Henry Harrison and had opposed giving lands to Vincennes University. Jennings had agitated to take all advantages away from the city, including its status as territorial capital. Still, statehood was something wonderful. Harrison had left Vincennes some time ago, first as commander of the Army of the Northwest during the War of 1812, and just this year as a representative in Congress—from Ohio.

Increasingly the village was English, as settlers filled the entire lower Wabash valley, changing the woodlands into farms. Still, the original French contingent remained and shared mutual interests. Honore Thoreau was at the center of it as a merchant importing his stock in trade from New Orleans, with some of it coming from Paris. He and his daughter Marie Thoreau, continued to try to preserve French tradition in the face of changing times.

Honore had been educated in France and was a man of culture and refinement. It was difficult to understand why he would have brought his family to this little out-of-the-way place, a trading post when he first came. But once he arrived, he entered into the spirit of the town and seemed to enjoy life among fur traders. Now, in the new state, his store was serving the increasingly prosperous Scotch-Irish farmers. Often finding success on their rich river bottom farms, these farmers and their wives were ordering such things as morocco leather gloves, delicate forty-piece china services, and pianofortes.

His daughter Marie had received her primary education in New Orleans and had then spent a year at a finishing school in Paris. At the time of the arrival of Koo-wa, Marie Thoreau was in her twenties, though she seemed older because of her maturity—and because she did not have the same interest other young women her age had in the newest fashion and frizzy hairstyles. Her hair was pulled back in a bun from her severe but kindly face; her dresses were simple gowns that flowed in a straight line to her sensible shoes. She taught school now because she wanted to work and be useful and had been educating and shaping such children as Virginia, Mary, and Joan Simpson and watching the career at the academy of Peter Morningstar Cooper.

She called herself and those in the small French community creoles because she was of pure French descent but born in America. Her people had lived in this land for more than a generation and had maintained their French identity. She disliked calling the half-Indian, half-white people in Vincennes creoles, as was the custom. To her they were uneducated, rude people, often shiftless and breaking the peace by gambling and drinking and fighting, not to be compared with the gentile French-descent people like her family. Each Sunday morning these "creoles" would be found sleeping in the gutter as God-fearing people were heading to church.

It is true that this uneducated creole population had its own pride, too, and not every one of them was drunk in the streets. These creoles separated themselves from the tribal Indians nearby and told their own stories of aristocratic beginnings. When they recounted their heritage of Indian blood, they did it with pride (and imagination), saying that their hard-working, well-off French coureurs-de-bois grandfathers came down the river from Quebec, found beautiful Indian damsels awaiting them, and married the Indian princesses, daughters of chieftains and of tender and aristocratic hearts.

The two groups of creoles in the town had one subject on which they could unite: anything French. They loved French customs and revered the French Catholic church and were willing to contribute for the good of France. In this time of transition on the frontier, many citizens still spoke French, maintaining it stubbornly in the face of an onslaught of often-corrupted, southern-derived English. Many stores still catered to the French trade, though Honore Thoreau sold to anyone who wished to buy his quality goods. In the mills and carpenter shops, instructions were given in French as well as English. Some educated men of French descent kept up with the times and read news of their homeland in the *Vincennes Western Sun* and in the Louisville papers. Those who could not read were dependent on others to give them the news from Mother France, and Miss Thoreau was glad to oblige. She spent several hours in the evenings in her father's home bringing her French compatriots up to date, reading aloud to those who gathered, translating the English papers into French.

They all rejoiced when Napoleon swept across Europe, even though they could not understand why his soldiers turned against him and allowed him to be banished to Elba. They sang for joy when the Little Emperor was recalled, mobilized a great army, and started once again to conquer the enemies of France. The creole townspeople sought papers from all around and handed them to Miss Thoreau so she might read of the happenings in Europe. They listened with rapt attention when the teacher read that allies were concentrating in Belgium under the command of unknown (to them) generals. They murmured, trying to pronounce the names of Wellington and Blucher. When Austria joined the English, they held out the hope that Russia would get to the battlefield too late. These "Friends of France," as they called themselves, threw their hats high and shouted words of encouragement when they heard that Napoleon had determined to strike quickly and before the allies could be reinforced, when Marshal Ney was back with his old leader and would help his old commander. News moved entirely too slowly across the roads and down the river to satisfy these news-hungry French sympathizers, and it was not until late July of 1815 that word came of the complete defeat of their idol at the Battle of Waterloo in Belgium. The paper which brought the news of Napoleon's defeat also brought the disgusting news of the possession of Paris by the allies and of the long lines of English soldiers marching down the Rue de Tuileries.

Gathering all in the French community together, Miss Thoreau read to her friends how the Little Emperor was forced to abdicate for the second time and how an English battleship was taking him to the lonely isle of St. Helena, where he was to be confined as a prisoner for the remainder of his natural life and guarded by the hated English soldiers. The tears in France were no more real than those of this small band of creoles on the banks of the Wabash. These distracted people got some consolation in remembering that Andrew Jackson had given the British a good sound whipping at New Orleans not all that long ago. Miss Thoreau scanned the papers to see which candidates for United States office would best represent French interests and act against the interests of the British, and she advised them. When they went to vote, they did as she had told them. Even though the capital had been moved, Vincennes was a hotbed of politics, and Miss Thoreau made that bed hotter. She could not vote herself; she was a woman, but she made her influence felt.

Before Jackson's victory, when the war with England was immanent, the people of Vincennes had supported President Madison in his attempt to reopen the seas for American commerce; they opposed the demand of Great Britain that America must send her wheat, rice, cotton, and fish to Liverpool. These people on the western frontier became sea-conscious, and anyone hearing them talk would have thought they were whalers or cod fishermen. Earlier, when Englishmen had boarded American ships and forced American citizens to join their navy, Vincennes citizens had held indignation meetings, and Miss Thoreau led a chorus which sang, "Free Trade and Sailors' Rights Forever."

Those issues had been mostly solved, and it was now a time of peace. Miss Thoreau continued drilling the basic skills and graceful abilities of learned young ladies into Virginia, Mary, Joan, and other girls, whose mothers seemed to have forgotten their indignity over the "Indian girl."

Chapter 15

The Children
1817

Joan and her family prospered in their modest way in the friendly cottage at the end of the street. The Battle of Tippecanoe, the War of 1812, had changed the Indian situation forever, and they enjoyed this time of peace. The Indians of Ohio and now some of Indiana had to change their homes, and they moved into other lives in lands reserved for them or were taken to the west.

Fort Knox was no longer needed at Vincennes; in fact, it was falling into disrepair, as were the other stockades across southern Indiana. Joan and her two sisters made the trip each day to the school still in Miss Thoreau's father's residence near the center of town and not far from the Wabash.

Joan was now eleven years old and had been in school six years. Peter Morningstar Cooper was seventeen and attended Vincennes University a short distance from the center of the town, which was itself ever growing out from its original core.

As the three girls passed the Cooper home, they were sometimes joined by Peter, and the group made its way together to school. It seemed natural to the neighbors that Peter and Joan should be together. Their stories seemed somehow linked. Neither the boy nor the girl thought of the situation of their coming to the same town in a remarkably different way, but it was not forgotten around the family dining tables in that town or around the evening fireside.

Joan was growing fast and being taught to do her part in the Simpson home. Peter was a manly young fellow with fine intellect and decent manners. As years passed, the two families often found themselves together, and though one went to the Baptist church and one the Presbyterian church, they enjoyed each other's company at socials, school events, and town lectures.

Their homes were very different. Jim made a modest living from the production of barrels and lived in the little white log house. Hiram maintained his prosperous mill and had accumulated some wealth. But the families were good friends. Hiram admired Jim and Sarah's strong character, industry, and determination to provide education for their girls, simple calico dresses and all.

Miss Thoreau may have had something to do with the children's advancement and enthusiasm for school. While she loved all three of the Simpson girls, her love for and interest in Joan was unbounded. Miss Thoreau had never married. Very few men had even sought her hand; she was a formidable and independent woman, unlike most in the town and even the state. She could have lavished love on her own child, but instead lavished it on Joan Simpson. She found herself laying plans for Joan's future.

Following an old French custom, these Vincennes creoles held a celebration called the King's Ball each January 6. People came from miles around, sometimes even from New Orleans. The people elected a king, and the winner was allowed to elect his own queen. Peter was old enough now to be king, and everybody expected his queen would be Joan. She was only still a little girl, but she would be a beautiful queen, and that had a lot to do with the selection. The festivities connected with the King's Ball lasted for six days, with feasts and a carnival spirit prevailing.

The creoles also conducted a beautiful Easter service in which the choirs from all the churches took part. At that time, and again at Christmas, the singers met at the public square and sang songs of joy and praise for the great gift of Christ. Peter and Joan enjoyed picnics at the Mounds and at the waterfront. Children, including the Simpson young people, took part, and although there were a good many Catholics in Vincennes, all joined together at these special times and exhibited religious tolerance. The priest of St. Xavier, at this time Father Chabrat, and the ministers of the various Protestant churches enjoyed close friendships; it was, after all, a small town. Only a few years ago they had clung together to wrest out their freedom in a new nation; later they joined hands to protect their homes and futures. Now they worshipped together and worked to build a good community.

As everywhere else, even in democratic America, and especially with the newcomers, various groups in town split themselves off, with an elite class developing. Several social clubs and literary societies called to those who were educated. Lodges, working men's associations, and church organizations served working class people. The Coopers were of the elder gentry, and the Simpsons were proud to be of the working class. A new elite was developing; the first bank in Indiana had been organized in 1814. Its president, Nathaniel Ewing, and agent, Benjamin Parke, were growing rich. Still, there was much mixing in this homogeneous society, and among its younger generation particularly. The young men from Vincennes University often attended parties at Miss Thoreau's school for young ladies.

Miss Thoreau conducted her school as a work of love and devotion, and she did it exactly as she wanted to. She enrolled young ladies of promise regardless of their wealth or social standing. Certain anonymous supporters made it possible for girls who could benefit from the school and truly wanted to come to enroll. Marie Thoreau wished her students to be good readers, observant of the times. Some of her graduates were now nurses for children or the homebound, and some were teachers in their own right. Many were the wives of successful young men. It is true that her goal was to prepare these young women to be good wives and mothers and in this way lift the moral stature of their own communities. She believed to do this a wife needed to be the intellectual equal of her husband, and she inspired her students to study and understand books on agriculture, medicine, and government. The pupils learned to be temperate in habits and speech. They were taught cleanliness, neatness, and comely dress; Miss Thoreau subscribed to, or obtained, magazines like *The Lady's Magazine* and allowed the girls to see proper fashions, even if she considered some of these ribbons and froufrou things extreme frivolity. She wanted these young women to understand simple personal appearance and health. Most of all was her favorite saying: merit should be rewarded without reference to sex, race, or social position. It was an attitude that would help to build the Midwest.

Chapter 16

The Spelling Bee
1821

The Simpson girls were growing up. Virginia was seventeen. The two younger sisters were fifteen. They were no strangers to physical work as well as needlepoint and biscuit making. Work never ended at the Simpson home and garden patch. In summer they helped their father plant seeds, weed, and weed some more. They made sure the young plants had adequate water and poured soapy water on invading bugs. This was in addition to floor scrubbing, wall washing and whitewashing, soap making, laundry tub pounding and wringing and hanging out clothes, butter churning, apple cider pressing and vinegar distilling, apple drying, chicken neck wringing, rug and mattress beating, and carrying of water. Man worked from sun to sun, but the Simpson girls were never even partially done.

Their father had been for many years the sole breadwinner, and the girls came to see that he could benefit from some support, along with the extra cash the family could use. Mary served customers in the Thoreau store, and Virginia served as a nurse in families where there was sickness. She had helped see the community through the great sickness epidemic of 1820, assisting (in spite of her parents' reluctance) the town's two doctors Elias Mc-Namee and Hiram Decker. All three of these agents of mercy had survived, thanks be to God.

Joan had for several years been assisting Miss Thoreau with the beginning class at her school. Even the littlest girls studied the basic school curriculum: reading, writing, spelling, and arithmetic. Spelling was diligently taught throughout the state now in subscription schools and contests held to encourage the subject. After the youngest students learned these basics, they would learn more of them along with English grammar, history, science, arts, ancient and modern languages, and, of course, French.

Those boys attending the academy with lower-level courses progressed to Vincennes University, with some few going east to college or, as of last year, to the state-organized state seminary in Corydon. Sometimes, as in the case of Peter Cooper, older boys did not go on to university work but took advanced courses right at the academy.

One day in 1821 a spelling match was to take place at the academy, which is how Vincennes University described itself when speaking of its younger students. Miss Marie Thoreau and Reverend Samuel T. Scott were to do the pronouncing. Each school had its partisans. Word had been passed around that fifteen of the academy's best spellers and fifteen young women from the girls' school would be competing. Other spellers in the town might enter at the beginning, but it was supposed that as the more difficult words were reached midway in the contest, the casual entries would drop out. However, sometimes these dark-horse spellers would finish high up in the race. This was especially true when an older student made an intensive study of words for the purpose of entering the match. Each good speller at each school and each dark horse also had his or her individual rooters who took their places at school desks in the center of the room to cheer on their favorites.

The would-be champions went to stand around the outer walls of the largest room in the academy. The two pronouncers were posted at the far end of the room and were supposed to keep distant from each other. The words were read, spelled, and if a mistake was made, there were groans, and the candidate who failed the word dropped out. The others filled up the gaps.

Miss Thoreau was a stickler for adhering to proper methodology. The spelling books which were used—for instance Noah Webster's American Spelling Book—started with short, easy words, and as the leaves of the pages were turned the words were harder and harder to spell. Sometimes the pronouncers would turn pages rapidly to get to the difficult words. Trick words, proper names, or foreign words were avoided, and so the spelling bees were in English. The pronouncer was supposed to know the pronunciation and meaning of the words that were presented. A teacher stood in the middle of the room with a dictionary in hand, ready to arbitrate any dispute or correct a mistake.

On the evening of this match, the spellers started well. No one was in a hurry. Page after page of the spelling book was turned with very few candidates having to step down, but after about half an hour, the spellers began to drop out. The contestants had studied the spelling book for days, and they were proving their worth. The word "syzygy" took a couple of contestants down. One boy asked Miss Thoreau for the meaning, and with much care she explained that it might be defined as a point at which the moon was in conjunction or opposition to the sun.

Joan relieved all the spellers beyond her by spelling it quickly, and the race then progressed at a more rapid pace. The race was settling down to about a half dozen good spellers. Reverend Scott and Miss Thoreau now discarded the book in favor of a selected list of words which the spellers had had no time to study. Soon two young people stood side by side before the anxious crowd. Joan was the champion for the girls' school, and Peter was upholding the reputation of the academy, Vincennes University's first-level program. Miss Thoreau and the professor were recognized as partisans, and it would not do for them to pronounce any longer. The former Catholic priest Father Jean-jean, who was visiting for the month, assumed that duty. He had prepared his own list of words, and there were no rules with respect to the words he had chosen—foreign words and proper names were acceptable.

Many in the crowd smiled. Peter and Joan had come to the spelling match together. They had talked of other things on the walk from "the house at the end of the road" (which was no longer the end of the road, as new homes were being built). The town knew that they were good friends on the way to being sweethearts and approved. The priest stepped into place. Joan and Peter looked all concentration. They could not sense the particular interest of the spectators, some cheering for one, some for another. Of course Minerva and Hiram Cooper were cheering on their boy, and Mary and Virginia Simpson and their parents clapped for the former Koo-wa.

Father Jean-jean, the priest called by this familiar name by all, pronounced the word "exegesis," meaning an interpretation of a text or passage from the Bible by analysis of its context. Peter knew it was spelled with a "c" or an "x" for the second letter, but he wasn't clear which. Joan felt the same way, confused. Peter spelled it with a "c" and was out. Joan spelled it with an "x" and was therefore proclaimed the victor. Miss Thoreau's school was the winner, and the priest grabbed Joan in his arms for a congratulatory embrace. Peter would have liked to have done the same.

"I'm glad we both got to the last round there," Peter said to Joan as they walked home. "It meant I got to stand next to you longer." He smiled, and she knew that would be the end of the conversation about the spelling bee.

Peter Cooper was of a serious turn of mind, and his dear friend knew this. She also knew that being a miller was his life and that he had grown quite good at it. He had been told that his father's ancestors had been millers near Kittanning in Pennsylvania. During his boyhood he had spent much of his time at the mill playing at, and later grinding, corn and wheat. As his father Hiram grew older, he sometimes said he wanted to put aside some of the responsibilities of running the mill. That day never seemed to come. Hiram was so accustomed to an active life and could not think what he would do with himself around home that he did not consider leaving the mill. Peter had suggested some changes and enlargement of the mill, but his father brushed them off, not seeing the necessity. They made a good living and supplied the community with corn and wheat, so what more could anyone want? Some of the Cooper flour went down the river in fine white ash barrels, but not enough to satisfy the son. "I can operate this mill by myself, Father, and I'm rarin' to go," Peter said, but his father only smiled. "The wheel is strong enough for two sets of burrs," said his boy, now such a fine young man.

"I could do a selling job for us downriver, I know," he insisted, but he could not persuade his father that the business needed to grow. Peter had long talks with Professor Scott, the minister at his Presbyterian church and head of the academy, though Peter would now be leaving, deciding not to take courses at the university but to pursue his trade.

Mr. Scott was of Scottish descent, and he believed in the old adages "Shielded sons never make strong men" and "Self-reliance is the pathway to success." Scott was good at adages. Peter had looked into the places where better, modern machinery could be bought. "Our Cooper brand of flour is and should always be the best, and it should be sold through the Midwest," he stoutly stated to his mother and father at home during their evenings, but his ideas fell upon non-interested ears. Only Joan thought these ideas for the future had merit.

Chapter 17

Independence Day
1822

The "Birth of the Nation" was celebrated each year in Vincennes, as it was in most American towns. No other frontier village had better reason to celebrate; Vincennes had participated directly in both the revolution and the War of 1812. Many citizens in the town on the Wabash could speak directly to the hardships and dangers involved in making the nation what it was now. Some older people recalled that time less than half a century ago when the Liberty Bell had rung and then the thrilling days when George Rogers Clark had recaptured the town from the British and the War of Independence really reached the Wabash.

This year the town would celebrate with appropriate feasting, contests, speechifying, and general rejoicing. Some of that rejoicing, secret perhaps, was over the fact that the capital of the state that had been taken from Vincennes had now been shifted from Corydon. That uppity little town was going to find itself having tit for tat: the capital was being moved to some small village in the central Indiana wilderness, in the upper White River boglands. The only roads to this place, which would be called Indiana-polis, city of the Indians, were Indian paths. The legislature was already talking of a road, a highway, to connect Madison with the Michigan border. Those who wanted work, and there were plenty of them since hard times had come in 1819, from surveyors to road builders, were interested in the project. It made Vincennes realize the future was fast upon them.

Vincennes would celebrate Independence Day on a favorite recreational pond south of town. Near this Otter Pond was a highland with shady groves, which made an ideal picnic spot. Descendants of the families who had delighted in taking food to the rebelling soldiers took delight in taking their baskets of food to the picnic grounds. Each year the Fourth of July event had become more of a civic affair, and Joan, her sisters, and her parents looked forward to it with eagerness. The Cooper family and the Simpson family rowed boats across the pond and ate together.

When the remains of the luncheon picnic had been put in baskets, the Vincennes Guards band played "Hail Columbia," "Jefferson's March," and other rousing songs. Then a local doctor made a speech in which he compared the young country to Greece and Rome and praised and read the Declaration of Independence, every word. He called it a flowing fountain of freedom. He spoke at length, in the custom of the time, reliving military achievements, particularly of the War of 1812, which many from the town could all too well recall. He predicted a glowing future, praised President James Monroe, and asked God for continued tranquility for the nation. As the speech went on, Joan and Peter found themselves rolling their eyes. They wanted to see the horse races and visit the circus stands further back behind the picnic grove, where ring-the-canes and the knock-down-babies stalls had been set up. If the constable were diligent, he might find a few games of chance with wagering going on in the thicket back of the grove and an improvised spirit bar where the thirsty could quench their thirst and drown their sorrows.

The game-play stands would be those of Pepin and Barnett's Circus. They had planned their circuit so that they could arrive at the Fourth of July celebration. They had come up the Wabash by boat the morning before and had given a trained monkey show in the town. Local people had seen the posters plastered on buildings and were prepared, old and young, to go to the small part of the circus they had brought across to the picnic ground by Otter Pond, just the performing horses and the games. The rest would be left near the town's center for a week or so of performances.

As Joan and Peter walked through the edge of the grove, they stopped in front of the ticket booth. "The *Western Sun* said the menagerie back in town will have a lion," Peter said. "We can see it tomorrow."

"Maybe a tiger, a lion, and zebra, too," Joan commented. "But I love the monkeys best of all." The wild animals had been unloaded in the common area the night before, but each cage was closed during the evening, so no one could see very much. "Get an admission ticket," the barker had said in a surly voice when the townspeople crowded round tried to get a free look. "But go ahead and watch the circus unload," he said to the children, who were looking crestfallen.

Today the crowd was ready for the horseback-riding show. The Simpsons had brought along Miss Marie Thoreau. She was particularly interested in the beautiful performing horses that were ridden bareback around the equestrian ring. Mary Simpson, being her usual exuberant self, said she could not wait to see the antics of the monkeys, particularly the one named "Dandy Jack," and the chariot races that would go on tomorrow at the larger show in town. Walking around afterwards to see the booths, they purchased candied roasted pecans in paper cones.

Young ladies wore their bright summer dresses, with slightly high waists and puffy sleeves, and young men wore trousers and cotton vests. A rude and puffing steamboat had brought the circus into town and was docked, ready to carry the crew on. The town itself was deserted during all the picnicking and speech-making and bareback riding.

As the afternoon advanced into evening, many were back out on the water of Otter Pond. The Simpson and Cooper families both had their own small boats and had brought them in wagons. Every member of each family knew how to take care of him or herself on the water. Peter was just developing into the independent stage of life when he must own his own boat; he had saved from his earnings enough to purchase one of those new light craft skiffs that were said to be safe and easy to manage. It had been arranged several days before this that Peter and the three Simpson girls would give the new skiff its maiden tryout.

The young people had a world of fun at the picnic and circus, but somehow Peter wondered how it could be arranged that he and Joan might come home alone. It was not a very proper thing for a young couple to be alone upon the pond in a boat after dark, and yet there would be many boats coming and going. Wouldn't it be all right? The town would probably suspend judgment for this one celebratory summer evening.

Virginia and Mary had plans of their own for going home. Donald Estridge, a young man in his twenties who was going to school at Transylvania College to become a doctor, was bringing Virginia nosegays and walking out with her, and he was here at the celebration. In fact, these two sisters had definitely put their minds to determining who they would like to take them home. They could also take home the Simpson parents, Peter reasoned.

As the afternoon wore down, Peter managed to slip the words to Joan that he hoped they could have a boat ride and take the Simpson family wagon home. Joan let him know that her sisters had made their own arrangements and probably could add the parents. Joan would, of course, have to ask her mother. She was young and had never had a serious beau, although for a long time remarks had been exchanged at the Simpson house that Joan was seeing no one but Peter. He was older than she, of course, but had been friends with this family for many years and now counted Joan as a special friend. And she was a blossoming young woman. Still—there was agreement in the Simpson family that this old friend of the family would be perfectly all right to bring Joan home in his boat. "Of course," said Sarah Simpson. "I'm not sure Peter can find his way across this pond, and you are probably needed to help him. With two oars and a determination to get across, I'm sure you will make it," she said merrily. She had a parting word. "Tonight is a special night. You must be sure to go to the other side by the time the fireworks display is over."

Joan and Peter rowed out, and the pond was full of boats. It seemed that every young couple at the picnic had the same notion. The fireworks lasted until ten o'clock, and the young couple did not need to hurry. It all seemed so natural, and the families thought so, too. Mrs. Simpson did not want her girls to see young men until they were sixteen. Joan was sixteen now and Peter would soon be twenty-two, and the other two already had more than one beau. They were all so fresh and beautiful that you could not keep young men away from them.

The current was not strong, as the pond was low at this time of year. Still, the canoe did not navigate the pond well. It had a tendency to go backwards; it would need to be looked at. The craft would make a good start and then get out of control and float towards shore. Peter would adjust the boat and make some headway towards home and then quickly lose all gains. The odd thing was it had not been so stubborn on the way out, but then the wind had come up since then. They did not worry; they were comfortable together. Something about the festivities of the day and the calmness of this starlit night made them realize they had a lot to talk about.

Finally, Peter rested his oars on the shore under the drooping branches of an oak tree. "Joan, I've never really talked seriously to you. We have had our fun, with others and by ourselves. Here, come sit by me. There's room for two here."

They sat together in silence a moment, and then Peter spoke. "I've watched you grow up. Miss Thoreau has always kept a watchful eye on you. She seems partial—no, don't deny it. I got jealous of her for she gets to see you so much and I so little."

Joan was silent a moment, then said softly, "Peter, we have promised my parents that I would be home tonight—right about now. The boat is still here on the other side of this pond, and is against the bank. I know what we should do. I'll row with one of these oars and you with the other. We better start towards home."

Peter nodded. "With the both of us working, perhaps we can make this tub go forward." She smiled and shook her head at his name for his new possession.

"You know I can go with you again in this boat when it is behaving better. My parents will let us ride—and do other things. I know they will."

"Joan, I'll get to the point. Your idea of us both rowing is working, and we will get to the shore, so I'll talk fast. I want us to be sweethearts. I want us to plan a future together." They both labored at the oars. "Talk fast, Joan, so we can row back home," Peter said. "What do you think of what I just said?"

"Well, you know it is said silence gives consent, so I suppose it isn't necessary for me to talk." She smiled. "It's also true you are doing quite well on your own, but—I don't know what Mother might think if you come often if, as you say, we are sweethearts. Yet I know she likes you."

They pulled together and the boat fairly flew to the opposite shore where the horse and wagon were waiting. Peter said, "Wouldn't it always be good if we could pull together, Joan? You haven't answered my question. What do you say? Sweethearts? And solve all of our problems together, as we have rowed this boat?" They had reached the town shore. Gently he helped her from the boat. The crowd had gone. They climbed the bank and walked down the road hand in hand to the horse and wagon.

When they reached the front gate, he took her in his arms and heard her say, "Yes. For always."

Chapter 18

Planning
1824

Spring came unusually early to Vincennes in the year of 1824. The vernal equinoxial storms were nothing more than gentle April showers. Winter had released her vise-like grip several weeks ago, and now in mid-April the sun had long since driven away the blanket of snow and changed the surroundings to bright green velvet. Last fall's leaves looked like lace as shards of grass pushed up through them.

Cold, clear water flowed from a brook, gurgling over little boulders and around larger ones. Joan and Peter strolled near it along the River Road, watching birds spring around. They laughed that robin husbands were building their new nest homes, aided by brown-clad, hopping wives. Blackbirds lined up on a low, thick branch of the tallest forest tree in their path scolded and chattered. As the birds left the one tall tree to wheel, circle, and then land on another nearby, Peter said, "It's all confusion today, but it will be only a short time until they divide in pairs and you'll see the couples building nests of sticks and straws and dry grass." He looked up. "They always seem to go to the highest limb."

Joan pointed toward a fallen log, and they sat down. At their feet, with squirrels hurrying nearby, were spring beauties, violets, trillium, and the last of the Dutchman's breeches. "The redbud is lovely," Joan said. "And soon we'll see white banks, like snow, of dogwood blossoms."

"You love flowers, don't you, Joan?" Peter said. "You must stop with me at my house. Mother has some bright yellow flowers she is raising for you, jonquils." Joan took his hand. His face was thoughtful.

"Father wants us to stay here and take over the mill. Do you suppose we should? He says he will turn everything over to us if we stay—if we will only stay—in Vincennes."

"We could do that," Joan said, "but the town seems to have stagnated. I don't like to say it, but it's true. I suppose it was because of the epidemic—people coming into Indiana or resettling are afraid of our marshes, unhealthy climate, with the doctors talking about the garbage and waste running into low places causing bad vapors—miasma which leads to disease."

"I know. Enterprises are settling in Evansville instead of here. Still, they keep saying that opportunities here are good and businesses will flourish again. And we have a mill already established and thriving." She sensed the doubt in his voice. She had heard it before. He finished his thought. "In spite of the steam mill which so flourished for a while. I try not to be glad it went under, like the bank. Both of them probably deserved it. I'll try to run my business in a fair and upright way."

"The old tried and true Cooper mill goes on. But in the future not you with it?"

He sat silent for a moment, then spoke. "When I came into their lives, Mother and Father took me as the very own son they could never have, and so I have been. When I was kidnapped, their life seemed to go out, like a snuffed candle, they said, and when I was returned, they could never express their gratitude except in prayer. When they say things like that—" he was silent, almost brooding.

"And you think it would be an act of ingratitude for you, us, to leave them and strike out to find a home somewhere else. Isn't that it?" Joan said, moving leaves aside with her shoe.

"Beyond that—my parents have been fascinated with you, your time with the Indians, your return here, your success in school. They have been so interested in you that they have invited Miss Thoreau to our home merely to have a talk about you."

"They often visited us, asking about me. They seem, like half this town, to continue to wonder about my natural parents, what they did after I was stolen. I too wish I knew, but I think I never will. My own family has filled my life." She turned to him with a sweet smile. "Along with you."

"I cannot allow myself to live in another time and with unanswered questions," she continued. "I might go insane if I dwelt on that. I have my life here, and I have you, Peter." He put his arm around her.

"My parents believe your parents are still living and will someday come to claim their little girl."

Joan looked earnestly at him. "But I am not their little girl, am I? I am a young woman of Vincennes, and my parents are named James and Sarah Simpson. And my love is Peter Cooper, here in Indiana. Nothing can change that. Still . . ." She was silent, then went on. "Sometimes I think of the north country, where they say I may have been born."

"I feel sure," Peter interrupted, "you did not come from Quebec. Miss Thoreau wrote all the papers in that area advertising, giving your approximate age and a general description."

"I too doubt it. But in our library at home are a number of my grandfather's books. In one is a picture painted by someone—General Wolfe scaling the walls of Quebec. I have loved to read how he arrived with his fleet to meet General Montcalm." Her eyes were far away. "How he found a path among the rocks and in the darkness climbed the steep cliff and at daybreak appeared before the French general on the Plains of Abraham."

"Well, the British took the city, and both generals died. You'd better not let Miss Thoreau hear you talk about that Englishman Wolfe as a hero. No, you are not from there."

"And you?" Joan said, looking at him with kindness and love. "You too were taken."

"That woman who took me for whatever reason loved me for only a little while. She yearned for me and then realized she had hurt others to get the child she took from them and then—brought me back. But perhaps she is still around. No one has ever pictured my mother as other than a proud, unfortunate woman. I can remember nothing about those days except those big, red apples. Sometimes I have a feeling she may be watching me, especially when I have been in big crowds or at times when I have participated in some entertainment before the public, like when the circus came to town. I have no doubt she lives near Vincennes. Think of it! There is a hole in my heart for that woman that can never quite be filled. And so I am always looking, looking, for a beautiful but sad woman I don't know and surely wouldn't recognize."

"And in mine for the parents of my birth." She looked into his eyes. "We are so alike. One's early childhood, whatever it is, marks us deeply, and if there was pain, we have a scar we carry for the rest of our lives. But"—and here she was very firm—"it is much grown over, and love makes us strong and living on with hope and a real future!"

As an afterthought, she added, "Still, you know, I have always believed, really feared, that my father and mother would one day come and claim me. What would I do? Father and Mother Simpson would never have given me up. Well, we will be married soon, and then all four will give me up to you!"

They walked back along the springtime trail, happy to be together.

"And as for our staying or going, I would be happy either way. I want you to know that your father and mother have asked me to persuade you to stay in Vincennes. I know you want to be independent. I know you want to own your own mill and that you are ambitious to make a superior grade of flour, to sell that everywhere. I do understand and sympathize with that."

"Joan, let's set the wedding date soon, before these beautiful summer days are over. Then let's take a wedding trip down the river. My parents always wanted to do that." She knew he was thinking of the day he had been left in the basket; often Minerva and Hiram had told the story of that night, sitting and talking of a trip to New Orleans, and afterwards hearing a noise.

He went on. "I'm not talking about New Orleans. I have arranged for a new boat, and I think we can take it down to Harmonie. We'll have a delightful time. Live out of doors, camp, free ourselves of care for a few days."

Joan considered this. She knew the town of Harmonie, farther down the Wabash. She wondered how she would do sleeping in a tent.

"And as for the future beyond that—of course I love Mother and Father. But Father is fixed in his ways, and as he grows older, he becomes more determined. It would break his heart to change anything out at the mill at all, even in the smallest particular. He does not utilize all the waterpower at the millrace and could improve the grade of his grinding as well as the quality of the grist, the cornmeal and wheat flower. We are working in the last century. We could easily place more burrs and grinders, but he will not even give it a serious thought. We could be supplying customers all the way down the river. The new steam mills in some places are working, in spite of the failure here, and they claim steam operation is more economical than water, even when there is an ample supply of water the year round. I hear they have the latest in steam machinery in Harmonie, not too far from us."

"And that is why—" Joan looked at him.

"Only part of the reason for the wedding trip there."

He seemed to still want to say more about his father and himself and their disagreement. "He often talks about advancement in the world and how he built up the business himself grinding better flour and building up trade, and yet he cannot see how I might want to do the same." He stopped and looked at her. "I don't want to seem ungrateful."

"You are not," she assured him.

"If he had his way entirely, I would stay and use the same old wheel and the same old machinery all my work life. That wheel is good for a hundred years, he says! He tells of the timbers and how they are joined, the name of the man who did the carpenter work. I don't want to hear that, Joan." He stopped while they watched a fox run up the path. He turned to her. "Joan, we must go away and try out our own hands and minds. If it isn't Harmonie, there are the wilderness lands. We need not go across the country. Transportation is improving, and we can see our parents. Roads are being built, and the stage now goes across the Buffalo Trace. Think of that. We who count Vincennes home are fortunate." His eyes were far off. "Still, the country is developing like corn sprouting up in the spring after rain. Just a few counties from us, over there north and east, is wilderness, land amidst hills and streams for mills. We could settle there." He smiled, thoughtfully. "Or risk it downriver."

Joan finally spoke. "Peter, I am glad you've said this so firmly now. Of course I couldn't have been with you and not known of your wishes and plans, but we will soon be married and decisions will have to be made. You know I will also hate to leave Father and Mother. When they took me in they thought I was a little Indian child. It turned out not to be that way, but I really think if I had had red skin they would have loved me the same. They are dear, kindhearted people. And how can I leave Miss Thoreau? All those years she came to my rescue and put me in the school and has been always at my side. She loves me not any less than my mother and father, although I do see that since you have often been with me, she has stepped aside lately. But as I dream for the future, I think of that land some are telling us about, where pleasant streams, mysterious rivers, hills that are almost mountains, and virgin woods and farmland are beckoning to us. Let us cling to our loved ones now for a while, even more than we have in the past, and then pursue our future. Ruth said, 'Whither thou goest, I will go, where thou lodgest, I will lodge.' That is what I will do, also." She smiled. "I didn't mean to quote scripture at you like Mr. Scott." They walked on, laughing. "First Harmonie and the steam mill—we shall think on that and make a decision when it comes to us that it is right."

In early summer Peter and Joan sat in the grotto which James Simpson had built in the flower garden of his home. Honeysuckles covered this bower, which had always been called by the girls their retreat. In summer the scent of the honeysuckle mingled with the perfume of the roses. It was a little paradise of greenery in June. The sweethearts often sat to talk in this little cove, and tonight they were deeply in earnest. They were planning their future. There were a couple of choices: to locate and to stay here, as well, but Harmonie was on both their minds. It seemed so adventuresome.

"Have you come to know more about Harmonie, Peter? That religious group there is certainly not of a traditional denomination. The Rappites, the Harmonists—they seem to me like the Shakers who are out on the road north of Vincennes and still holding on to their community. But rumor has it that they are not flourishing. That they will be gone, disbanded here. What a flurry they have caused!"

"There are plenty of Shakers elsewhere, but they are a bit like the Harmonists in that they believe Christ is coming in our own times and that men and women should be separated. It's a celibate society, no need for children at the Second Coming." He looked up, then thought to correct himself. "There are children there—some families came in with them to join the sect. And they do take in orphans. But the Rappites are said to be restless again, thinking of moving. They hold everything in common in their community, and they are trying to get someone to succeed them there at Harmonie on the Wabash, a group which believes in common ownership. I hear there are great opportunities awaiting those who will join this new society. Rumors are that Father Rapp has sent his representative to Scotland, negotiating with a man named Robert Owen of New Lanark."

"What is Owen's religion?" Joan wanted to know.

"He does not believe in God. That I do not care for, but…I noticed a statement made by Owen and published in our paper which sounds very interesting."

"What did it say?"

"Owen said that he was coming into this territory to introduce an entire new state of society, to change it from an ignorant, selfish system to an enlightened social system. He thinks that his new common community system will gradually unite all interests into one and remove all conflict between individuals."

"That would be good if it could happen," Joan said uncertainly.

"Well, I never had any faith in the old owner. After ten years of apparently successful operation of the communal plan, the old man up and sells out at a handsome profit. When George Rapp came to Harmonie in 1814, he had a large amount of money, and he is still flush with cash and going back to Pennsylvania to try it all over again where he started. "

They had stopped to look at the river. "You doubt his motives?" Joan asked.

"He knows how to work his people, that is certain. He seems to have gotten his original ideas in Wurttemberg, Germany. He crossed the ocean and formed a religious communal society in Butler County there in Pennsylvania about twenty-five miles from Pittsburgh."

"Not too far from where my mother says my grandparents grew up," Joan said.

Peter went on. "Rapp moved to the Wabash with nine hundred men. He built several strong and even beautiful buildings. It's reported he had a good architect. Separate dorms for the men and women, yes, and a brewery, a distillery, and granaries."

"I seem to have seen some goods they made sold in stores here."

"Yes, they put up factories which made shoes, hats, saddlery, linen, cotton goods—many other things. Robert Owen has many of the same ideas as Rapp, but he leaves out the religion. 'All things will be held in common and no one shall own property. All shall work for the common good.' They will need a miller, and seem to have the money to supply one in the latest ways."

"Common ownership? How will that work out in practice, Peter? Lots of us here in town, including your own dad and mine, have made a success because they wanted to get ahead of the pack."

"They say money will be held by one treasurer, all things shall be sold by one agent, and everything shall be cleared through the one head office, Owen. All will work together in the fields and factories. Owen has tried a factory system like that in Scotland." He shrugged his shoulders, then smiled. "I wonder who will fork up the manure."

"Well, Peter, let us take our wedding trip there at Harmonie, or New Harmony as it may be now," Joan said. "You can see the steam mill. And if we do not like it for our settlement, then there is—the deep forest." Soon it would be time to ceremonially seal their union.

Into the Deep Forest, 1825

"Joan, when did time begin here? When was this land formed? What a shame we have no recorded history, so that we can learn more of this land. How many thousands of years of silence lie before us? Will the wind or the trees or the stream ever be able to tell us what has gone before in this beautiful valley"? —Peter with the Conestoga train in the Deep Forest
Photo: Hoosier National Forest at sunrise.

These settlers were seeing a forest which had rarely been viewed by the eye of a white man. . . If the forest trees could have spoken, they might well have said, seeing these newcomers, that they realized the time had come for their destruction, as their fellows had fallen in other parts of this area. Where their shade was deepest, the men would choose spots for their homes. . . These stately giants would wonder, should they be able to talk, why in a short time this enemy who claimed to be civilized would lay waste that which it has taken centuries, eons, to produce.—The Author

Photo: Giant tulip tree, 1920s from the Sycamore Land Trust

Chapter 19

The Wedding and Vistas Beyond the Wabash
1824–1825

Joan and her parents had thought the wedding would be a simple one at the Simpson home. Miss Thoreau, though, insisted that the people of Vincennes would be as interested as the family were; townspeople were a part of the larger family of these two. It had been thirteen years since Koowa had appeared as a little Indian girl and was led up the street by her two new sisters and twenty-four years since Peter was found on a millstone in the early hours of the morning, but the town would never forget.

Friends wished to be part of the nuptials and volunteered their services, hoping to be invited. Marie Thoreau offered the big porch of the home that was now hers. "Joan and I often taught on this porch with the little girls, and it is a beautiful place for a wedding," she said. "And in addition I want to give Joan a gift of the wedding dress and the wedding bower where they will be married." The Simpsons were pleased, realizing that this woman was more than an aunt to their daughter.

Miss Thoreau came to the Simpson house every day as the plans unfolded. Joan's schoolmates would attend and would sing a little French wedding song. The wedding would be held at dusk, under the giant old elm tree in the front yard, with the flower bower placed so all could see. Flowers from the Cooper yard would furnish the side decorations. Minerva and Hiram were included in the planning and were selecting the types of blooms from their own garden. All the town could attend, inside if rain came, but a small family reception would be held afterwards. Pastor Scott, who had been Peter's teacher, would unite the couple in the bonds of wedlock. The old professor entered into the plans as if he were a youngster. Joan's sisters were her bridesmaids. Sarah Simpson and a dressmaker in town, donating her services, were busy sewing lace and ribbon onto satin.

The day came in late summer. Bouquets of flowers grown in local gardens and donated by well wishers lined the path, adding to the Simpsons' flowers, and through them Jim Simpson would lead his daughter to meet her new husband. The minister, in a long, starched white robe with an ecclesiastical band of linen and a black scarf-tie around his neck, welcomed the pair under the tree, the bride in a light lavender dress as simple as her life had been beautiful. The pair said age-old vows and were declared man and wife. The crowd lingered until nightfall came in full, then slowly left with a prayer in their hearts, and, indeed, the evening star did shine on the scene with blessing.

New Harmony was unusual and pretty as a site for the wedding trip, in spite of rain flowing into the tent, but not as a permanent home for settling. Both felt it immediately: the atmosphere of the communal town, now in the process of change, was interesting to witness, but not what they wished. They inspected the site for the steam mill and talked to its engineer, then bade goodbye to the community. And so it was they set their eyes and their course toward the deep forest and a new life. As Joan's parents had struck out into new vistas and opportunities, so would they. Thus has it been for many in every generation.

They were going to build a new community in the hill, river, and spring lands north and east of the old licks, where the Indian camps had been. They would start at daybreak on the anniversary of Bastille Day, July 14, 1825, still celebrated by a few people in their town. This might be the last time these travelers would be affected by any French customs, for there would probably be few Frenchmen in the new settlement. Land was available in a few good spots in the timberlands, and they would find and secure it.

Twelve families with all their earthly possessions were to be on the commons at the east edge of the town to begin the pilgrimage to the land of promise in one of the counties established in 1815 or 1816. Two extra wagons would come along to carry provisions and tools to build the cabins of the new community. Most wagons were covered with white canvas, which was to protect the voyagers from rain and sun, each wagon drawn by one or more yoke of oxen. Some of these wagons were new, painted blue with red wheels and fully equipped; others were farm wagons in a poor state of repair and hardly fit for a long journey. Some families had extra horses for emergency, and these were usually ridden by the guides. Cows, goats, and sheep were tied behind the wagons, with chickens, geese, and ducks in cages attached to the outside of the wagons. The dogs ran loose. Furniture, cooking utensils, farming implements, and provisions left little space for the old grandparents in the wagons. Everyone else walked. Some of the families had camped at the outskirts of the town for some time before the starting day, for a number them had come from several miles around.

Peter looked at the sorry state, thrown-together looking, of a few of the wagons. That some of these families would need help was evident from the first day. Peter and Joan, living as newlyweds in the Cooper house, had made their plans for a year, and they were starting well equipped. Peter had two good draft horses, two yoke of oxen, several cows, sheep, and plenty of tools to start work from the first day. It would be necessary to have all kinds of carpentry tools to build a cabin. Of course, Peter intended to start building a mill as soon as the settlers were housed. He had purchased a large covered wagon in which to make the trip. The white canvas-top wagons were conspicuous this morning. He had urged all the settlers to avoid the largest wagons because they would be clumsy to maneuver on the narrow roads to the east. The preparations, shouting from wagon to wagon, and quacking and whinnying and oinking of animals and general excitement in the air attracted the attention of the crowd assembled to see the party leave.

As the party was to start at sunrise, it meant that each team must be harnessed or yoked by four-thirty. There had been little sleep the night before, so it made little difference how early the train would move. Friends and relatives had assembled around the campfires the evening before because the settlers were going a long way and would not be seen again for some time. As the bonfires blazed, the voyagers were serenaded. The singing and frolic went on all night. All were ready when a large red sun began to show on the eastern horizon, overcoming the lights from the embers of the campfires. It made no difference that the day would be a long one; this was a farewell party. The travelers could sleep some time later after bidding their friends goodbye. Although many tears were shed and many hands squeezed, all felt that the new home would not be too far away, that roads would soon be built, and that relatives would visit them before many years. These people felt that family ties need not be broken, for the land of promise which was to be their new home was only a little more than a hundred miles away, and possibly less. Merchants would soon follow the settlers. The home-seekers would be sending their products to all markets. Peter and Joan felt sure the stage would soon follow. It had already reached Paoli, and efforts were being made to extend the stage road through the hills to Hindostan Falls and on to Vincennes. Already a new road was in the course of construction from Madison toward the new capital of the state.

Land for miles about Vincennes had been patented by the government at an early date, so those wanting more or better land must go into the interior of the state or west to the prairies. Many settlers were coming from the east and south, claiming the rich land of central Indiana and of Illinois. Wagon trains with people unwilling to battle the forests were passing through Vincennes, bound for farther west. The ferry at Vincennes was doing a good business helping these homesteaders cross the Wabash, where they made their way to the broad fields of tall grass. The big drawback to the prairies was the lack of building materials. The settlers had to be content, at least at first, with rude cabins. Those who lived in this sort of lean-to were soon dissatisfied, and the sawmills east of the Wabash were doing a big business cutting timber, producing two by fours, and carting them by ox teams farther west. The land through which Peter and Joan were to travel was mostly forest, but settlers for a long time had been trying to make a go of it among the trees. Some were succeeding, but many had given up and moved on. The land even beyond the forks of White River had been settled in a large measure. New cabins and farmsteads were spreading out in every direction. But a little farther north, amidst an area of caves and springs and tall hills, there was land that could be good for farming and it was still almost empty. They would buy land when they found the spot of promise.

On this morning the friends and members of the different groups were standing around the wagons, offering words of cheer and encouragement. Advice was freely given and quickly forgotten, but all the folks knew that the bystanders intended to be helpful. Those heading into the wagons made promises to write soon, for the relatives and friends left behind would want to know about the roads, the new homes, the dangers of the trip, the wild game, and encounters with wild animals.

Peter and Joan's family stayed all night at the camp. Around this family circle were many of their friends, but those who stayed through the night were the closest relatives. Jim and Sarah had little to say, but there was a big lump in their throats. Virginia and her husband Donald Estridge, a doctor, would like to have gone along, but Donald tried to be on call at all hours. Mary's husband Ellis Vyborg had an established provisioning business in

Vincennes, so somewhat sadly, Mary said goodbye to her sister.

Miss Thoreau was almost silent all night; she had hardly a word to say. Tears were more common than words with the Simpson family at this hour. Joan was going into the great forest out of which had come so many weird and strange stories. When the big trees would close around this couple and when they were lost from sight, the dear ones felt that their little girl would be going into another world, that she would not come back again for a long time, if ever. Never was a long time, and life would never be the same without the ones going off in the wagons. A hundred miles down the river didn't sound frightful, but a hundred miles into the center of the big forest seemed as if Joan were entering a cave of unknown size.

Hiram and Minerva Cooper were, of course, in the farewell throng. They watched their big boy as he gave directions. By unanimous vote of the party on the evening before, he had been made captain of the caravan. Peter would drive one of his wagons, and a neighbor boy would drive the other. On that morning, as Peter moved among the homesteaders, he seemed so confident, the parents proudly told each other. Many were coming to him for directions and encouragement. As starting time came nearer, Hiram and Minerva reproached themselves for not turning the mill over to their boy and letting him have full responsibility. Peter had never made complaint. He did not want his father to know the real reason for seeking a new site, but Minerva, at least, seemed to know by intuition. "Would it have been possible," she whispered to her husband, "to have him back in our home as our boy, or married later, down the road, if we had turned the mill over to him?" That opportunity was gone. He was married now, and this couple needed their own life path. Of course, they would go to see him, and he would return home when he could, but that big dense forest they spoke of seemed so black and far away.

Miss Thoreau was always brave when courage was needed, but this morning when she realized things would never be the same again, there was a load upon her heart. Someone else had claimed her little girl. She had not slept a wink all night, although she went to the big wagon and lay down for a time. She took no part in the singing and hilarity that kept up all night, never could lose sight of the fact that Joan was going away where she could not see her often and where she would no longer have her as a confidante.

Just before dawn, as there was a reddish glow in the eastern sky, Miss

Thoreau had climbed out of the wagon. Joan was not going nearly so far away as Louisiana or France, she told herself firmly, but it seemed so much farther. Miss Thoreau debated whether or not she would have courage to go on with her work with the school as in the past. She had planned for Joan to be her assistant for the years to come. In all of her plans, she had thought of a capable and good man who would claim her Joan for his wife, but she had pictured Joan and her husband on the streets and by the river in Vincennes. She had thought she would walk down the street to visit Joan often, see her in her own home and with her own babies. Perhaps at some point she could visit in their new homeland, but it seemed so far away. She knew Joan was strong in mind and body, that she was capable and courageous, and that her future would be bright, but she was not ready for this moment of separation. A girl who was more than her niece and best friend was moving out of sight and into the deep forest.

Some of the party had joined because of their confidence in Peter's judgment. Even before Peter had been selected as the captain, others had come to him with their problems. There were plenty of troublesome details to solve even before a wagon turned a wheel. All had been told that if they expected to complete the journey, they must extend a helping hand to others day after day when help was needed. This was a communal undertaking. This morning, the hopes of the party were high, their intentions were good, and all were determined to succeed.

Each wagon had been assigned a position in the train. This would be a lengthy trip, although only a hundred miles. Horses could ride over it in a few days, but a wagon train lumbered on slow and steady, through rutted and often impassable roads and often bogged down. It was well known that the speed of the caravan would be determined by the slowest member. The positions had been assigned and taken last evening. Every wagon would be in place as soon as the whips began to crack. It was not necessary that the wagons be in close formation, for each family was to keep its wagon moving and in its proper place. Some of the outriders, who had the best horses, were assigned places in the rear. A number of these horses were already harnessed, so they would be quickly available if needed. The signal was given, and the entire train began to slowly start down the road.

The long white train began to move eastward along the only road leading toward White Oaks Springs at the forks in the two branches of White

River, the road taken years ago when Peter was missing. Some older people in the crowd thought of that trip, when the Indians had been insulted. The people of Vincennes were scattered along the route for more than two miles. Some had driven out along the highway to be able to bid a goodbye to their friends, lining the track. All stood in silence except for the waving of hands and the calling of "Goodbye" and "Good luck." The drivers felt proud. The sharp crack of the long whips which whirled above the oxen's head could be heard like the report of a pistol. What seemed to be rising was a communal prayer, silently said, beseeching that God would guide them and protect them on their way. The well-wishers not only hoped for a safe voyage but that these home-seekers would be brought to a country of rich fields and a land of plenty. As the train moved by and the last wagon faded in the distance, those left behind were loath to go back home. They gathered in little groups and poured out to each other all the information they had of the lands in south-central Indiana. James Simpson separated himself from his family and walked quickly ahead to watch the vanishing vans of the newly-weds, now leaders of the train. "Goodbye, my little Koo-wa," he said softly.

That old highway leading toward the forks of the two rivers was well worn on the end nearest Vincennes, but as the train moved on, the travelers found the road less worn. It was not a graded highway but one made by voyagers, following the buffalos' track, the herds who had gone to and from White Oaks Springs. It had seen much travel since the days of the bison. The much anticipated and delayed state road from Madison to the Michigan border had yet to be begun. It had waited for a treaty with the Potawatomi, which would, they hoped next year, cede the Indians' land to the federal government. The road would go north and south through the whole state. All other trails were rough and often muddy.

The road to the forks wound its way along the best path available, sometimes along the valley of a small stream, sometimes around a hill or gully, making due allowance for big trees and obstinate stumps. There were few bridges, and most that existed were mere logs laid crosswise on log sleepers. At this season of the year, midsummer, there was little mud, so soft wet ground did not hold the train back. This old road, which was used by early travelers going to Louisville and coming from it to settle in Vincennes, was used now much more than formerly when lurking Indians might pop out from behind any tree. In earlier days those who traveled this road were not sure of returning.

William Wright's ferry had been near White Oaks Springs for many years. The settlers expected to follow the well-marked route to the ferry crossing. Beyond that they would be obliged to carve much of their own way. Many settlers had gone north along the west fork of White River. A number had gone east along the east fork, but neither road was well marked. Travelers had said that it was sometimes a long way between cabins.

Winding along the trail on this summer day in 1825, it seemed that each family maintained itself as a single unit of the train. First came the wagons pulled by oxen. Then came that family's livestock, the older children, and finally the dogs. The head of the family walked behind and to one side, driving the oxen. The old folks and the babies or expectant mothers of a family might have a place in the wagon, but all were expected to make their way on foot whenever they could. Pulling these heavily weighted wagons over the rough unimproved roads was a big task, and it was not a quiet pilgrimage most of the time. Axle grease did not entirely remove the squeaks, much less the noise of heavy wagons over rocks and ruts and fallen logs. The company had no fixed schedule, for there was no hurry. All knew there would be many delays and mishaps. Impatience would not be a virtue on this trip over unchartered ways. They journeyed on, they stopped at night.

Log cabins at the west end of the road were fairly well kept. The inhabitants had done what was necessary to keep the cabins habitable, to make them homes. The word was passed down the line that further on and beyond the forks, settlers sometimes gave up, unable to make a living or worn out, and left their cabins to the birds and wild animals. In the homes passed the first two days, the settlers were making good. They welcomed the new homesteaders as they passed by. The satisfied homesteader could be easily detected, for his home would be in repair with roses and daisies growing in the front yard and in the garden. The despondent or homesick homesteader allowed the weeds to grow in his yard, and everything looked tumbledown and neglected. The progressive settler worked a large patch. His crops were free of weeds, and his livestock was in order. His farm showed the effects of industry and determination. Joan noted daisies and black-eyed Susans growing in the cabin window boxes, potted plants placed on stumps, clean churns hanging in the sun, family pants and shirts on lines, and all household effects ready for use.

The ferryman was the first to welcome the party as they pulled up near White Oaks Springs after a strenuous four-day journey. A group of settlers lived at White Oaks, and since the Indians had left, they had been building up the community. The gristmill and sawmill were busy all the time; the tavern furnished good food; the general store was well stocked and flourished with a thriving trade. There was rivalry and questioning about how the town would grow. Some enterprising lot salesmen were insisting on calling the village Petersburg. Peter Cooper, responding to good-natured jibing that this town was being named after him, was interested in hearing about the gristmill, the burrs, the race, and the supply of water. Only a few years before, the mill had been burned by the Indians. It had been dangerous also in times past to run the ferry. Many of the settlers remembered when a former ferryman on the West Branch had been murdered in his bed by the Indians. All was quiet at this little village now, although the deserted blockhouse had not been altogether abandoned. The tavern was a busy place, for here congregated trappers, fur traders, and salesmen who were introducing new kinds of merchandise into the community. Manufactured cloth, carpets, dishes, and all kinds of tools were hauled into this center by ox teams.

Word had reached the village that a caravan of homesteaders from Vincennes was to pass through the village. A committee of citizens had been selected to meet the train and to entertain them while they remained. They introduced themselves as Justice of the Peace Hozea Smith and settlers Wolsey Pride, James Brenton, Henry Brenton, Moses Harrell, and Jacob Chappell. This committee upon horseback met the train and escorted them to the campgrounds on the river. Big white oak trees formed a wonderful canopy overhead, and well-pastured bluegrass afforded a rich green carpet. After two days of dirt, dust, rocks, and ruts, it seemed as if the party were pulling into the fields of Elysium. The residents of the town furnished some fresh meat and brought it to the campgrounds.

General Walter Wilson was in charge of the militia stationed at this post. In his blue uniform, he greeted them after they arrived in the grove. Squire Smith, while telling of the forests and groves lying up the forks, did not fail to emphasize the rich soil near this village and to give an invitation to the travelers to make their homes in the vicinity. The river was low, but the slow, clear water moving into the one big stream was a beautiful and welcome sight. Campfires were soon started. Roaring blazes settled into live coals ready for the kettles and cauldrons. The women were quick to set out the cooking spider ovens, the coffeepots, and the frying pans. Cornmeal soon filled Dutch ovens. It was not long until the ovens were covered with live coals, producing in a short time cornpone with a rich brown crust. Meats were broiled over the fires this first evening, from the villagers' supply, while a few of the voyagers had been lucky enough to catch some quail and grouse, and that was shared. All had pleasant dreams the first night while sleeping in this beautiful grove after a feast fit for a king.

A resident who did some Methodist circuit-riding preaching came to the park the next morning and upon the stump of a large tree conducted religious services, encouraging the home-seekers in their undertaking and asking the blessing of God upon it, but not forgetting to leave the thought that they were welcome in this community.

White Oak Springs was the "jumping-off place" for most people who had not bought land in advance, like the party Joan and Peter led. The choice as to which branch of White River would be taken was to be made at White Oaks. The company needed to question hunters, merchants, and settlers before deciding which fork they would follow. Both branches of White River were about the same size. Each led off in an almost opposite direction into the unbroken forest. To stand and look up the river of one branch would give no more of an answer than looking up the other. Both branches at the forks were wide. Good clear water indicated that each received the water from vast tracts. Hunters coming in from the different branches would tell much the same story. A partisan for one fork would have his story matched by a partisan for the other fork. More furs might be brought to White Oaks from the west, only to have some fisherman upon the east branch bring to the tavern fine strings of fish. Some of the settlers themselves were partisan for one or the other branch, but, of course, they could not support their positions with convincing arguments.

A few days would be spent here. The townspeople were kind enough to loan the visitors canoes that they might make trips of inspection. Not much could be learned in this manner, though, for little could be told of the soil from a boat in midstream. These home-seekers would have to go scores of miles before they would be able to find unclaimed land. There were good farms here and there in almost any community, but it would be difficult to find land enough for the entire group to start a new community of their own. They were insistent they would be together.

The home-seekers were in no hurry to leave White Oaks Springs, for the villagers were kind to them. The beautiful oak grove was made available for the party for the time they needed. They found the old blockhouse in exploring the ground near the town; it was not used now except as an arms depot. The children from the group, who had only heard stories of Indians and forts, explored its ruined stockade and went within its gates.

The few militiamen stationed at this post, being citizens who served on call, did not live within the stockade, and the premises had an unkempt appearance. The soldiers preferred to stay at the tavern, where they received good food and plenty of spirits and rum, and had little to do. Even this lazy life would not hold the militiamen for long. They wanted to get out and be about their own business. Some of the early settlers had built their cabins under the protection of the fort, and these cabins were in use. Most of the newer homesteaders had also built cabins upon their own lands and liked the name of the community: Petersburg. Among the families who had "stuck and settled" were some Dutch from Pennsylvania who had been followed by newcomers from Virginia, New Jersey, and other eastern states.

Gratefully, the group thanked their hosts and moved away from White Oak Springs and onward, in a steady rain. As the original twelve families moved forward, they were joined by other families from other states as well as by some who wanted merely to change their home in Indiana. Some home-seekers were natural movers and would never be satisfied for long in any one place. Among these joining the troupe were a couple of Scotch-Irish families, whom Benjamin Franklin had called the Movers. Others were dissatisfied with their former stops. Some, it must be said frankly, were disgruntled because the soil would not produce without work on their part. A few families could not resist the temptation to move whenever they saw a train of covered wagons going by. The stories which were told of fertile lands further on never lost any of their fervor in the retelling. These newcomers to the train, as a rule, had no definite destination in mind but were willing to be led on into new territory.

The lazy and the laggard were marked before they were long with the train. All on the train were required to do a part of the common work. Perhaps fifteen miles could be covered in any one day. As they proceeded, there were no roads now, for the last road had been left about twenty miles from the forks. The guides found a short distance from the river a path which had evidently been made by the Indians and later followed by hunters and trappers. To enable wagons to get through, men with axes went ahead and cleared a way wide enough to allow the wagons to pass. Underbrush was simply crushed under the heavy wagons. The paths were far from straight. The company was often led aside from a true course because the route must follow high ground and avoid gullies and steep banks. As the days wore on, the travel became more difficult, the trees larger, and the forest more dense.

Campsites were selected before sunset, for there was much to be done before the weary travelers would be able to lie down for rest. The first thing to be done after halting was to build the fire and to prepare to hang over it a soup kettle supported by a quickly made, crude tripod constructed with nearby saplings. Two strong men carried the pot from the wagon to the tripod. It was essential to find cool drinking water, also. Each family was supposed to arrange their own campfire, but before the company had been on the route many days, agreeable families grouped together and surrounded a single campfire. The men collected fuel, helped get the food ready for cooking, brought water, and if they were not too weary, prepared rough log tables. The women cooked and arranged the supper. Potatoes and corn were baked in the ashes, while other foods were fried or boiled. "Hot bread," (biscuits) could be made in the spider pot (Dutch) ovens. Soup was kept bubbling all evening. The last thing to be done before stretching out for the night was to enjoy a bowl of hot soup.

The men on horseback were assigned the task of finding the way and supplying the party with wild game. These men could shoot a deer while in the saddle, for most of them had a good deal of experience as frontiersmen. After the first day out from the forks, it was not difficult to find deer, wild turkey, grouse, quail, and opossum. The wild game was divided among the families according to their size, and the big common pot was never neglected. The pot was carted from one campsite to the next and was never empty or cold. Wild game of all kinds and vegetables were soon boiling together and were kept boiling all night. This pot served the company at breakfast as well as for supper. Its meat stew, boiled for hours, was choice for hungry palates. The Scotch-Irish settlers who had joined the group called it burgoo.

The shiftless father was often the best shot. He therefore did his part in keeping the company pot full of good stew. Cold meat on cornpone made for good sandwiches.

After supper the home-seekers gathered at a central point. There the young, who never seemed to tire, would engage in games, while the elders looked on, talked, or just sat. In the evening around these campfires, the family heads would discuss the events of the day and plan for the next. Stories were told of other days. Men told improbable, exaggerated tales as jokes at the expense of some other member of the company. Fifty alligators had been wrestled by a man who had joined from Kentucky, and the others had to make insulting or humorous comments about that. The settler who could not stand a joke about himself might spend a miserable evening. Bear stories, fights with wild animals, and escapes from Indians were favorites, even if some of these stories caused women and children to have nightmares during the rest of the night. The work following ox-wagons all day, cutting trees, and helping the wagons over streams, through marshes, and up hills put the men in such physical condition by night, that no story would carry over into their dreams.

The evening usually closed with singing of frontier songs, creole epics, spirituals, and gospel hymns. The settlers from Kentucky could sing songs of great pathos and human feeling. Stories complete from birth to the time of wooing and love affairs usually ended unhappily or with tragedy. In this company most of the home-seekers were earnestly hunting for a place to make a good home and were generally of a religious turn of mind. Thus they closed the day with a deeply felt prayer asking for God's guidance. Many in this company of pioneers were God-fearing men and women: Methodists, followers of Thomas and Alexander Campbell (Campbellite), Presbyterians, and Baptists. They believed that all good things came by following in His footsteps. They wished to give their thanks for His guidance.

Most of the wagons had little pretense of having springs or anything close to them to ease the bumps, so most of the company were glad for the opportunity to walk and follow the wagons. A true Conestoga wagon would have allowed the most comfort, but these were impractical on the rutted paths they were traversing. They were all using some form of wagons, covered with some sort of canvas, with no springs and little room to store straw or grass to ease the jolting. These wagons would plunge, bob, and buck like wild colts. One day, after covering much rough territory, the company drew near a river. Upon the opposite side of the water, the bank was high like a granite wall. The tall banks formed three sides of a natural amphitheater. As the day was nearing its end, a shadow was cast across the river and covered the wagon train. Wildlife played on the rim of the high bank and was seen in relief. Near the top bank, swallows flew from little holes in the cliff. In their swift flight, they flew close and twittered at the new company. As the sun sank low, the shadows surrounded the weary travelers and cooled their hot brows. With the high banks upon the opposite shore as cathedral walls and with a large flat water-worn rock as an altar, Peter was called upon to conduct religious services and to thank Almighty God for the life and health and promise of the future.

The leaders soon noticed personal characteristics of the different members of the company. Industrious and serious-minded men were up early ready for the march. The laggards needed help and prodding. Some of these were changing their assigned positions in the line of march and falling behind. It was often necessary at the close of the day to send horses to the rear to help the slow catch up. Some parents saw that their families were well provisioned, while others were continually borrowing and annoying the industrious ones. No one in this company was permitted to go hungry, although some of the families had made little provision for themselves. Joan was especially active in seeing that children were cared for, and the dainties of her larder extended to other families. Some who had joined the caravan after its start had been living in the woods for a long time and depended almost entirely upon wild game and fruit. The men and women of these careless families were in their way helpful at this time, for they were expert in shooting game and finding choice blackberries and elderberries.

Peter Cooper was a natural leader. He encouraged the discouraged, helped the unfortunate and shiftless, and was able to get some work out of the lazy. Each family respected the words of Peter and Joan, who helped make the careless members useful to the entire company. Family disputes and quarrels among different settlers were explained to Peter and Joan so they might settle them. Joan had a good influence upon the women and children. She found some in the company at this point, well into the trip, were destitute of almost everything but children and dogs. If any children or mothers were sick, Joan called on them. With her supply of simple remedies known to pioneer women—acacia, St. John's wort, castor bean oil, and foxglove extract—and with cheerful words of advice, she gave relief. As the trip was being made in summer when the members of the company would be comparatively free from colds, she found the most common complaint came from overeating.

As the days went by, progress became slower, the trees larger, the undergrowth more dense, the hills higher, the bluffs steeper, the valleys deeper, and the land wilder. Slow-moving oxen were continually trying to feed as they moved along. They were too tired to browse overnight. The moving days were so long that the animals, horses or oxen, were continuously hungry. The train must keep a mile or two from the river, for the deep gullies and washes along the main stream prevented consistent progress. At some places the wagons could move forward only after a temporary road was built. The hope of the leaders of the company was that the train would advance as much as ten miles each day, but of late, they were falling far short of expectations. The guides needed no compass, for the sun was bright almost every day, and they were following the river. Although the party rarely saw the stream, the scouts kept them posted as to their distance from it.

The land was not without some human habitation. A venturesome settler, a hunter or trapper, had built a cabin here or there and was attempting to live, subsist, in it. Such a lonely family was sure to welcome the train and give information about the next few miles. Occasionally they passed an abandoned cabin, where the patch had gone to weeds, with the yard grown up in burdock and ragweed. Generally this was dilapidated, speaking without words that the lone settler had sadly given up his forest home and moved back from where he came. In some of these deserted cabins, they found notes of discouragement, which told of trials and hardships and utter loneliness. None of these notes discouraged the finders, but they read the messages with interest and pulled their belts with new determination. The sad notes warned about the cold winters, the wild animals, the mischief of predatory animals and varmints, the chills and fevers, and above all, the wearying lonesomeness. At one or two spots where there were single settlers and their families, eager settlers came out to urge the company to stop and to make their homes. However, in two instances, a pioneer quickly collected his earthly possessions and his wife in his own wagon. Hitching his own horses or oxen and with children, stock, and dogs, he followed the train.

Peter and Joan had questioned the fur traders and trappers for several months before leaving Vincennes and knew something of the locality as well as the nature of the territory for which they were searching. The travelers who had come out of the forest had told of the giant trees of oak, beech, poplar, and hickory. They told of walnut and maple groves and of rich valley bottomlands where the grass grew high. The company was finding the forests of huge trees and beautiful groves, but the tracts found so far were not large enough. The territory lacked a stream big enough to support a year-round millrace. The land of their search lay some distance ahead. Peter and Joan had mental pictures of their new home. They would not stop until they found land and streams which tallied with their dreams. Peter had heard of, and was looking for, a particular large valley just beyond a high range of hills, where land was rich and broad enough for the entire company, and where a fair-sized stream came down to meet the river. He also believed this valley to have knolls upon which the settlers might locate their cabins. His plan was to grow corn, wheat, and vegetables in the bottomland and to provide each settler with an eighty-acre tract.

The train started a little later each day, for the going was getting harder. Travelers and teams were becoming worn. The company was not discouraged, but the physical exertion of traveling through the forest with heavily laden wagons, striking camp, and preparing food became more wearisome each day. The oxen and horses were showing the results of pulling heavy loads over bad roads. Peter with his extra team of horses repeatedly had to help some straggler who could not keep the pace. Those who started late in the morning did not have much trouble in following the trail, but the dilapidated wagons and decrepit oxen were usually behind. The advance teams were sometimes several miles ahead of the last wagon. Peter had admonished the slow to close the line and keep closer to the leaders. He feared an accident might happen in the rear, unknown to the leaders, and much time would be lost in going back to give relief. Except for the cloudburst leaving Petersburg, there had been little rain during these late days of summer. The train was having no trouble fording streams. Many creeks and even larger streams were dry at the sand bars, but as they neared the hill country, it was expected that the deep valleys would keep the streams running. Scrub trees grew upon the high hillsides. Boulders and gullies were appearing. The traveling grew harder. More help must be given the tired oxen.

While in this hill country one afternoon, the leaders noticed a black cloud hung low in the western sky. Soon fleecy clouds broke from the black one. These white feathery clouds seemed to be hurrying before a wind. The order was given to halt the advance team and allow the rear wagons to close formation. All coverings of wagons were ordered closed and tied. As fast as the oxen pulled in, they were ordered staked, just as the horses were tied to trees. The sky became darker. Lightning began to play. Thunder started to roll as the storm drew ever nearer. The flashes of lightning and crashing of thunder became frighteningly loud, with the sky as dark as night. The settlers pointed and cried out at a large spiral seen in the air with each flash of lightning. A cyclone was coming their way.

The wagons were separated, for a number of the drivers could not crowd their oxen fast enough to bring the company into one corral. The black spiral cloud dipped from the sky down to earth and started east directly toward the wagon train. As the rain came in torrents, wagon coverings were of little use. When they were not whipped from the wagons, they appeared to be no more than sieves. The trees bent low and then snapped, and the downpour was terrific. Cannonading thunder drowned out the crashing of trees and the cries of children, women, and livestock, with water rushing by on every side. Sewing chests, tables, and bed clothing were blown and washed from the wagons. It was hard to breathe, for the water dashed in faces with great force.

The cloudburst did not last long, but great quantities of water covered the earth and filled the air. Then the sky grew lighter. The rain slackened. Water underfoot was deep, and the current swift. Peter gave the order to rush the women and children into the trees, for the water seemed to be growing deeper. Men waded into the current and floated along on logs trying to recover lost articles. Within a half hour, the swift current had spent itself, but the wagons were still in deep water. The contents were thoroughly soaked. Clouds disappeared almost as quickly as they had appeared. The sky became clear. The sun, before it set, got one good look at the havoc of the storm.

Not a twig moved. The depressions in the streambed and paths were deep with water, while the higher ground cleared. This was certainly the calm after a storm. The oxen, sheep, and horses were scattered, and some wagons were overturned. Quilts and small three-legged stools were seen floating with the currents or lodged among the trees. The underbrush was dotted with pots and pans. Children clung to their parents. Some families were separated. The orderly caravan of two hours before was in a state of confusion. As the sun hid its face, the settlers were able to determine that no lives had been lost. Many articles packed in the wagons, however, were irretrievable. With cooking utensils swallowed up by the waters and the wood hardly dry enough to burn, supper was late this evening. Women were obliged to work at it alone, for the men were busy hunting their livestock and rearranging their wagons.

As the first wagons had advanced before the storm, they had hardly noticed that they were crossing the dry bed of a small stream. This bed was now a raging torrent. The wagons in the rear would not dare to attempt to ford this stream, so the caravan was divided into two camps for the night. The family groups made themselves as comfortable as possible under the circumstances, all tired and excited. They could hardly think of sleep, so it was midnight when the two camps, still without much supper, settled for the night.

In the middle of the night the rear company heard an unearthly scream which seemed to come out of the hollow. No one afterwards seemed to know the hour. A long, deep growl followed the scream. One of the tethered calves began to bawl in fright and pain, and the dogs were aroused and began to bark and howl. The sleepers sat up, startled from their uneasy sleep. Finally the racket of the cattle and the snort of horses indicated the location of the disturbance. Men grabbed their guns and rushed toward the spot where the cattle had been tethered. Glowing coals from a dying campfire enabled the men to see a large animal dragging a calf from its mother.

The light from the fire shining in the animal's eyes disclosed two bright spots resembling live coals. Several guns cracked. A snarling mountain lion let loose its prey and started to run. The animal's legs failed him. He was hardly able to drag his hind parts. With growls, he seated himself on his haunches to fight the dogs that were after him. Men were afraid to shoot in the darkness, for none of them wanted to lose his dogs. The men rushed in when the lion was in clear view. One more shot from a frontiersman's musket finished the animal, and the dogs were upon him. They were hungry. A mountain lion's meat is never fit for human food, and at this season of the year, his hide and fur were worthless, so the dogs were given full play and would muss over him the rest of the night. It was hard to sleep after this experience, and it wasn't even worthwhile to try. It would soon be morning, and the settlers were anxious about swollen streams and ready to press on, if they could.

The sun broke bright and clear to find the torrent of last night now only a little stream flowing gaily along as if it had caused no damage. As the last wagon bumped through this little stream, the women especially said a prayer of gratitude and gave a sigh of relief. They soon found a suitable camping place and spent the day making repairs to wagons and harnesses. Some furniture and clothing were recovered and identified, but many articles, including family keepsakes, had floated into the river and were gone forever.

"Only a few more days, but be prepared for the hardest pull of all," was the word passed down the line. It took but little urging hereafter to keep the wagons in closer formation. No lives had been lost thus far upon the trip, but three had come into existence. This morning while the caravan was quiet for repairs seemed to be a good time for another pioneer settler to enter the world. There were no doctors in the train, but every married woman was supposed to be a midwife if she needed to. When the sun went down that evening, every wagon was in place. The home-seekers were ready to conclude the journey.

They comforted themselves with the thoughts of the future, of the cabins they would immediately be building as soon as they arrived. All of them knew the details; they had spoken of the cabin raisings time and time again around the campfire. All the cabins had to be put up within a few weeks after the settlers determined the valley should be their home. The neighbors would help each other in cabin-raising bees, and the little log homes they put up would be one-room basic living cottages. Winter was not far off. Not a moment could be lost in providing shelter for each family, and each cabin must conform to the same one-room pattern, each house built by the community one at a time and together.

First the trees must be cut. The logs from the forest trees would be laboriously felled and dragged with sledges and oxen into place. The floorboards of the cabin would then be whipsawed from the logs by a crew of men in a process which took two days before the day of the cabin raising. One side of the floorboards was to be made smooth. The boards would then be laid upon four foundation logs. By means of pegs in holes, the boards were to be made fast.

Then the day of the cabin raising would dawn. Promptly at sunrise on the building day, the dinner bell would begin to ring. Workmen and their families would assemble, with the men ready to move the heavy timbers of twelve to eighteen feet, and all of the same circumference into place at the command of "the boss," who would be Peter. Some neighbors would be told to bring hammers, saws, and planes. Others would bring adzes, hand spikes, ropes, pulleys, crosscut saws, and pike poles. Each man knew his place. The logs were notched on the job to insure a perfect fit. The "saddle" or upper log was cut at the end, so it would seat itself or fit tight in the "seat" log just under. A derrick, brought with great trouble from the Vincennes homelands in the special tool wagon, would be used only to lift the heavier logs and those that must be hoisted high. Each man knew his own skills and was assigned to use them for the good of the project.

The women, too, would know their jobs. Big tables were prepared from the lumber available about the build. Whatever food they could assemble would be set upon the tables. A good spirit of fellowship prevailed, but the mood was, "We must get this done. We have one day here; this family must complete the job, and we all will move on to the next cabin." Some days the roof could be completed, others not, and the chimney was the job of the cabin owner and his good friends—or family.

So the log community would go up before the snow set in. Could it be done? They had come this far. Here, this night before they mounted the last ridge, they murmured among themselves that they could, they must do it. Pray for good weather, they told each other.

They could see a high range of hills in the distance, appearing to be covered with a mantle of green. It was evident that the trees upon the summit of the ridge were not large. From this distance, Peter thought them to be hickory saplings of stunted growth. Erosion for centuries had washed away the soil from the tops of these hills and redistributed much of the earth in the valleys below. As the company advanced, they could see that the higher hills were skirted by lower ones. From now on there would be much climbing. Sometimes the smaller elevations were steep and hard to climb.

Sometimes the hills would afford a long, gentle slope.

The teams heaved, pulled, and strained in their collars, dragging the wagons uphill, over boulders, and through gullies and ravines. The train advanced at a slow pace, with horses used as extra teams because they could make the return trip more quickly. By hard pulling, much perseverance, and a good deal of urging, the last wagon was brought to the foot of the big range by sundown. The hills ahead now looked like sizable mountains. In this country they were called knobs. The next pull was sure to be the hardest.

Around the campfires that evening, they could discuss nothing but the pull for tomorrow. Scouts who had been sent to find the best road were not altogether in agreement except to say that the hills were high and the road poor. They had found a pass which had been used by Indians and lately by hunters and trappers. No games were played around the campfires this evening and the customary songs were omitted, for the company to the last man and child was dog-tired. The oxen and horses were ready to lie down in their harnesses. No unnecessary movements on the part of animals and humans alike were made because muscles ached and joints were stiff. Beds were hardly made before families were ready to stretch out and sleep. A full moon shone down upon a peaceful company of home-seekers who were determined to save every ounce of energy to go through the pass the next day.

At break of dawn the trumpet sounded. The settlers arose from their beds and began to limber stiff joints in tired bodies. The horses and oxen had lain in their tracks all night, too tired to eat. Now each pulling animal was given a choice feed, and ham and jerky and coffee for the settlers was soon over. The anxiety of the moment caused the workers to forget their tired muscles and stiff joints. They greased the wagons, carefully yoked the oxen, placed the extra horses, and passed the word down the line that all wagons should reach the high ridge by sundown. Slowly the wagons began to ascend the hill. Boulders were avoided, gullies negotiated, and paths made wider. Chocks were held ready in case a wagon halted or a team faltered. Every foot gained was saved, for no wagon was to be allowed to run backwards. Foot by foot the wagons climbed the hill. At five o'clock every settler and his wagon was upon the highest ridge and looking beyond.

With the wagons locked and the animals staked, the settlers gathered in a little group. Sixty-one souls, fifteen families, peered into the valley beyond and wondered if that beautiful tract ahead was to be their future home.

The settlers were at last looking over their land of promise.

At a lower elevation on the tableland, green giant forest trees covered the land from the hills to the valley yonder. From the high ridge the settlers could see over the tops of the trees ahead, a vast velvet carpet with different shades of coloring. These settlers were seeing a forest which had rarely been viewed by the eye of a white man. For many centuries the tribes had used this beautiful forest as their game preserve.

If the forest trees could have spoken, they might well have said, seeing these newcomers, that they realized the time had come for their destruction, as their fellows had fallen in other parts of this area. Where their shade was deepest, the men would choose spots for homes. Their bodies would be burned that the fields could produce grain. These stately giants would wonder, should they be able to talk, why in a short time this enemy who claimed to be civilized would lay waste that which it had taken centuries, eons, to produce. Perhaps the men now coming down and gazing at the trees could have answered, the God of the Universe has saved this paradise of trees, so that civilized man can now build his home on a beautiful spot and be able to provide for his family and for others. Cities may spring into existence near here, useful arts, education, industry. What before supported a few will now supply many. But, some thoughtful one might add, some day my descendants may come to regret the sacrifice of the deep forest trees.

The great hill ridge upon which the home-seekers were standing was in the form of a crescent and appeared to surround a valley several miles in diameter. In the distance they could see the high river bluffs, while at the feet of the bluff wall flowed a silvery stream which did not appear large from this distant viewpoint. Extending back from the river and toward the tableland covered with trees was the meadowland.

Not a soul could be seen in all this vast panorama. Black spots, which the settlers took for water birds, appeared over the low ground. Truly this was the land hoped for. As Peter and Joan stood hand in hand and looked across the valley, they thought of another group of settlers four thousand years ago fleeing from an oppressor and looking from the hills of Moab into the land of Canaan. Finally Peter whispered to Joan, "This will be our home, and the land we shall call Canaan."

"We will camp on the ridge tonight," Peter thought. "We will watch the sun tomorrow morning as it comes over the treetops to the east and casts its first rays upon the meadow. We will all sleep well tonight, for our journey is almost over. In that valley yonder we will build our homes and cultivate our fields. I wonder if the Lord has been saving this land for us." At the practical level for the morning was also the necessity of visiting the land office. He had been told of its whereabouts by the last settler they had met, some miles and some time back.

The wagons would not be heavy going down grade. All horses were released for scout duty. Men on horseback were ready at dawn to scout the outer edge of the valley and to report to an anxious group descending the hills. The scouts were directed to observe the first and second bottoms as well as the midland.

The settlers adjusted the rub-locks on the rear wheels, for the wagons must not run over the oxen. In a short time all were down to the midlands. Here were the tall forest trees, which covered the earth so densely that sunlight could hardly penetrate. The shade did not give encouragement to undergrowth. The tall, straight trunks looked like so many pillars supporting a vast canopy over an amphitheater. Here in all their glory stood the mighty forest oaks, the tall slender poplars, the spreading elms, the graceful ashes, and the ragged hickories. Across the river could be seen the white, mottled bodies of the sycamores. After leaving the midlands, the company found maple and walnut groves. The leaves of many winters were packed in layers underfoot until the mass was much like a cushion. Here was a paradise for elves and the Elysium of dreams.

For some time the wonder-struck company walked through this leafy paradise until the second bottoms opened up as far as the eye would see. All was meadowland. A few deer and some partridges could be seen lazily making their way through and over the tall grass. The company then turned to the right and away from the river, intending to remain upon the elevated land overlooking the bottomland. They reached the smaller stream, which came out of the hills in the distance, and marveled at how it leisurely found its way to the river. This would be the stream of Peter's visionary plans. It would fill the race that would bring water to the big mill wheel.

There might be several thousand acres of rich soil in the valley, for it extended forward as far as the settlers could see. The tableland near the foot of the range followed the hills far back to the right. The river in the distance seemed to circle two sides of the valley, and the forest groves completed the encirclement. As the tired but enthusiastic settlers stood in wide-eyed admiration of the panorama, they could see gentle movement of the grass and rushes in the meadowlands, while the green canopy of the treetops was perfectly motionless. Their journey was at an end. Here they would build their homes and futures.

Peter called to Joan and pointed to the rich land ahead. The two could trace the stream from the point where it came out of the hills to its union with the river. Peter said softly, "Joan, when did time begin here? When was this land formed? What a shame we have no recorded history, so that we can learn more of this land. How many thousands of years of silence lie before us? Will the wind or the trees or the stream ever be able to tell us what has gone before in this beautiful valley? Was there ever a civilization or a people older than the Indians who inhabited these forests?"

Her eyes lost somewhere in the past or future, Joan replied, "The wild animals know more of this land than the most learned historians, and even the animals will soon be gone. Indians have told of giant elephant-like creatures with mammoth tusks whose bones they have found on the ground. They say giant cats larger than cows trod the hills. Our scientists are finding chieftain burials in mounds in the hills, and some may be near here. Will we ever be able to learn the ancient past of this country? Has the ripple of the water ever meant music to the souls of men in these meadows? Or have the winds howled among the trees and gone unnoticed? Has no human being ever stopped to admire these flowers? Has any people ever called this home? If not, all that will change now."

Chapter 20

The New Home
1830

How quickly time seemed to pass! It amazed Joan that what had been a wilderness, no living habitation in sight, could grow so rapidly to a town. Peter told her it was ever thus on the frontier. "Look at Hindostan Falls," he said, referring to the town they had seen further back on the road to Canaan. "A company started land sales and within four years pioneers descended. By 1824 Hindostan had a huge inn, a blacksmith shop, a tannery, a mill, a provisioning store, land sales office, and even a doctor from the east. Where did all these folks come from? That's what I wonder about our settlement. How has it grown so rapidly. Word must just get around, on the wings of the birds." Joan smiled. She knew that Hindostan had just as suddenly become a ghost town, when the "yaller fever" had hit it a couple of years ago, and now it was a few moldering cabins, everybody gone, moved up the hill to Mt. Pleasant just as quickly as they had come. That would not happen here. Still, it was amazing to see people pouring in and starting up enterprises—a store, church and school. And in the hills, Kentucky people had seemed to bring whole clans to live together out there beyond the town.

From the beginning Peter and Joan had been living with some dissatisfaction in their log cabin, and as they had made more room, they had started plans for a much larger and more substantial home. They would need expertly sawn wood, and that was available at the sawmill, which soon went up near Peter's gristmill. These people from Vincennes knew how to make kilns and use river mud to make bricks, and they did so early on as they settled. All was in place for real houses, and Joan and Peter were almost from the beginning determined to have theirs. Every extra to the first cabin had been placed so that it might be transformed when the day came for the new big dwelling house; for instance, the big brick bake oven had been placed with the idea that it would be useful in connection with an expanded kitchen. They erected the summerhouse complete with the oven, which would also serve later. In this building Joan could make soap and apple butter. She could also do the family wash, quilt, spin, and sew out there and do so many other things required of the pioneer housewife.

Joan had lifted many golden brown loaves of white bread from this big bake oven. As the miller's wife, she was expected to bake the most delicious bread. When large pieces of hot bread were broken from big loaves and generously supplied with golden yellow butter, it more than compensated for some inconveniences. Saturday had always been bake day, and appetites were always ready and waiting on that day particularly. These big bake ovens were community ovens, supplying pies, cakes, and even the huge roasts of beef or hams that would feed a group. Members of a family would gather around to wait for the big "lumps" of bread to come out of the oven. Joan always baked a supply of yeast biscuits that were to be eaten on Sunday. There were sure to be a few loaves of salt-rising bread.

All summer through, this summer kitchen with a bake oven also served as a dining room. It was boarded up and the room was free from rain and heat except that given off from the fireplace. Some distance farther back toward the garden, Peter added a cave where vegetables could be kept all winter and some cured meats during summer. The Coopers were regularly acquiring new furniture, dishes, silverware, and linens—all to be used when a new house was ready. Joan and Peter spent some time inspecting homes in other communities with a view of incorporating the new and modern improvements in their new home when it was ready.

The location of the original cabin had to some extent been determined by the spring of flowing water at the foot of the hill. As the community evolved, the pioneers found it to be a simple matter to dig a well and to wall it with flat stones. The water in these wells was always cold and protected from the elements. The wells were dug square and thus easy to be lined. Around the top a solid box curb was built, with a frame constructed above the curb that supported a windlass, by means of which the oaken bucket could be lifted or lowered. At some wells the owner preferred the long well sweep, which was a long pole held in place by a forked post. The long handle permitted the dipping of water from the well, and with these contrivances it was no longer necessary to consider a spring in locating a home.

Homes could now be built along the road and need not be built at odd places upon the land. The Cooper family collected a number of pictures of southern homes from the books which had come with them, for Peter and Joan preferred the broad fronts, wide verandas, and large white columns of some Georgia or Carolina farmsteads. Joan wanted a covered porch across the entire front of her new home. There must be a railing, she said, both upstairs and down. Peter knew where to find long white poplar logs that would serve as columns. The upper, as well as the lower, veranda would have a white picket fence around it for the railing. Big, deep-seated front doors, both upstairs and down, would make the home a welcome retreat. Large windows, two on either side of the hallways, would admit light and add dignity to the house. Green shutters would cover each window and keep out glaring sunlight. Weatherboarding was now available, and the whole house would be enclosed in it, with insulation of soft bricks under it. The carpenters under Peter's direction would raise the roof with clean, sawn clapboard, and wrought-iron nails would be brought in to finish the work. The two large rooms in the rear of the house were built so the roof extended to the base of the upstairs windows. This building, when complete, would be the most substantial home in the Canaan Valley and would rank high in the county. The miller had prospered financially in the five years since the group had arrived, footsore and anxious, but marveling at the beauty and appropriateness of their newfound home. Peter and Joan's neighbors rejoiced that the Cooper family was to have a large modern home; they were major contributors to the prosperity of this little community.

The home would be complete with a full basement that would be lined with flat limestone serving as foundation for the house. Choice flat stones recovered from the millstream that extended back into the hills would cover the basement floor. A big chimney would push upward from the basement at each end of the house. With this double chimney arrangement, there would be six fireplaces, two on each floor and two in the basement. The cellar fireplace was a wonderful place at which to work during the cold winter weather; both of the Coopers had seen it in Grouseland, the Harrison home, and other stately homes in the Vincennes area. Joan would be able to make her soap earlier and her apple butter later than in the old home. Peter would see to it that the fireplace they planned for the living room would be big and roomy.

Much of the winter living must be before this fireplace. A long crane would allow the pot to be ever ready. The children they hoped to have could pop their corn and bake their potatoes, and Joan could broil meat. Andirons were to be large to hold back the burning wood so that the hot coals would pile high and hold heat. One of the family members or the servants they had now hired from among the hill people, especially the hired girl every-body called "Blabbering Minnie," would toast the bread over the coals for breakfast using the long-armed toaster with room for two pieces of bread. A Dutch oven would bring forth delicious cornbread and hominy, and Joan could turn fried potatoes in bacon fat until they were crisp and delicious. Nuts of all kinds would taste good cracked before this fireplace.

The women of the valley prided themselves upon their cooking, but it had been conceded that Joan, as the miller's wife, was first in baking. At every opportunity the farmers' wives asked her the best method of preparing food. She had learned the art back in the Simpson home. With the best flour and a good bake oven, she could prepare bread, pies, and cakes that would always be in demand at weddings or church fairs.

Still, there were problems to solve in building a new home. The wide hallway, both upstairs and down, would be hard to heat from the fireplac-es, especially because this hallway had big doors in front and rear on both floors. Doors separated the hallway from all the rooms. When the weather was severe, the hall could do little more than serve as a place to remove wraps. Winter winds would have a hard time finding cracks in walls thick with hewn logs well laid together, sealed with plaster and hidden under the weatherboarding. Skilled carpenters, expert joiners sent from Louisville, would carefully encase all windows and doors so they did not allow air and were strong and resilient enough to withstand high, whistling winter winds. A carpet weaver in the county seat town had already spent many months in weaving carpets for the new home, but in the parlor a large flowered Brus-sels velvet carpet imported from mills in England would grace the polished wood floors. Peter and Joan and their hired helpers were already trained in the way they would enter this favored room. In a vestibule in the rear end of the hall they could pull off their mud-covered boots so they could be cleaned up and lined up on a hempen mat. In the center of the parlor would be the family Bible, given honor by being placed on a hand-carved table that was to be covered with satin drapes. The holy book was more of an ornament than a book to be read, for there was a smaller Bible, well marked, that was used by the family and which had a concordance. The family generally read the Bible each winter evening.

Joan was determined that the parlor in her new home should be some-thing more than a dark, musty room. She had noticed that in the homes with parlors the window shutters were generally closed, the blinds pulled down, and the curtains drawn tight. She did understand and had grown up knowing that the reason for that was that sunlight should not enter the room lest it fade the carpets. Still, she reflected, entering this forbidden room, the visitor was met with the smell of stale air. The sun and ventilation were strangers who were not allowed to enter this part of the house. In winter the parlor was cold, and in the summer it felt dank, like a cellar. No one dared to enter such a room except upon special occasions. A young lady might entertain her beau in the parlor upon Sunday evening, and, of course, all weddings and funerals were conducted in it. The minister was ushered into the parlor, and he might read a chapter from the big family Bible, but family and close-by neighbors only rarely saw inside this stately place. Joan would not have that at all; she planned to make this room a central gathering place and would be calling it the gathering room.

A big spare day bed would grace one corner. The guest who was invited to stay overnight could lose himself in the comfortable downy nest. Children would be able to romp and play in this room, and it would not be sacrilegious to make too much noise and to toss balls or small hoops .

The family honored its religious heritage. In some homes, families would gather in this spare room for bedtime prayers. Father, mother, and all of the children were supposed to get down upon their knees. Peter often told the story of what happened at the home of Elder David Jackson, one of his customers at the mill. David had four children who had great respect for their father but dreaded the long prayer at bedtime. The oldest son brought home his young bride. She was not accustomed to much praying at her own home, but she knew she must be upon her good behavior at prayer time. The second son decided to have some fun and prepared himself for the occasion with a turkey feather. After all were down on their knees, this young man proceeded to draw the feather across the bride's neck. The young lady, who had always been afraid of mice, gave a scream which broke up the prayer service. The second son bravely hunted for a mouse or even a big rat. The groom "smelled a rat" himself and located the feather and the next morning gave his brother a good "cussin'. The offending brother never confessed, but the remainder of the family apologized the next morning.

Both Peter and Joan hoped their gathering room religious exercises would be a little more dignified but still pleasurable.

Chapter 21
Housewarming
1830

The new Cooper home could not be built in a day, but the couple wanted to observe as many as possible of the old customs, in particular the cabin, or in this case home-raising. Peter and Joan clung to the old practice of neighbor helping neighbor that had built those cabins at Canaan in such a short time. It would take weeks, even months, to build their new house, and there would be no such thing as coming at sunrise and leaving at sunset as in the first days, with a house built from foundation sill to comb rider. Masons would be some time in building even the foundation that would provide for a cellar under the entire house. Skilled carpenters must fit the foundation. There would be many more weeks before this house was ready for a roof. What could be done to preserve the old custom of friendliness among neighbors, and yet keep the neighbors no more than a day?

Remembering those first days in Caanan, they had an idea. "Let's move ahead with our new home. As we are about to finish it, we can invite the neighbors in to come and celebrate with a real housewarming. They'll stay a day and see the house, then feast the way we used to." The Coopers were known for miles around, so their new home would excite interest. People would come out of respect and through curiosity, but all would be willing to take part in festivities. They could see the new things and offer suggestions. Someone suggested to Peter and Joan that the housewarming invitation be announced early, for the second week in June, from the church pulpits and in the county paper. Communities in the whole county were well underway when they had arrived and had continued to grow rapidly. Some of these folks would want to see the new "mansion" that was being built out in the hill country.

There were many delays in building and more delays in obtaining furnishings. At last the day was near at hand when neighbors might come to see the new Cooper home. Country stores and blacksmith shops offered good places to tack posters telling of the welcoming party. Ministers in the churches spoke of the Cooper housewarming and warmly issued invitations to one and all. Big wagons were made ready the day before, for it would take twenty-four hours for some of the families to reach the Canaan Valley. Fathers and grandfathers and the ladies of each home made ready to drive to the big social event, preparing food for the families, hay and corn for the team, and chairs for the old in the big wagon. With picnic food in a traveling basket, visitors should reach the new home just after noon, already having lunched. This would give plenty of time to inspect the building and the modern equipment. Supper would be served in the evening, and festivities would last until the "crack of day" the next morning. And Peter and Joan would proudly show the upstairs room that would now be a nursery. Joan was expecting a baby.

Jim and Sarah Simpson were coming from Vincennes. Mary and Virginia, without their families, would be on hand. Peter's father and mother had not said whether they were coming or not. The Vincennes party would be arriving by stagecoach. Miss Thoreau had been invited, but no one was sure she would come. Sarah had written that Jim was going to examine every joint in the house to see if the city mechanics could make a good fit. The Vincennes party had also been working and saving to bless the house. New silk quilts, heavy comforters, and all kinds of fancy work had been made to grace the rooms.

Some settlers had brought tents to shelter them if they arrived a little early, and early in the morning the wagons began to pull in. Before long it would have been hard to tell whether the new home was being surrounded by a circus or a camp meeting. Every woman had tried to make the best as well as the most beautiful cakes and especially pies: apple crumb, peach and rhubarb cream, raisin and pumpkin, lemon, and sugar cream were in their pie pans in baskets, with pieces already cut. Every home in the valley would help to entertain the families who came from a distance to attend this housewarming.

The hill settlers, those who had come in so quickly after the valley land was taken and made their homes in the hills, sauntered in wearing clothing of homespun, colored calico, and bright silk sashes. They came in two-wheel carts pulled by oxen and, in one instance, by an old cow. In each cart was an entire family and one or two of their dogs. The people from the hills were of little value at the ordinary house raising, for their teams were not first quality, and these settlers did not know how to get the best out of their stock.

That didn't matter at this housewarming, where the work had been done, so the hill people, the hillbillies as they were called in Kentucky and by many here also, were right in their element and welcomed. They had their own food baskets to contribute. Much of the food coming out of the hills was delicious and much prized. The hillbillies knew how to cure game meat. The wild hog that lived upon mast was not in demand on the farms, but these wild hogs, killed late in the fall when they had filled themselves for weeks upon nuts, were delicious if the meat was cured properly. Hillbillies could make prize cured bacon, and the hams in their lean-to smokehouses were tasty, if a little salty. Hill people depended much upon venison, and smoked deer meat was appreciated by the farmers in town who had little time or opportunity to hunt deer. Pickled or smoked venison tongue was saved for special occasions such as this.

A housewarming was not unusual in the valley, but the Cooper house-warming was sure to be an especially memorable great affair. Peter and Joan had made friends throughout the county in the short years they had been in Canaan, and the miller was admired generally. This new house was unusual because it was big and had all the modern conveniences that might be found in the residences of city folks. Word had been passed from one end of the county to the other that the Cooper home was stately, worth seeing. Most people would be admiring the stained glass in some of the windows, the glass panels, and even glass transoms over the doors.

The weather was ideal. Those who had traveled during the night before had found a big, round full moon looking down upon them, beaming like a joyful face determined to grace the happy event.

Joan had been saving ever since Canaan was founded to refurnish her new home. She wanted feather beds filled with only breast feathers of white geese, none of the coarse duck feathers in her beds or pillows. Comfort-ers and quilts had been accumulating; they had been wedding gifts from Vincennes. Gourds and earthenware were giving way to new and beautiful white china, which was in boxes still. Pewter plates were also to be obtained from faraway big cities. Each family longed to have at least a few of these beautiful plates or dishes which Joan had ordered.

Something new had been added just six weeks ago. To supplement the kitchen and downstairs fireplaces, Peter had ordered one of the new cook-stoves he had seen advertised in one of the big city papers. It could serve for quick meals until they saw how it performed, leaving the traditional fireplace cooking arrangements for most large meals. The cookstove had four removable plates and a warming oven as well as a bake oven, and the women gathered around it to ooh and ahh. Reservoirs to maintain hot water were attached to the rear of these new cast-iron cooking stoves. Few people were willing to give up their Dutch ovens and fireplace cranes, but after testing the merits of the new cooking stoves with ovens, some forward-thinking farmers' wives were giving up the old methods. Joan told the visitors she would be using both her summer kitchen and basement fireplaces and this new cookstove. Sometimes one could not keep up with progress, and as soon as one thing was finished, another would be advertised in a Cincinnati paper. Some men were looking carefully at this new marvel of a stove, advertised to make the housewife's job easier. One of the hill men could be heard saying that a johnnycake could only be baked upon a hot board. "I'm not a-gonna have my wife to make a change in her way of cooking our victuals," he said smugly.

One old lady, Granny Whitehouse, speaking in a loud, shrill voice, agreed, insisting that her man would not eat hoecake unless the cake was baked upon the blade of a hoe. "Where do you put the hoe?" she wanted to know. Some of the friends of the granny laughed. "Your old man wants an excuse for having no handle on his hoe. Without the hoe, he will be saved hours of work, even if the weeds do take his corn," one of the old couple's neighbors ventured.

Many of the women came to the housewarming for the express purpose of commenting behind Joan's back. The drapes and rose carpet would be too high falutin'. These new methods of cooking were foolish. Viewing the stove, and out of sight of Joan, they sniffed, "How can she make hominy or broiled venison steaks on that thing?" They would be watching to see how this contraption handled fried squirrel or chicken or roasted a goose. "She'll soon be back to using that big fireplace instead of this stove," one neighbor whispered to another.

Joan did not listen to these comments; she had eyes for only one carriage, rented at the store's small livery stable after its inhabitants had disembarked from the stage. Now stepping down were her father, mother, and two sisters. Her sisters' husbands, fulfilling the needs of business, had stayed in the city, taking care of the children along with nursemaids. "Father," Joan said, warmly embracing James Simpson. She pulled back to look at him, white-haired now, with a face lined with cares of work over decades.

He laughed. "You are pulling back just as you did so many years ago, when I first saw you on a misty morn in November by the Wabash. Staring into the faces, wondering about those around you."

"But not with such joy did Koo-wa examine the faces of those soldiers," Joan said softly and with a smile, "as I do today to see these parents." She went to her mother Sarah, now a little portly, and kissed her and Mary and Virginia. Peter was told his parents were ill with the grippe.

"Furnish me with an apron," her mother said to Joan, handing her a large crock of watermelon pickles. She smiled and pointed at Joan's growing girth: word had come to them that the Simpsons were going to be the parents of a new baby.

Supper would be served early, for many people had come to the housewarming with good appetites. Neighbor women were prepared to help. The visitors brought their baskets of food; it was a country pitch-in, with dishes varying from pickled cabbage to lemon drizzle cake. There was sure to be enough for all. For days Joan had been busy, and her sometime hired girl from the hills, Blabbering Minnie, was actually helpful on this occasion and was managing to keep her mouth shut. Big tables were arranged, white cloths spread, crockery pots of flowers placed in the center as children stood around dancing first on one foot, then on another. "When will it be time?" They would have their own jobs swinging tree branches over the food as scores of flies tried to attack the delicacies.

The groaning board drew them all up to fill their plates and take them to the picnic cloths spread under the trees or small tables set up in the wagons. As soon as one group had eaten, the tables were quickly cleared, and the women trundled out with more food. Each was keeping an eye on who was delving into her own special dish: the Indian succotash of corn and beans with bacon bits, the mile-high spice cake with applesauce filling between the layers, the jelly roll with blackberry preserves. No one would leave this feast hungry. Men were served first, beginning with the older gentlemen and then the young. The older women supplied the food to the table, and the younger women served the guests. Next to eat came the women, and finally the children. Occasionally some mother would slip her youngsters a chicken leg or some dainty bit while they looked on hungrily. The supper began at five and must be over in two hours. While the women and children ate, the men gathered in the front yard and discussed the architecture of the new home. Those men who were not interested in newer methods of buildings could find their own group with whom they might discuss crops, horse races, or recent turkey shoots. Politics and religious news were always a subject of conversation as pipes came out and snuff was taken: what the Shakers were up to now, or the Indians probably getting ready to actually move across the Mississippi. Some fearless people were thinking about chucking it all and heading out to the area of Oregon on a new trail that was being laid out and could be finished soon. They could go at least the first lap and then wait for completion to take their wagon trains on. The men began interrupting each other to talk about the Sauk and Fox Indians led by an Indian named Black Hawk fighting this very month in Illinois. "Pshaw," old Mike Bigger from the hills said. "I thought we got ridda all of them."

The Baptist minister wanted to know if anyone had heard of a man named Joseph Smith who had supposedly had a vision in New York. Heads were shaking no. "This gentleman says that an angel came to him and gave him books of prophecy and even the history of Jesus visiting—you will not believe this—Mexico after his resurrection. He has published a book about it. So the eastern newspapers say."

"Do tell" and "sacrilegious hogwash" could be heard between spittings and snufflings.

Promptly at seven the musicians arrived with their fiddles, took their places, and began to tune up. These woodland orchestras were not obliged to practice much together, for every fiddler knew the tunes common for dancing purposes. The party would go on until dawn, and so the fiddlers carefully seated themselves, settling in for a long grind. As the dance progressed, the old and the young took part, but by midnight the oldsters and youngsters would grow tired and slip away quietly from the party. They would seek the soft hay bed in their own wagons and would soon be fast asleep. The young adults seemed never to grow tired. The longer they danced, the merrier they became. Before dawn the horses or oxen were harnessed. All would be in readiness to leave at dawn. As the sun began to show over the hills back of the valley, the fiddlers would play "Home Sweet Home," which meant that in a few moments the party would be over. The words from this new, but already beloved, song rang in the guests' ears:

A charm from the skies seems to hallow us there
Which seek through the world is ne'er met with elsewhere.
Home, home, sweet, sweet home. There's no place like home.

As the last strains of the tune died out, the young men and women broke and ran for their wagons, all the time shouting and yelling and bidding each other goodbye. They had made new acquaintances. They had forged new attachments, particularly the young men and women. The drivers of the teams with reins in their hands gave the command to go as soon as the last late arrival climbed in the wagon, returning to their own home sweet homes or staying over with neighbors. Before daylight all vehicles deserted the barnyard. There was little left to denote there had been a party. The revelers of the night before slept the sleep of the exhausted. Rough roads and no springs to the wagons meant nothing to these tired souls, who had had a good time and must now pay some penalty. The housewarming at the Cooper home would be long remembered. Peter and Joan felt confident that their visitors had had a good time. They ushered Sarah and Jim Simpson and the sisters into the cabin, which still for a few more weeks would be serving as their home.

"A pity Minerva and Hiram could not come. The grippe has laid your father low, but I hear he is recovering," Sarah said to Peter, as he ushered her into the bedroom of the cabin and showed her the rope mattress bed, soon to be replaced by a new bedstead. She had just kissed her daughter and proudly patted Joan's stomach, where the grandchild-to-be nestled.

"Yes, I very much want to show him my new machinery at the mill," Peter said.

"I believe Miss Thoreau has planned a visit, also," Sarah said, looking questioningly at her daughter.

"She did not want competition with all the housewarming guests," Joan said. "She wants me all to herself." The family members smiled. They knew exactly what she meant.

Chapter 22

Lincoln
1830

Vincennes, Ind., August 25, 1830

Dear Joan and family,

I was glad to receive news of your successful housewarming from the several from here who were able to attend. Joan, I spoke to Virginia and Mary; they felt the entire event was "high on the hog," as they say where you are. Yes, it appears I missed quite a festivity.

I received your letter telling of the arrival of little Jimmy. Your wish is fulfilled in having a boy, and your father is delighted that you have named him James. Your whole family called at my home, and we all were happy and drank a glass of elderberry wine. Jim Simpson has always been proud of you since the day you stepped from his boat and you were led home between your little sisters. I can see you always in my mind's eye as that little helpless child. I wish some of us might have had foresight enough to have kept the little deerskin which served as your only garment. It was so tattered and torn, though, that your mother could hardly wait to get it into the fire.

I am anxious to see the little fellow. I was hopeful he would look like his mother. I do not blame you for rejoicing "that he is the very image of his father," but you know I always admired Peter more on account of his intellect than his good looks. I will say, however, that your husband is better looking than some men. I hasten to make this last statement as a matter of my own self-defense. You know I am honest; that you must know by now.

The old town has changed much since you went away. We are especially proud of the building of the new St. Francis Xavier Church. It is such an impressive brick structure. Many new faces are coming into the town, though, who know little, and care less, concerning the old traditions of the place. The creoles are being fast outnumbered. At the last election many creole candidates were defeated for county offices. The new people coming to live here care for little except their own conveniences. I dislike seeing the old customs discarded or even fading away.

I am still planning to drop in upon you. Don't be surprised if you see a buxom lady alight from the stage some day before long and make straight for the new Cooper home. Perhaps in the fall. I know how rapidly your community has developed. In a few short years have come all the accoutrements of a town: inn, general store, a couple of trade shops, and two churches, more on the way, so they say.

A few evenings ago I called upon Colonel Vigo, who now lives at the home of Mrs. Betsy LaPlante. He is in distressed circumstances. You will recall what a wealthy landowner and fur trader he was, but he lost all and now has no one to care for him except Mrs. LaPlante, his former ward. When Colonel Vigo came to Vincennes, he was unmarried. He soon acquired a beautiful home, owned the finest boat upon the river, and entertained General Clark and, later, Governor Harrison. Governor Harrison made his home with him for a time before Grouseland was finished. By the way, the general has returned from being minister to Colombia and some say—hold on to your bonnet—he is considering running for president of the United States!

Colonel Vigo's wife, whom he married here, lived with him for twenty-five years. He has never had children, and as you know she has been gone several years now. I feel sorry for the old colonel, for he has no kin in this country. At this time not many seem interested in him except for Betsy. He has done so much for the Catholic Church, and some of the church members help him a little. If you have time, I wish you would write the old colonel a letter.

I will say the town tries to honor him from time to time. He presided over the Fourth of July celebration a couple of years ago, and you know that is an honor. And after all, a county has been named after him!

Many home seekers are passing through this place upon their way to the wide prairie lands of Illinois. Some of the settlers are making for northern Illinois, which, I understand, is good homestead country. I wish you could have been here earlier in the year and seen a typical pioneer family going west. In this group of settlers there were three families, more or less related. In all there were thirteen souls. They were not immediately able to cross the Wabash by fording at the winter season of the year. There was some ice upon the river, and it was a little high, so they decided to tarry a short while. This group was of all ages ranging from babes to old men. There was one talkative fellow in the group by the name of Dennis Hanks. Since they had paused in their journey, I invited him to tea. He was ready to give much family history. He said they started from Pigeon Creek,

Spencer County, Indiana, and were upon their way to Macon County, Illinois. He told of unusual hardship on the way, as it was cold most of the time. They had followed a route that took them through Jasper, the county seat of Dubois County, then to Petersburg, the county seat of Pike County, in the same general area in which you live, and finally to this place.

This fellow Hanks said they had heard that there was a good bit of the country over on the Sangamon River waiting for settlers. He said he got good reports from a relative, but he wanted to see for himself before he pulled stakes and moved. He related how the families came from Kentucky to Spencer County about fourteen years ago. The land in Spencer County didn't suit, so he wanted to make an inspection for himself. The talkative one then said that after he saw the Illinois land, he knew it was good. He returned and advised his people to get ready and to move at once. That's why they were traveling in winter weather. Hanks said the river over in Illinois was named by the Indians and meant a land of plenty to eat. This story reminded me of the stories we heard five or six years ago, when land to the east and north was called "the land of promise." Your Canaan land. It seems only yesterday my dear girl and her new husband were so enthusiastic about a new home not upon an open prairie, but in the deep forest.

Some of the citizens of the town were attracted by the "gift of gab" of Hanks. I was asked to meet the group when they pulled up at the courthouse to ask permission to stay outside for a day or two until the river conditions improved. There was one young man in the group who attracted my attention very much. He had a serious countenance and an intelligent look. They call him Abe Lincoln. His father, stepmother, and other members of this family were in the group. Part of the time the women rode in the wagons, but the men walked. This young Lincoln fellow was tall and ungainly. He wore heavy boots, and his buckskin trouser legs were much too short. His hair was black, long, and shaggy, and the blouse coat he wore was short in length and at the sleeves. I am not sure but that this fellow wore a slouch hat. I know you have many of this sort out in the hills near you. They are good people, many unschooled, but this Lincoln lad has struggled on his own to read and write, loving books more than hunting or fishing in the wilds.

I had a talk with young Abraham before they pushed on. He said he had just reached his majority a few days earlier. When he finishes this trip he is going to strike out for himself. The young man so attracted my attention that I wanted to hear him talk and asked him questions. He used the peculiar dialect so common among the poor people in the hills of southern Indiana. You know we call it Hoosier dialect, as it is different from our dialect so much influenced by the French language. This young Abraham told me that the "milk sickness" is again raging in the neighborhood of Pigeon Creek, killing livestock and striking some of the farmers. He told me that his family has had more than their share of the sickness. His mother was taken away when he was a mere lad. It didn't take much persuasion from the roving members of his family to convince them all that they must move on. When I got this young chap to talking, he was very interesting. I think it is the schoolteacher in me. He related how the family had made every part of their wagons, save the iron tires, which surrounded the solid wooden wheels. The whole of the wagons are made from native wood. The tongue and coupling pole are seasoned hickory. The wheels and the bolsters are of oak. The wagons are held together with hickory pegs and cleats. They use slippery elm bark to make ties, and hickory withes are bent to suit by boiling them in hot water. It is evident this group is poor, for all of their furniture, cooking utensils, and farming implements are stowed in the three wagons.

I must tell you more about young Abe. He is so gawky and yet so bright. He told me he had bought a supply of "jim-cracks" at Jones's Store before leaving Pigeon Creek. He intends "peddling them out" as they move along. I was anxious to see his pack and asked to see his merchandise. In his pocket he had needles and pins, buttons and thread, tinware and suspenders. He had other small articles which I cannot remember. I asked him if he thought he could sell these articles. He replied that he has already sold some, and he would do a hard job trying. I bought a few buttons just for the sake of remembering the young man.

Young Abe was anxious to see the printing press of the newspaper, so I volunteered to take him over to the office of the Western Sun, where he met our old friend Elihu Stout. Mr. Stout took an interest in the young man and told him some of his early troubles in starting a newspaper. You know he delights in reminiscing about his early experiences. He told young Abe the story he has so often repeated of how he procured his press and printing equipment for the papers at Frankfort, Kentucky, and how he had to transport everything by keelboat down the Kentucky and Ohio rivers and up the Wabash. The editor told the young fellow that he often took rags with him on each trip to Kentucky on three horses, one of which he would ride himself. He would load the other two with paper and barrels of ink on the return trip. He never forgets the storms, floods, wild animals, and Indians along the Buffalo Trace that made his trips exciting adventures. I knew he would not be able to resist telling of his fight with the wildcat, and sure enough, he told the whole story, often stretching it out a little beyond the way he told it years ago. But we've had our own wildcat stories, too, haven't we? I recall the one from the posse all those years ago to find your Peter!

Mr. Stout told Abe that although he had to do all of the work in the beginning, nowadays much of the mechanical part was now being done by young apprentices. Elihu did not fail to impress this young fellow with the idea that he still writes all of the editorials and directs the policy of the paper. Young Lincoln was much impressed with the setting of type and the printing of the newspapers. He seemed reluctant to leave the place.

As the group left our town, we could not help feeling sorry for them. The weather was so cold, and they were so poorly equipped. The group had three wagons and seven yoke of oxen. The Hanks man bade me goodbye as the group finally pulled out, the men walking beside the wagons. They seemed to take a pride in the way they managed their oxen. They had long rawhide whips and would curl them around the oxen's heads, and with a sudden jerk of the hand the whips would straighten out with a loud, sharp report. They seemed to be able to play their whips wherever needed. The drivers yelled at their droopy-eyed teams, and the steers would bawl and squirm in their yokes.

I later heard that that group, moving on, camped at Emison's Mill upon Maria Creek. The men were much exercised when they were told how they would cross the river. The ferry toll seemed unusually large to them, but the ferryman explained it would cost more to carry over three wagons with teams and livestock than the usual fare. This letter is long, and I have said more about the Lincoln family than I intended, but they have so much reminded me of my own dear Joan when five years ago she moved east instead of west. She was going where she would be all covered by the big trees, while they will arrive at a prairie.

Give my love to your husband and a big, no, a small bear hug for the little son.

As ever M. T.

Chapter 23

The Billies
1830

From time to time Judge Walter Ogden dropped in to see the Cooper family in their new home. Judge Ogden, a tall, lanky man with a drawling voice, was one of the best jurists in southern Indiana. He lived in lodgings at the county seat, but his heart was out in the forest lands. He particularly liked to hunt and visit the hill people, and as he sat in the parlor of the new house, conversing with Peter and Joan, he was not averse to giving his opinions of the people he called the "Billies." He would often stop to chuckle. Joan wondered if he really felt this way about these folks, grouping them all together and discussing their idiosyncrasies, or if he cared about them and just liked to have fun at their expense. It gave him subject matter, anyway, on a rainy day in Canaan to speculate about others. This was his view of the hillbillies out in the "holler":

Back in the hills not far from Canaan (he said) lived the hill people, the "hillbillies" or "billies," as the settlement's Kentucky settlers had called them. The name stuck. They were a distinctive type content to hunt, fish, trap, and loaf. Some of the settlers coming into the valley in the last five years as the community was being built could not stand the dull life of village living. To prepare the ground, plant the seed, cultivate, and harvest and store grain and vegetables was too monotonous for these folk, as it required energy and time, so they moved back into the hills. While the thrifty farmer was hard at work, the hillbilly could be asleep or, at most, taking it easy by the stream. What was life for, if it wasn't to enjoy yourself?

Some of these folks decided to live free, without benefit of government records, thinking it a waste of money to pay the government price for land when they could go up the hollow and become squatters. These people up the hollow raised a little corn and beans and some sweet potatoes and pumpkins. Their meager crop was gathered about frost time and lasted until the first hard freeze. When the weather was cold, they killed some game and depended upon charity. Listening to the old Indian legends, they believed that the two spirits North Wind and South Wind fought each other all winter. When the South Wind won, perhaps Indian Summer or Blackberry Winter, they could crawl out of their huts or holes, fill their bellies if possible, and stretch like they had been in a long sleep. When the North Wind started down the hollow, they would again dive for their holes and pull their bearskins over themselves, living on dried jerky, apples, and cornmeal or one huge ham from which they cut slices for weeks.

The only money they needed was to purchase fishhooks, hunting knives, and powder. For these articles they would often trade a valuable fur. Each family cleared a small truck patch of never more than two or three acres. The heavy rains over a long period of time washed the soil from the hilltops. So much of it as did not go down the stream in flood-time, was deposited in spots in the valley. These patches were unusually fertile, and if given an opportunity, would have produced a good crop, but the "billy" was indifferent to the chance.

They cleared their patches of underbrush and chopped down trees less than a foot in diameter. The larger trees were "girdled" by removing the bark in a band around the trunk. Then, after burning the brush and removing felled trees, they plowed around the trunks and "jumped" over the roots with a light "jumping plow," taking always the easy way.

In the spring of the year and before the weather got warm, the head of the family would draft his entire bunch. They would start out with good intentions to prepare the patch for a crop, but these good resolutions never lasted long. With an old upright "furrying plow," the father would force the ox back and forth until the ground was all messed up. The good intentions would then extend themselves until the patch was seeded, but from then on it was a struggle between the crop and the weeds, with the latter usually winning the race. When the days got long and hot, it would be hard to find a hoe up the valley, but in spite of all the neglect, the soil was so fertile that some corn and sweet potatoes could be located by frost-time.

These hillbillies lived in quite crude cabins, especially if they were new arrivals, by which title they could have been known for at least a couple of years. Small saplings were selected and driven in the ground in front of a steep hill. A fair-sized cave was dug in the hill, and these saplings formed the three sides of the hut with the hill side as the rear. Saplings were piled up on the tops of the driven-in logs, which in turn were covered with boughs, cornstalks, and finally dirt. These huts were called "dugouts." They had one door, sometimes a window, and possibly a stick chimney. Most cooking was done outside, except in the extremely cold weather, when the first fire was built on the floor in back of the front door. Dirt was mounded against the outside piling, and the "dugout" could be really warm.

A visitor back in the hills would attract attention and usually was not welcomed by the hill people. Judge Ogden was an exception, showing that in spite of the way he talked he was a true friend to the Billies. Others they accepted warily. If there were sickness in the cabins, and Doctor Eldridge, the village physician, or Joan or another charitable lady acting as midwife visited the section, they were escorted to the proper cabin by a number of the inhabitants. The visitor would find first the patch, where he could usually see some stunted corn or stray vegetables. Near the home was the pigsty that held the shoat, which would stand upon its hind legs and reach the top of its pen and squeal if a visitor came near. Over to the other side was a fodder-covered shelter for the old milk cow, a lean-to for the old plug, which fortunately for himself, spent his time away from home foraging, and of course, a rather well-prepared house for a hound, who had the place of honor. With the complete equipment, the hill family was prepared to meet all of life's vicissitudes.

If anyone "up the holler" was able to shoot a stag, a wild hog, or a "bar," there was sure to be plenty of food for a few days. Every neighbor was generous and took pride in being able to divide with his friends. This was a time to pay back folks in Canaan who had done favors. These hill folk could be generous and grateful and had their own share of pride. After a neighbor had had "luck," and the families had had a good feast, it would take a quantity of "yaller root" to bring him back to normal. A jug of moonshine whiskey could usually be found in the dark corner of each home. It was kept only to be used in case of snakebite or protracted sickness. Empty gallon jugs could be bought at Trowbridge's general store in Canaan, but the contents of these jugs during the remainder of their existence was far too strong to be imbibed by one not accustomed to it. A test for moonshine was to see if a saucer of it would burn blue for a half hour. And of course, the more staid members of the community, down in the valley, were also often tempted by spirits, coming to the hillside stills or imbibing higher quality spirits without quite so much wallop but also the ability to get them intoxicated too often, to the detriment of themselves and their families.

The hill people came to Canaan occasionally, but they wouldn't tarry long. The men, wearing homespun clothes, flannel shirts, broad-rimmed hats, and high boots, were invariably followed by their long-eared, sad-eyed coon dogs. These dogs were lean and hungry looking and could give forth an unusually long dismal howl at the least provocation. Each family in the hills had one or more of these dogs. The standing of a hillbilly in his community was determined by the value of his canine attendant, and an owner would take great pride in telling how his dog treed a coon, each tale full of adventure. In spring the hillbilly would display upon the south side of his own barn many coon skins drying so as to be ready for market. The settlers up the "holler" could talk for hours concerning the relative merits and wonderful accomplishments of these splendid canines.

The coon dog had followed his migrating master from the hills of Kentucky and it was these canines that made Judge Ogden particularly eloquent. As many of the hillbillies came from south of the big river, the habits of the hill country of Kaintuck had conditioned them, he said, and then went on again. Some of the coon hunters preferred a bright, full moon-lit night for hunting, while others wanted dark, rainy nights. The bright-light coon hunters would tell of treeing the coon and then waiting patiently until the coon came out upon a limb, where they could get him full in front of the moon. The crack of the rifle could bring him tumbling to the ground. This method of hunting was called "mooning the coon." Some coon hunters considered it unfair to the coon and would no more take advantage of a coon under those circumstances than they would shoot a rabbit while sitting. They had their own code of honor, the judge affirmed.

The billy would almost go hungry himself in order that his dog might be fed. People in the valley said the children up on those hills came in for affection only after the dog. One often wondered how the dog could see around his big ears. There is no question but that the ears got mixed in the dog's food when he was trying to eat. The dog loved to lie in the sun and sleep. His lips would draw back, exposing his teeth and big red gums, and the slobbers would bubble out of his mouth as he breathed. The lower eyelids drooped, affording a splendid roosting place for gnats and flies, which he occasionally wiped off with one of his front paws. This dog looked sad and forsaken even while being admired by his owner. Perhaps he was happy in his own right, but that could not be determined from his looks while lying in front of a cabin.

Of a full-moon night this coon dog showed off to best advantage. He would put his front feet upon a log, looking at the moon, and bay. The long dismal sound would carry for miles. The "beller" was sure to be answered in other directions by the same kind of a dog until the dogs could be heard the length of the hollow, making music in more than one octave. There was something in the moon that reached the soul of the coon dog. While the mournful howl was hardly a pleasant sound, the dog seemed to enjoy it in a peculiar sort of way. One thing was certain: the dog was never required to cease howling, and his owner was satisfied with his vocal efforts and seemed to enjoy the concerts.

Several of the hunters who lived "up the holler" were proud of their foxhounds. These hounds were smaller and more trim and alert than the sleepy old coon dogs. A foxhound had more sense than his half-cousin, for he kept his mouth shut part of the time. But when upon the trail, he sent forth a bellow that struck joy into the hearts of the hunters. Fox hunters would congregate from far and near when word was abroad that there would be a fox chase back in the hollow, and it was Judge Ogden who often spread the word. He was at his best on a horse among the Billies at the chase.

It was not necessary to follow the dogs, for the hounds would bring the fox around. Each hunter knew the bay of his own dog, and he could tell his position in the pack, even if he were a mile away. The hunters would seat themselves in the saddle of their horses, turn the dogs loose, and wait for the fun. The hounds ran in a pack. If one struck a scent, he would start his unearthly yelp. Soon he would be followed by others. Hunters could tell by the bark of their dogs just how they were progressing. The men on horseback would chide one another, for the dogs in the rear were in disgrace, and then the betting would begin. If a man was really proud of his dog, he would bet freely and liberally. When the younger dogs were out-distanced by the old faithfuls, the owners of the old dogs would shout with laughter. Some of the hillbillies owned good dogs, and they would invite their friends in town to come out and enjoy the chase. Many would come.

Judge Ogden would leave any business matter to join with the fox hunters for one of their chases. His voice grew more animated as he described the chase. As the hunt progressed, it seemed that even the horses sensed the spirit of the chase, for they became nervous and would prance and neigh. If the sound of the dog chorus grew fainter, the marshal would sound his cow-horn bugle, and the horses would bound away in the direction of the baying hounds. The moment one of the dogs discovered the scent, he would announce the fact with a sharp bark that was to be immediately followed by long howls. The pack would then give "full tongue," and every dog would join in the chorus. Each yelping hound had his own particular key to be followed by a variety of expanding barks, all depending upon the age of the scent. Yet amid all the confusion, each horseman knew the voice of his own dog. Some bayed a deep, mellow bass, others a sharp, shrill staccato, while some of the older dogs gave forth a long "foghorn beller." The high and the low yelps, when tempered with the deep and the shrill, would create in the ears of the hunters the finest symphony.

A clear, frosty, full-moon night was the choice of the veteran hunter. The men from town came late, because there was little use of unleashing the hounds until after the dew fell. With the grass and leaves dry, it was hard to pick up the scent. If the hunters stayed until morning it made little difference, for the runs were usually held upon Saturday night. If the hunt was on a weekday, it was not much trouble for a fox hunter to find some excuse for not working the next day.

These long-eared foxhounds could easily have outrun a fox upon a fair field, but the cunning old Reynard usually took to the hills and streams, darted under logs, and through "stake and rider" fences, until Mister Fox could almost laugh at his tormentor. Most foxes had a habit of crossing and recrossing their own trails until the hounds often found themselves in confusion. At break of day, many hunters have seen the sly old fox silhouetted before the morning sun, running along the ridge, staring down at his enemies in evident glee. Upon such occasions the smirk upon his face meant that he had outwitted the swiftest fox-dog. Rarely did the hounds ground their prey, but if they did it meant that the hunt was over, for the smart old fox knew enough to select a hole in the ground among the roots of some big tree. Sometimes the hillbillies' dogs would wait for days to grab their prey when hunger forced the sly little fox from his hole. It did not seem a bit cruel to the hill people; foxes could cause real mayhem in chicken sheds, thus destroying the meat for an entire season.

The billies had a cure for everything. Many of their remedies included some black magic and sorcery. Old Granny Whitehouse knew more "cures" than anyone else. Sometimes substantial farmers in the valley would out of desperation rely upon her strange prescriptions. Granny advised that if you would rub a wart with a stolen dishrag, then bury the cloth, the wart would disappear. She advised against handling toads. She caused many a child to go for months with a bag of asafetida tied to a string and hung around the neck to keep off childhood diseases. Doc Eldridge said it would be hard for the miasmas that caused disease, bad air currents, to drift past that smell, especially if the bag were worn for a long time. Granny insisted that a poultice made of jimson weeds would reduce swelling. She stated that burning a piece of yarn would cure croup and that a buckeye carried in your pocket would cure rheumatism.

Some of these old brown-skinned cave dwellers may have had Indian blood in their veins. If they had high cheekbones and straight black hair, they could not have been told from Indians. Many of the hillbillies, however, had light hair that was usually faded by being sunburned.

These people of the back country had their own politics, government, and business. At election time they would yell for Andrew Jackson, whether he was a candidate or not. Old Hickory had an appeal for them; he loved the common man and was even opening the White House to them. "You know, they trooped in and tore the place up," Judge Ogden had opined on one of these country fox hunts, and the billies gave him looks that could kill.

The men smoked long-stemmed corncob pipes, and the women were fond of snuff. When the hill dwellers went to town, they yoked up two steers if they could be found and filled the box bed of the wagon with straw, and the whole family was ready for a two-day jaunt. The family would hold the wagon back going down hill until the valley road was reached. Then they would all jump in, ready for the oxen to pull the rest of the way while most of them snoozed. They liked to spend one night in the county seat or the smaller town of Canaan, sleeping in their wagon, so they would start from home early in the morning and would take all the next day going back. The hillbillies paid no taxes, had no schools, were scarce on churches, and cared little for local politics, but were ready for an argument any time, taking the side of the poor man.

The average household consisted of a couple of quilts, some frayed bedclothes, plenty of furs, a few pots, spiders, a table, and a few homemade chairs. Outdoors the menfolk kept the ax, a hatchet, a saw, spider pots of various sizes, some knives, a hoe, and parts of old harness. In the barn they kept the plow and a few chickens. All farm stock and poultry were supposed to forage for themselves, and they were scrawny; as a rule there was little to eat on the side of the hills.

The billies' houses, after they left the lean-tos, were built up the hollow, along the sides of the hills. It would never do to have the hut too close to the stream, for the water came boiling down the gulley at the time of the spring freshets and would often be swift and deep. Some of these hill dwellers avoided open springs, for they thought dreadful diseases like milk sickness, typhoid fever, and malaria were hidden in the white sand which lay at the bottom of clear, cold springs. They avoided the level land because jack-o-lanterns or will-o'-the-wisps hovered over the meadowlands. It was dangerous to live where the nightshade plant grew, they said. These people also knew that where the land was fertile, the settlers were expected to use their plow and hoe, whether they liked it or not. They slept warmly, because they were generally provided with the skins of buffalo and other heavy furs from a former generation.

Judge Ogden knew his recent history. Some of the hill people, he said, had come through Cumberland Gap, passed Lexington, crossed the Ohio at Madison, and traveled on north. Some followed the west bank of the Kentucky River, crossed the Big River at Ash's Ferry, and then came north. Others came by way of the Trader's Trace, but most of them came through Kentucky and out of the big hills.

Those in this community had no regular doctors and didn't believe in education, but old Mike Bigger was recognized as knowing the most about the things connected to feeling poorly and living well. Mike advised that soft lye soap must be used in tanning deerskin fit for buckskin breeches; that all planting of grain must be done while "the sign was in the head," that is, figuring by astronomical signs, the sign of Aries; that the first thunder in the spring awakens the snakes; that a cold winter is always followed by a hot summer; that fruit is never killed by a frost in the light of the moon; that it's wise to bathe only in the dark of the moon; that fish bit best in the dark of the moon; that cucumbers should be planted on the sixth of July and turnips sowed on the twenty-third of July, wet or dry; that it is bad luck for thirteen to sit at the table; that a hoe or ax should not be carried through the house; that it is bad luck for a black cat to cross your path; and that if you break a mirror, you will have seven years of bad luck. He advised, don't sing in bed; never be married while it rains; throw rice and old shoes at the wedding party for good luck. He also said to hang a horseshoe over the door for success and hunt for four-leaf clovers if you want to do well. A mole on the neck means money by the peck. Never let a cat near a corpse; plant corn when new leaves on the trees are the size of a squirrel's ear. When sun's rays come out from under a cloud, that is a sign of God's grace. Old Mike was consulted many times to find a sign that would bring good luck.

Diet was a subject these folks cared about: they often filled their plates with country food. They loved cornpone, sow belly, sweet potatoes, and molasses. A pot of "biled" cabbage with a "hunk" of fat meat was "mighty fillin'." Biled ham bone and sour dock was not bad eatin'. Dandy-lions could be picked and et during the early spring. Cucumbers were planted "just to see them grow." No one would eat a pickle, for it was sure to "bring on summer complaint," chills, biles, "yaller jaunders," cholerymorbis, cancer, or maybe consumption. If you must eat pickles, be sure to soak them for a long time in strong brine, then chuck them down in strong apple cider vinegar. If the pickle would make a pig squeal, it was safe to eat. Some epicures of the hills cut their pumpkins into strips, threaded them upon a cord, and hung them in the attic until they were ready for pies.

Joan and Peter were not sure how they felt about this discussion, but they were able to add to it a bit.

Joan raised sage and red mango peppers in her garden. Often when passing the billies would ask for a few peppers to tone up their sow belly or, as they said, "to cut the grease." In the rear of the Cooper home, Peter raised his garden vegetables. Billies would stop and hint for some choice article. In the fall, Peter lined barrels with clean straw and carefully stored his apples, turnips, parsnips, carrots, and potatoes. These barrels were placed in a deep furrow on their sides and covered with straw. The open end of the barrel was covered with boards, and the whole covered with earth. By Christmastime, the opening board was removed and fine fresh fruit and vegetables brought out. The hillbillies were often helped with their Christmas dinner from Peter's cold-storage barrels, usually with his permission.

The hill people, for their part, shared what they had, Peter reminded the judge. They raised gourds that were used the next summer as homes for wrens, bluebirds, and martins, and they gave them to friends in town. They taught Joan how to raise medicinal "yarbs" such as mullen, pokeroot, calomel, mint, horehound, senna, pennyroyal, and elderberry. She already knew, as a good housewife, many of these; others she came to regard for their efficacy. Old Mike Bigger told Joan his friends up the hollow were partial to the sycamore tree, as it was good for nothing, which just suited them.

He said, "You know the sycamore is common along streams and their white arms reach out over everything. They have no nuts or fruit and do not even make good lumber. Squirrels and coons stay away from them because of their treacherous bark. Crows and eagles sometimes build nests in their high bare limbs. Owls like to build nests in their holes, and the holes and the old hollow trunk furnish a nice place for the old sow and her pigs. The old hen will sometimes nest a little high, and ducks and geese will crowd around the tree at nighttime. And you know, Joan, little girls can use the hollow trunks as a playhouse. It asks nothin'; it gives a lot."

Mike would close his remarks with much satisfaction by saying, "I tell you, Missus Cooper—we have the only sensible life. We the folk of the earth can only eat so much. We need only a few clothes, so what is the use of work and worry? Some of our young folks break away, but born amongst the hills you want to cling to them." Joan could nod her head at this sentiment.

When the going was tough, the winter long, the children sickly, and the mother ready to give birth, it was Joan the hill people came to, and she gladly went to help them, as they helped her from time to time. She had become attached to them, and was not sure she enjoyed listening to the judge go on about the folks, making them all seem the same and—rather stupid. Down deep, there wasn't much difference between the men on the hill and those down below in the village. A generation or so before, many of those in the nice cabins and houses in town had been wearing homespun, eating coon meat, and letting the hogs sit on the front porch.

Chapter 24

Canaan, the Promise Fulfilled
1832

Peter and Joan had now lived in the Canaan settlement for more than seven years, and were "a," if not "the" leading family in the village. Fine farms had been developed, and the soft, rich, loamy soil produced abundantly. Peter's dream was now coming true, for in this valley a grade of wheat was grown that made splendid flour. Also he was able to handle large quantities of grain; big, solid ears of white corn made good meal, and bushels of corn were used in making hominy. Big ox teams hitched four to the wagon hauled Cooper products in the four directions. Even the old route back toward home in Vincennes carried bags of "Cooper Best Brand of Flour," as big wagonloads went south toward the Ohio River. Some were even delivered to the new and growing capital of the state at Indianapolis.

The state was encouraging building of good highways, but in the Canaan community the roads could not be used for commerce much during the winter and spring months. It was necessary to get the products of the mill to the markets while the roads were firm and solid. Most road building was in the hands of township road supervisors, and these men, without public funds, could not do much building. The county gave little road assistance, and the state was centering its efforts upon a few main highways and canals that hadn't been completed and seemed to go nowhere.

Farmers in the Canaan neighborhood, caught up in the drive to prosperity, were demanding roads so they could get their products to market. The road that led to the county seat, the Canaan Road, could be used only part of the year. After leaving the valley, this poorly graded road followed winding streams. Farmers constructed small culverts, but where the road crossed Big Creek, there was no bridge, and the ford was treacherous. Wagons stalled in the marsh. Heavy loads were ordered off the road whenever there were big rains.

The Canaan road had been a path made by the Indians upon their ponies. Settlers followed this same path on horseback, then with ox cart.

Later trees were cut, some grading was done, and gravel was used in mud holes, until this winding route was the best road out of the valley. Since road supervisors had been given the power to order able-bodied men out to work upon the roads, some things were being accomplished. Each farmer would bring his plow, his grader, and his team to work together. After the roadbed was made, they would haul coarse gravel, which packed and made a passable road. Those settlers knew that as soon as the Canaan Road reached the Michigan Road they would have better markets.

The Michigan Road was still working to complete its route from Madison upon the Ohio River to South Bend, Indiana, and on to Michigan. Land for it had been given to the state of Indiana to improve. With the job, a strip of land one mile wide upon either side also went to the state. Contractors were given every other section of land, checkerboard fashion, provided they would clear the highway of trees and improve the roadbed to a width of thirty feet. The right of way for the highway was made one hundred feet and retained by the state. At this time of construction, work was progressing well south of Indianapolis, but only the southern fifty miles of the road were usable throughout the entire year.

The Cooper Mill had been built, as Peter wished, along new and improved lines. Engineers had developed waterwheels that collected the maximum of power from the water in the race. The water in the millstream never ran low, for it was fed from many springs. It flowed, traveled, out of the hillsides for miles down from the gullies. These tiny feeders united to form a constant flow of water into the creek that came from the hills. Peter had installed big burrs that ground fast and fine, although the steam mill idea was still in the future.

The mill was big enough to allow a number of the burrs to be maintained. Clear, cold water ran down the millstream to the dam. There a large pond was formed, which in turn supplied the race, which carried the water under the wheel and caused the wheel to turn. It then flowed off and over big, flat boulders and wandered back into the millstream. The pool below the wheel was deep. Big fish hid from the many anglers who sat with pole in hand trying to lure some fat bass toward the bait and then into the frying pan. Of a warm summer day, nothing could be more restful than to loiter down by the old millstream. Peter often dreamed of himself, a little boy, watching the same sort of water and fish at his father's mill.

Nobody knew where the millstream started. The hill people who came out of the hollow gave varied stories of the origin of this beautiful stream of clear, cold water. The hills were high, and the hollow seemed to follow the bases of the hills for miles. As years went by, big stories also came down with the water, and nobody knew just what to believe of the millstream tales. Some said the millstream flowed out of the side of the largest hill. Some said dark caves fed the stream. Many of the billies believed that a subterranean stream flowed under the hills, finding its way out and into the millstream. The forest trees were not large, but they were dense along the banks of this stream, making it hard for travelers to follow it. A boat could not go up-stream because of boulders and shallows, and the pools were too deep for wading. Paths followed the streamlets up in the hills, but none of these ever ran to the source of the flow of water. Mystery came with the water out of the hills. If a true story had come out of the hollow, no one would have known whether or not to believe it. Peter often remarked that sometime when he had the time he would follow the millstream to its source.

The high hills back of Canaan were rough, rocky, and covered with stunted vegetation. The land on the hills was so poor that trees never grew tall. As more squatters came from the South, it was necessary for them to push farther back into the hills and onto even poorer land. At first the new-comer who went farthest back was content with a path down to the road. As other home-seekers came, the path became a road used by ox carts and mud boats. As each hill person was satisfied with one patch, it was necessary only for the latest arriving squatter to follow the hollow to the next level patch. There he would dig in, or if he were energetic, he and his big family would build a cabin of small logs and daub abundantly with the yellow clay that was easily obtained in the side of any hill. The longer this yellow clay mud was exposed to the air, the harder it became, and rains had little effect upon it. No cabin up the hollow had ever received a coat of paint or bit of whitewash, so the hut always looked about the same. The squatters wanted neighbors, so the cabins were spotted as close together as acre tracts of valley could be found. If given a little encouragement, the men from back in the hills could tell an exciting story of a fight with a wildcat or a "bar," but Joan Cooper could never get information from these people concerning the ferns or flowers or birds that were abundant along the millstream.

There were two types of people seeking homes who inquired at the Trowbridge store at the Canaan crossroads: those who wanted to go back into the hills and those who wanted to buy rich farmland. Most land had been entered and patented by the government years before, but there were always those who wanted to move onto what was left. Usually, also, there were some farmers who would "give it up" for various reasons and move on, ever on. Good land in the valley was at a premium. If a family came searching for a home, and if they carried good references, Trowbridge would direct them to the farms that might be bought. Trowbridge claimed he could always spot a squatter; he would send them up the millstream road. These people, when inquiring, usually used the name of some hill relative who lived up the hollow and who was known to Trowbridge. The fact that their wagon was in a bad state of repair, or their horse was old and poor, or that their cow looked travel worn was not always the determining factor. If the inquirer were followed by several long-eared, sleepy-looking hound dogs, that was all that needed to be known.

The billies also followed the millstream road in the opposite direction, down to the Cooper Mill. There they traded their grain for flour and meal. Peter saved this usually inferior grain to make meal especially for the billies, and they were satisfied with it. Peter treated these people with kindness and consideration, and many of them came to him with their troubles. These lowly people generally walked to the mill, leading their "hosses," upon whose backs were a few sacks of poor-grade corn. Hillbillies traded the corn for meal made of the same grade corn.

Peter kept meal in stock for these people. There was no difference if their grain was mixed, for it was always the same grade, and the hill people didn't want to wait in line for their turn. "These people are always in a hurry to get back up the hollow where they are not crowded or rushed," Judge Ogden, who knew them, told Peter. "Coarse meal is more to their taste than is the finer milled you do. Hoecake lacks something, they say, if the meal is too fine."

"Up the hollow," the judge went on, tamping his pipe, "time means nothing. In the valley everyone must hurry back home to tend to things. The drummers and lawyers and tradespeople who are increasingly coming to our town are always rushing around." The judge lived at the county seat but seemed to prefer being in Canaan. A bachelor, he was always welcome at the Cooper house.

Peter told him, "I myself have been working harder than I had expected to as my business demands growth. I had expected to revel in the beauty of the woods, but there is little time." Peter sometimes wondered, he told the judge, who had the better life, "us or the billies."

"That sense of country serenity, slow pace, that's what I like up there with my friends," the judge said, funneling more tobacco into the pipe. "The lawsuits that I have to deal with in this area would shock the hair off your head. Prosperity brings litigation."

Signs of progress were obvious in the town. Canaan school was in full operation. Two churches, Baptist and Presbyterian, had regular Sunday services. The Catholic church was up the road. Trowbridge's general store was well stocked with merchandise, with teacups and saucers, bolts of muslin, clocks and watches and blue pill, and even children's dolls and horehound drops coming in from the north and south. The blacksmith, a man named Rube Stockbridge, had done well from the beginning of the settlement. Farm implements were coming into the valley, and the clear ring of the smith's anvil told that the farmers were busy these days. The plow had been improved, and the old wooden mouldboard was giving way to steel. The best scythers in the county lived in this valley, but they welcomed news that a man in the east by the name of Cyrus McCormick had invented a machine that would cut the wheat and bind it in neat rows. One prophet in the valley even went so far as to say that he believed before long this machine would bind the wheat into sheaves. There were always men who liked to talk, sitting around the stove in the store in winter and on the benches outside in summer. Their wives said they were good at avoiding work. Not many gave credence to the thought that there ever would be a machine that would cut wheat and bind it at the same time, but these men listened with interest.

In this community each farmer helped his neighbor at harvest time. The cradlers would go into the wheat fields, one following another. With this backbreaking work, fields of wheat would soon yield. Cradlers would lay the grain in neat bundles to be tied by the binders who took some of the wheat stalks and, with deft movement of the hands, would securely bind them. Not a great deal of wheat was planted by each farmer, for caring for the wheat was a difficult process. When the wheat was well dried, it was brought to the flaying floor where the wheat was whipped out of the straw.

Then the grains went on to Peter Cooper's mill.

Corn was the grain of the gods, as indeed the Indians had said. It was planted by hand and covered with a hoe, but with the blacksmith's new shovel plow, the ground could be furrowed out and later covered by the same plow. Later this plow was used to cultivate the growing corn. In the fall the cornstalks were cut and shocked. Still later, the corn was husked with the help of an iron shucking peg that fit in the farmer's hand. Some in the town felt they were on the edge of something good, but then people everywhere have always wondered what ten years down the pike would bring to them.

Chapter 25

Blabbering Minnie
1836

Joan had hired help with the house warming, if it was indeed help, and she continued to have a hired girl to assist her with the large amounts of daily chores a woman faced. That help was unpredictable. Minnie, everyone's hired girl from the hills, often showed up and took over the kitchen in Joan's and other people's houses. That was the way she operated.

Minnie lived with her parents and about a "baker's dozen" of brothers and sisters back in the hills. She seemed to be related in some way to Mike Bigger. Minnie was not timid, and as she wanted to talk all of the time and sometimes tripped up in her speech as she raced along, she acquired the name of Blabbering Minnie. Just what her last name was made little difference to her or her friends, for she was well known in Canaan. She came out of the hills frequently and stayed for irregular periods, usually to visit and work for two weeks at one place, but her favorite period of work was two days. Minnie had worked in practically every home in Canaan, for she liked to get around, to look around. About the only thing that would keep her from working in a home was that she couldn't get in. If the housewife saw her first, the homemaker might decide not to be at home to the willing worker.

The moment Minnie arrived in any home, she removed her hat and coat and announced to the housewife that she had come to work a spell. No one ever sent for Minnie, even if hard pressed for help, and no one asked her to stay. It wasn't necessary. She took it for granted that she was welcome and wanted. Sometimes the first announcement of Minnie's presence was the rattling of pots and pans. Minnie had no thought of leaving if she was not needed and paid no attention if told to leave. She had a certain mission to perform, and she used her own notions about the performance. She could, in her best mode, work very hard.

There was always work to be done in a house, especially in the spring. Braided rugs had to be taken up and beaten out on the line or a tree branch.

The straw under them had to be replaced. Floors should be scrubbed with sand and soapy water. The soap itself had to be made from the rendered fat and lye water. Candles needed to be dipped and whale oil lamps cleaned. All, and any, of the other tasks of a household she could do. To give her credit, Minnie entered a home and worked night and day until she was finished. Then it would have been inhuman to let her go without paying her something. She had no regular charge but left it to the woman of the house, who generally figured on giving Minnie enough money for her own immediate needs but not enough to share with her non-working brothers. There was no cure for Blabbering Minnie and no way to keep her out. The housewife usually threw up her hands but practiced patience and endurance. And it didn't hurt to get the spring, or fall, cleaning done with some help.

Minnie preferred the Cooper home to all others in the valley. Joan treated her kindly and supplied her with plenty to eat. When she left for home, she was given a large bag of meal for her family, which meant pone for many a day. She stayed longer and did more work in the Cooper home than in any other and was especially fond of young Jimmy. He would listen to her tales of goblins and ghosts, even though the stories came with much gesturing and a frightening voice. Minnie lived in a world of make believe, and the little creatures in her imagination could be seen in the holes of trees or in dark, shady places.

Magic and charms were the frequent subjects of her conversation. She had native intelligence and a good deal of folklore about her that had come down through many generations in the mountains of Tennessee and before that, Ireland. She knew where goblins lived and how they played, and what displeased them. She had seen many ghosts, although she was dreadfully afraid of them. Graveyards and caves were to be avoided at night at all costs. The dancing glens of sprites and fairy folk were known to her. She had sure cures for many ailments, such as sore eyes, baldness, pains in the back, toothache, and bad tempers. She carried a rabbit's foot tied around her left wrist and a buckeye sewn in her undergarments.

This hill girl was deeply religious and prudish. She observed the strictest rules of etiquette for herself in her association with young men. She insisted that the safest rule was to look in the opposite direction when passing a young man. This actually seemed to meet the approval of most young men of Minnie's acquaintance. She came to church each winter as soon as

protracted meeting began and generally joined the church that started its
meeting first. However, she had some prejudice against those denominations
that took their religion quietly. She liked a loud display and thought there
was no use having religion if you could not make a lot of noise with it, if
you couldn't have long meetings and shout a little. She had no use for the
Catholic Church because they had no protracted meetings or revivals and
not much loud noise, though she did like the incense.

Minnie never failed to "give testimony" at church services if any opportunity presented itself. She liked Brother Cummings better than any of the
other preachers, for he could shout and pray louder than the others. Minnie
said he "seemed to understand her soul better than most." By the time his
yearly long revival meeting had been in full blast for about two weeks during
a given year, sermons would be getting longer and the shouting louder. At
one during the past year, church members were really feeling the true religious spirit, were reviving, and new members were being called upon to give
their "experiences." Minnie might be considered a new member, because it
was only during this "spell" that she had "jined" this congregation. Minnie
listened for a long time before she felt the "spirit moving" her, but finally
she decided she must do her part. She rose. People turned around to see her.

"Sompin dredful is goin' to happen in this valley," she started, hand in
the air. "The people are becomin' more and more sinful. Right in this community we hear swearin' and see drunk-ness. The people fight, swill whiskey,
play cards, dance, and play the organ. The Lord has given them warning, but
they won't stop. They keep on their sinful ways, and He has tried hard to
stop 'em. You remember just three years ago this very evening, after one of
our meetings, the Lord sent thousands of stars down upon this Earth until
it looked like a storm of bright lights right out of heaven. The people knew
what had happened. They rushed right back in the meetinghouse and fell
down upon their knees and began to pray. The people prayed so long and
so loud that the Lord decided to give 'em one more chance, and the stars
stopped fallin'.

"Then comes along that long black-whiskered schoolteacher a few days
later and tells the people the Lord was not mad but that every November
about the twelfth the Earth goes through the path of a torn-up comet. He
called the falling stars "meat-ors," or some such name, and said that upon
this occasion of November 12, 1833, that there was the date, that the earth

got right in the mess of these things. He said them shooting stars was about the size of peas and couldn't hurt nobody. He said them gravel stones get red hot moving through our air. Immediately the people took a long breath and begun to sin again."

Minnie pointed her finger at the revival congregation. "This old teacher showed a place in the sky he called the lion and said the stars come from that direction. He called the stars 'Leonids' or somepin' like that. Nobody ever saw so many stars fall before or since. I am glad they run that old teacher out of the community. Sin soon was going as fast as ever.

"For two years the Lord stood this sinnin'. Then he tried to give 'um another warnin'. Only last year, or the year before, I fergit, the Lord put a bright star out there in the heavens with a long tail. The tail was bigger and brighter than the star. He started the whole thing right after us and the people got scared again. They begged and prayed and shouted and sung songs until finally the Lord decided to give 'um another chance and moved the queer star out of the sky. The people breathed easy again. As soon as the star was gone, this valley went back to fightin' and drinkin' whiskey, and worst of all the playin' cards and dancin'.

"The old black-whiskered schoolteacher was gone, but that newspaper which comes into the valley every Saturday ups and makes fun of the Lord and tells the people that it was a comet. It said it comes back every seventy-six years and that it has been coming back for more than a thousand years. Wons't it helped a wicked king from France capture England by scarin' his enemies 'most to death. That paper said it was Howley comet. What is worst of all, Peter and Joan Cooper believe that stuff. I ast 'em when I was a-workin'. They didn't see it as a warning from the Lord. Nobody listened; people now sin again. I have seen the moon cover up its face so it couldn't see the sin. Once the sun almost covered its face. Some of these times the Lord will not be called off. He'll come right down and grab the sinners. He will make the world come to an end. We must all make ready to hear Gabriel's trumpet. Thankee. I may have testified too long—I know they call me Blabbering Minnie. Now I am a-gonna sit down."

Peter and Joan were devoted Presbyterians and had been since their childhood days and their association with Reverend Scott back in Old Vincennes. Now the much-admired reverend was gone. Some winters the new Presbyterian minister could not complete the circuit. There would be no

services in that church for weeks. On these occasions Peter and Joan attended the Methodist, the Hard Shell Baptist, the "Campbellite," or any other
service that might be available in theirs or some other nearby town.

A Methodist revival had been going for some time in the valley a year
or so after the time of the Halley's comet tirade, when Peter and Joan were
down with colds and unable to attend. Minnie had come to work at the
Cooper home so she might be able to go to church every night. One evening
Joan said, "Minnie, I want you to go and to pay particular attention to the
minister's sermon and to report both the text and what he had to say. You
can tell me when you get home. I thank you, as I hate to miss the meeting."
Minnie looked at her uncertainly. She did not want to displease "Missus
Joan."

The minister took his text from the third chapter of Daniel. Minnie
certainly liked to hear about Daniel. They could never find the Bible at her
house, she thought; "mebbe it had been et by one of the goats." Only a few
nights before, the minister had told how Daniel was thrown in the lions'
den because he would not obey Nebuchadnezzar's edict to worship only the
king. Minnie was ready to shout with joy when the minister told how the
lions refused to harm the hero. She was much pleased to hear that when the
king called at the den the next morning, Daniel was alive and well, and that
God had closed the mouths of the lions.

This evening the minister was preaching about the three Hebrew children who were thrown in the fiery furnace. She wanted to listen intently
and be able to report all to "Missus Joan." Nebuchadnezzar was a wicked
king who wanted all of his subjects to worship his strange golden image.
Minnie was delighted that the three Hebrews would rather allow themselves
to be burned alive than give up their Lord. Minnie felt she must make a
good report to Missus Joan and pronounce the names of those Hebrew children. She thought it strange that they should be called children when they
were grown-up men. The old bad king had a hard name, but somehow she
was having no trouble remembering the name "Nebuchadnezzar." The three
children, however, had horrid names to remember.

As Minnie left the church, she resolved to keep repeating the names all
the way home. She wondered how the preacher could pronounce the names
so easily. She began to say, "Shadrach, Meshach, and Abednego." She kept
walking faster and faster and repeating these names as fast as her tongue

would work. It began to sound to her as if she were running the names all together. Just as she was about to enter the front gate at the Cooper home, she stumbled and fell flat. She skinned her knee, and the names of the children completely left her. She sat there ignoring the injured knee and trying hard to recall the names, but she was helpless. Not a single name would come to her mind. What would she do?

Missus Joan would want to know the names of those children, and she would disappoint her. She decided to slip in the back door and go quietly to her bed to avoid making a report until morning. Possibly the names would come to her mind in her sleep. She might get someone to read them to her next morning before she saw the missus.

Peter and Joan had been waiting for Minnie. They had put Jimmy to bed and were reading to each other in their favorite armchairs. The moment the back door opened, they called for her to come in and make a report. Minnie resolved to do her best. She began to stutter, then to blabber, and finally she got started: "The preacher, he, he was surely all het up tonight. He says a lot about Daniel being a wise man and he could read dreams. The bad king, he wanted them three Hebrew children to get in the dirt on their hands and faces and worship that golden calf the king had his men to make. I don't see how they could worship nothin' with their faces in the dirt, but his solders kept callin' 'Get down. Get down.' Them children couldn't git down. The king said he would show who was boss around there, and he said, 'I'll fix you.' Then that old king told his men to take dry wood and poke it in the furnace and heat it up seven times hotter than it had ever been aforetime. He then told his soldiers to tie up these three children, their heads to their foots, good and tight, and when the furnace was red hot to chuck the hull bunch in the fire face fust. The preacher said not one of them was burned, not even a hair on their head singed. The king come a-runnin' up all out of breath and saw them walkin' around on top of the fire and they weren't getting' hurt, and the old king sees another feller in there with them which he thought was the Son of God. My, the king was skeered and mighty nigh blew up. The three children jist smiled and waved their hands at the old rascal. He was afraid they'd come out and git him and throw him in the fire. The king to save his own bacon, he says to his governers, if anybody says anything bad about the children's God that they should be cut to pieces and their homes made a manure pile. Then all ended happy and they danced around. The preacher then said everybody in this valley must worship the Lord. That was all."

"But Minnie, what were the names of the three Hebrew children?" asked Joan.

Minnie was caught; she could not make it after all. She began to blubber around and with a snort and in tears, she shouted, "Short-shirt, no britches, and into bed we go." With that she ran for her bedroom. Joan followed her to tell it was all right; the main thing was that the Lord got the three out and all was well.

Chapter 26

The Country Store
1840

"Peter, I hope you are not going to that old store tonight." Joan put down the county newspaper and looked at her husband. "You have a habit lately of going down there every Saturday night and listening to idle talk. I know in reality you have no respect for anything those old blowhards may say." Their son, a light-haired, good-natured boy of ten, sat at their feet playing with blocks his expert wood carver grandfather Jim Simpson had made him. Some of the pieces of wood had been shaped like boats, many were made like bricks, and a few had the faces of animals: a pig and a cow. He had stick soldiers and was building a complete fort on what he called "the river." Peter Cooper smiled. This child's peaceful stick fort was better for them all than Forts Harrison or Knox.

Joan looked at her son. "Jimmy and I are left alone here when you go down to Trowbridge's store. We get lonesome while you listen to the silly gossip of things those loafers know nothing about. From the things you've told me, their talk is just so much wind. I know you don't consider the judgment of one of them worth a fig."

"Well, Joan," replied Peter, "The way they spout off is a great show, better than a mime's. I do really enjoy their talk. You never know in which direction it will go. Talk about hot air: I admit it is fun to hear some of them make assertions which are wholly without foundation in fact. Some of these men cannot read or write, yet they offer advice about how every great problem should be solved. I wonder if it was a good thing our founding fathers permitted them to vote, because they have no conception as to what should be done for the good of the country. You know, Joan, the less men know, the more they pretend to know. I wish you could hear Steve Harrigan and Bill Savage in an argument over politics.

"Steve is the Democrat and Bill a Whig?" Joan asked.

"Yes, and neither has any conception of what those party platforms are all about. Steve's daughter, Mary, reads to him all the sayings of John C. Calhoun, and Bill's wife keeps him posted about the latest on Henry Clay. I want to go down tonight and hear what they have to say about election time. Then I will use some judgment and stay at home in the days to come. The fact is I am due to finish *Robinson Crusoe* for Jimmy."

"Somebody told me that you joined in one of the arguments when you thought they were hitting too close at Henry Clay. The idea of Steve Harrigan knowing anything about a national bank! I'll wager he never had two silver dollars at any one time. Why, his wife shares her egg money with him so he can buy tobacco. His grown sons have said time and again that if he couldn't work he couldn't eat, but still he hangs on. His family haven't got the nerve to drive him away."

"Well, Judge Ogden will be there, too. I hope Doc Eldridge can drop by. So there may be a little sense in the room."

Trowbridge's country store on Saturday night was the center of community interest for miles around. It was strictly a stag affair. No woman had ever manifested any interest in attending one of the meetings anyway. Those who came from a distance drove in, hitched their horses at the rack, and told their wives to visit their mothers or friends for a spell while the menfolk gathered at the store.

The long counters on either side of the store were soon full of men who dangled their legs and bent forward supporting their chins with hands while their elbows rested on their knees. Others had brought the outside benches in. The arguments were sometimes slow in starting. Some man would send a bantering statement across to those on the opposite side. Sometimes the jibes were cast off and produced no results. After a time some loafer would settle down to an earnest explanation of his ideas. This was sure to bring forth sallies from those of opposite views. The store arguments were always warmest in cold weather. The choice time of the year was late in the fall, just after corn-husking time. In the spring during corn planting, during the harvest period, and until after a good killing frost, the arguments did not have the proper zest. Saturday night meetings were not always well attended in summer. But when the wind howled outside and a few flakes of snow tuned up the air, then was the time problems of state must be solved. Not many religious men were regular attenders, but how the store sages could argue the fine points of difference between the different religious denominations! When it came to the proper method of baptism, each local wise man knew much more than the scholars who had translated the Bible into English.

On this night Peter Cooper eased into the store and, after greeting Judge Ogden, who had also just come in, he took a seat in the shadows by a large pickle barrel. He looked to see if it had been made by his father-in-law, and sure enough, there were the initials branded into the side near the bottom: JSV. James Simpson Vincennes.

Lou Trowbridge kept a little of everything in his general store. If he didn't have the article called for, he would try to lay in a supply the next time he visited the wholesale house in Cincinnati. Lou advertised that he kept everything from toothpicks to farm plows. On one side were bags of rice, sugar, lemons, apples, spices, and other groceries. On the other side were several bolts of cotton and even silk, clocks, iron skillets, and stew pots. In the rear of the store was the hardware, ranging from nails to the new cook-stoves. In the front and to the grocery side of the store, this merchant kept a good supply of apothecary distillations. On the other side in front were to be found the tobacco and candies. In the spare room under the lean-to could be found whale oil, vinegar, and molasses, all kept elevated on a low platform with a spigot in each barrel to fill your can.

Lou as host welcomed and enjoyed his friends, even if they didn't buy anything much. A good warm fire in a big barrel-shaped stove may have had something to do with the enjoyment of the evening, for when the fire went down the arguments cooled. Both died out at about the same time. Lou did not expect to do much business on Saturday night, for the loafers bought little but tobacco. They laid in their supply early in the evening. Snuff was kept handy. If one of the men ran short of Indian plug chewing tobacco, he was there to cut off another five-cent piece. Tobacco came to suit each customer. Plug was thick and heavy and was cut by measurement. Fine cut came in bags, while smoking tobacco was offered in neat oil paper pouches.

The evenings were long, and darkness was coming earlier. It was hard for some of the farmers to get to Trowbridge's store in time for the opening arguments, but there was much repetition, so it made little difference if the visitor missed the first round or two. Feeding and milking were usually advanced an hour or two to make schedules work. As for corn shucking, people like Harrigan and Savage were glad to quit early. Cornhusking was a backbreaking job, especially if the corn was down. Frost on the corn and tight shucks made rough hands. It was not uncommon at this season of the year to see hands chapped and cracked up. The hands were made even more unsightly by an application of pine tar salve.

As this was the week before the election period began, everybody knew that politics would fly tonight. Peter stayed in the back, observing, by his large pickle barrel and kept his opinions to himself. He had come on a good night. Andrew Jackson was not a candidate for president of the United States anymore, but his policies were always top on the agenda to be attacked and defended. He was either the county's icon or its devil, depending on your party choice. In this county the slogan "To the victor belongs the spoils" was almost gospel. Jackson's policy of going after the nullificationists of South Carolina must be explained properly. Some of those present, naturally, were ardent Whig Henry Clay supporters. Yes, as usual Joan was correct, and there were the two farmers, Steven Harrigan, Democrat, and Bill Savage, Whig, who lived almost across the road from each other. There were plenty of men in the two factions. Some here believed in a protective tariff and thought that Americans had no business in Texas. Others were ready to go to Mexico and clean up on that place, when word reached Canaan of the massacre at the Alamo. They all rejoiced when the Texans retaliated a little later by giving the Mexicans a good sound drubbing.

On the evening of Peter's visit, it looked as if Martin Van Buren might be re-elected president, but a majority of the people of the community were not favorable to that white kid-glove aristocrat from New York City. Judge Ogden was sitting in one of the few chairs in the place, tilting it back, reading the *Vincennes Western Sun*. Staying out of controversy, like Peter, he commented a little on some of the social happenings in the old city. The group grew quiet.

Old Pappy Thorn, who was unable to read or write, led off the debate they all knew would come. Nobody knew where Pappy got his information, because his young'uns and wife would not read to him, but he knew more gossip and slander than any other ten men. Worse than a woman. The black-bearded schoolteacher had boarded at Pappy's home before he left town, and some believed the teacher read the papers to the old man, who had a good memory and listened attentively to anything that was read to him. Pappy started by saying, "I like Little Van. He may be Dutch, but he is smart as a whip-cracker. His old dad was a farmer and a tavern keeper, and now look at the old man's son. He hasn't been bad in the top spot. Arrangin' for Indians treks out west."

Peter, hearing that, thought of Joan and wondered what she really thought of the "removal" of the state's Indians in various stages. She had not said much. What was her view of the fate of the people who had taken her, who, now humbled, humiliated and often suffering, were all being marched away from the lands of their fathers? She had no memories of that time when she was kept hostage, captive, a strange little child in a strange land. Still, she had murmured, "Poor things." That was Joan for you.

Pappy was still holding forth about Van Buren. Somebody across the room, recognized by Peter Cooper as Pap's brother-in-law, provocatively called out the name, "Aaron Burr."

Pappy cleared his throat. "This stuff about 'Little Van' having been a friend of Aaron Burr is all nonsense. You know, Van Buren was 'lected senator twice from the state of New York. He had also been a gov'nor before he headed to the White House. Little Mac believes in states' rights. Even though he has some wealth, he is a-gin the National Bank, and so am I. Mac was Jackson's choice, and that's enough for me. Democrat heir to the throne. And he won the election! I'm for anything Jackson is in favor of. I'm a-gin any tariff, except for revenue."

His brother-in-law, the heckler across the room, called out with a hee-haw, "What's revenue, Pap?" Pap shrugged his shoulders with an embarrassed smile, but then went on. "I'm for letting the rich manufacturers take care of themselves."

"What about this yere money panic we have had in Van Buren's first term?" demanded Bill Savage, a slight man with a huge bald spot on the middle of his crown and shreds of corn shucks on the back of his pants. "We have all had some setbacks there, and only bein' out here on the far reaches of the nation has saved us from disaster."

"Aw," Pappy said with a wave of his hand, "It is getting better already." Steven Harrigan, the lanky Democrat across the room by the door, gave an affirmative whoop, then looked around rather sheepishly and was quiet. He was a rough carpenter specializing in privies.

Pap went on. "They accuse Van Buren of being the father of the spoils system," he said. "If he is the father, I bless his heart for it. He's 'ristocratic. You remember they sent him to England as our prime minister, no, not prime, not that, just minister. And you know he couldn't have held that job unless he knowed how to dress like a duke or a prince, or some other kind of a nabob."

"The Senate didn't like him 'cause he wore a red vest," added Harrigan. "They refused to 'prove his appointment, so he had to come home. Then we sent some dad-ratted jackass over there."

"You're a jackass," some Whig offered from the other side of the room.

"Look here, you old rooster," said Bill, pointing at Pappy. "What have you been yappin' about? Van Buren is a flop as a president. Now he wants us to give him another chance to flop like a dead chicken—again." He put his arms into his armpits and flapped them like wings. Everybody laughed.

"Better'n the general who has up and left Indianny for good," Steve grumbled. "I wouldn't vote for him in this election if he promised to run the Michigan road right past my farm."

"Would you be so mean, Harrigan, as to be against Harrison, one of our own men?" Bill shouted. "Old Tip, the Governor, has lived among us, has kept the Indians from murderin' our families, has made it possible for us to live in this valley in peace and security, and you would turncoat against him for a man who wouldn't soil his white kid gloves by shakin' hands with you? Just think, less than twenty years ago you were afraid to go out on your doorsteps lest you be shot down by Indians. Now you are fighting the men who braved the cold and Indian arrows for all of us. And as for you, Pappy I will say one good word for you. You have a good wife, and so mebbe your two sons will vote for 'Old Tip.'"

"John, John Stevens," the store owner called out. "You had been with William Henry Harrison at Tippecanoe and in the War of 1812. Now speak up about this election." Old John raised his hands in front of him in a "no" gesture. He mumbled that he wanted to listen and not to talk. But the group persisted. Although he might not be well posted on current issues, still John knew his old general, and he was respected because of his reputation of being a brave soldier. He finally consented.

Old John began by saying, "Look here, boys, General Harrison was born in a log cabin, not a tavern, and what if he does prefer hard cider to hard liquor. We know what hard cider comes from, but nobody knows much about Washington champagne. I wish I had a drink of cider right now. That reminds me that Trowbridge put away a barrel of winesap juice only last week. It may not be ready yet, but I like it best when it begins to bite." He spat towards the corner.

"It may be that Van Buren will be re-elected in the election that comes up Tuesday, but I'll bet the fellows down Vincennes way will stand by their old friend," he went on. "What are kid gloves good for, anyway? My wife says they're colder than having no gloves at all, and I believe Van Buren wears them to show the public how cold he is. Pappy's Little Van is only a politician, a New York slicker. He's too polite to suit me. He's so afraid he'll lose a vote that he's wishy-washy. He wanted to be popular. Old Tip Harrison is not afraid to say what he thinks, and he thinks of somebody else besides himself."

Rastus Coffin, one of the men from near, but not in, the hills, stood up on his feet and waved a corncob pipe. "He waren't born in a log cabin! That's a truth-stretcher! He's an aristocrat from Virginny." There were grumblings about this; Harrison was still popular in spite of political errors, and the log cabin story was a stretch.

The large cast-iron woodstove Trowbridge had purchased and placed in the rear of his store could, when properly fed, get unusually hot. Those in the rear of the store were now sweating. As they mopped their brows, they were obliged to move nearer the front door. During the whole week, except Saturday night, the two counters were full of groceries and merchandise, but when Saturday night came Trowbridge piled the articles back of the counters so the sitters could have the room. The counter on the general store side was unusually filled with trousers, heavy work coats, heavy boots, and fur-lined caps. On the other counter dried beans and dried fruits and pickled fish were moved back. There was no danger of the hot men repulsing others with body odors, for you could see only a short distance through the blue tobacco smoke which would kill any other odors. Every inch of the counter space, all the nail kegs, and the one-arm chair were full of men in full political mode.

At this point Rastus, whose real job no one seemed to know but who maintained the whiskey works out along the ravine, could hold himself no longer and shouted, "You know, fellers, the onlyiest person I really admire is Old Hickory. They don't make 'em like that feller any more. He shot one cussed rat for talking about his wife. You remember he married her before she was divorced. It looked like he was in a big hurry, but I will say this for old Hic. When his wife got old and rheumatic, he left her at home. Then he picked a real-for-sure bloomin' young gal and had her at his parties. He gets tired of them old hens in their silks and satins and red paint. He wants sumpin' around him young and purty. I like a man if he's got spunk, even if he is crippled with the gout. The more my old woman gives Peggy O'Neill hell, the more I like Old Hickory. He hasn't much longer to live, so let him have a good time." He was winking and leering around the room and responding to laughs and chuckles from all sides.

Peter shifted in his seat, out of view of most of the men. The smell of the pickles was getting to him. He knew what they were talking about; Peggy O'Neill was a flamboyant and attractive woman who had disrupted with scandal and pursuit of politicians Jackson's and now Van Buren's administration.

Rastus had only started. He didn't know much about tariffs and banking, but he did know the ladies, he said. Now was a good time to show his spirited qualities. "There is another thing," he said authoritatively, "that I want you fellers to know. Peggy O'Neill can hold her own with the best of 'em. She may have been born in a boarding house, but she gets all them big boys on their knees. Of course, Old Hickory gave her a start, but she gets around under Van Buren as much as she ever did under Old Hic."

"Look here," piped up one of the young bucks from near the front door. "Rastus, if you don't be careful and quit being excited, your chin is liable to knock the end of your nose off. You have talked about Peggy so much, you have blown all your tobacco out of your mouth. And with no teeth in your mouth, you are gummin' that plug."

"Say on, young fellow, if ya dare," Rastus countered. "I can tell you some things, too. If that hired girl down at Muffins' hadn't give you the mitten, you wouldn't be here tonight. What's a young buck like you doing on Saturday night among married men, when they're discussin' the affairs of the nation?"

The young man pulled himself up a little higher and prepared another salvo. "Say—is Pretty Peggy a parsonal friend of you'rn, Rastus?" he asked, winking at the crowd.

"You bet your boots," continued Rastus. "We're best friends on my many trips away from here to Washington City and Peggy is smart and purty. She looks good and she smells good. The men in Washington like to get close to her and get a whiff of that French cologne. The old hens would like to scratch out her eyes if they dared. They would give anything if she would tell them where she gets her sweet-smelling scents. I got a pitcher, a drawing of her pinned up in a place where I can see her purty often, but maybe you think my old woman don't cork."

"She knows that Van Buren had to shake heads together to get Peggy O'Neill out of the light of day and the newspapers," the young man said in a lofty way. He was on a trip touting land up north and bragged that he had been to the university at Bloomington.

Rastus took the floor again, looking around cautiously. "Now there is one point that I haven't mentioned that seems a little strange to me, I must admit. There's no wimmen around here, and we men folks must keep this to ourselves. I hope I can speak frankly. I wouldn't want anybody to know I told it. I heard it said that Van Buren wears a woman's corset. I wonder what he does it fur? He's been a widower for a long time. I just wonder who pulls the strings for him when he gets into that 'er harness. Well, anyway, it's hotter n' Hades in here, and I am a-goin' outside." He moved through the group.

The crowd began to stir around a little and pull away from the stove. Rastus cuffed Pappy lightly as he went by. The judge stood up and, sighing, prepared to leave.

Rastus stopped to remark that if Trowbridge wasn't so stingy, he'd have a bigger box of sawdust for a spittoon. "Since I've lost my front teeth I can't hit the box every crack, but I guess it don't make no difference if I miss the box. There's an open keg of salt mackerel just beyond. The mackerel won't care. If it changes their taste any, it will be only to improve them." He pushed through the door and closed it.

Outside, the loud crack of a blacksnake whip was heard. The party rushed out the door just in time to see Molly Coffin whipping Rastus back home. Peter came out from behind the pickle barrel and, shaking his head and smiling little, started for home.

Chapter 27

Sassafras Bob and Tinkering Tim
1840

Sassafras Bob lived alone in the deep woods. He preferred himself, the squirrels, and the birds to the company in Canaan. Still, he would be seen from time to time, appearing when least expected and disappearing in an equally bewildering way.

Sassafras Bob was never known to take a bath or to change his clothes. His clothing was of a durable quality and lasted him for a long time. He sometimes gave his hands and face a few strokes with water, but that effect only emphasized how badly he needed soap and plenty of water. When some thoughtless person accused him of being dirty, he showed his resentment by saying that the "old meddlesome Matty" knew nothing of his personal affairs. He would insist that almost every summer he went back to the creek and took a good swim. "If I never went into the water, how come I know how to swim?" he would answer to someone questioning his cleanliness.

"Some people think they know so much when they know very little," was Bob's stock reply. "Soap is hard on the skin and never did nobody no good," he would soliloquize. "Of course my hands get dirty, for don't I have to dig these sassafras roots right out of the ground? Don't anybody dig for me, so I get my hands dirty. Here's another thing some of those people don't think about. When I sell sassafras, I have to handle it. I can't wash my hands every time I make a sale." There was actually some reason to that. Sassafras was his business and his life.

Sassafras Bob wore brown trousers, probably colored with butternut juice, and these pants had seen years of service. He wore a blue hickory shirt. His galluses were wide and strong. The age of his two garments depended upon how long they would hold together. He wore heavy leather shoes with a brass toe tip and a strong buckle that brought the facings together. Socks and underclothing were of no value and, of course, never worn. In real cold weather Bob had an old overcoat fastened securely about himself with a strap and buckle. He made his trips to the north to peddle sassafras only in the spring of the year. Therefore he had no need for the overcoat, which he left in his cabin.

In the community of Canaan, sassafras grew in abundance, so Bob looked for customers in other communities farther north. He could carry in a big sack upon his shoulders an unusual amount of sassafras roots. In the spring when he started out on foot with his bag, it was full and heavy. As he stopped along the roadside or in villages, he sold a little here and there until the bag grew lighter. Farmers' wives supplied him with food. He was welcome at their cabin doors. He was always able to peddle a little news, make a prediction as to the weather, and check upon the changes of the year. Sassafras Bob, in spite of his personal habits, was genial and would do a chore or two in return for dinner and entertain the children with stories. He did no harm; he knew very little evil.

Sassafras is a wonderful purifier of the blood. Bob would tell homemakers how after a long dark winter, they needed this "nature's remedy" to start the blood flowing more freely. He said it would put a spring into their walk. While Bob could tell them of the many virtues of sassafras tea, he did not need to do much talking, for most farmers' wives knew it was the time of the year to give the family sassafras tea.

Lately Bob had been meeting with some sales resistance, for some of the farmers' wives who had come from the East were singing the praises of "boneset" as a blood purifier. Sassafras Bob said, "Boneset is used only by ignorant women who don't know no better. Some of these mothers make their children drink that nasty, bitter boneset juice, when they could be drinking sassafras tea that has a pretty color and delicious flavor." Again the salesman would go, "Joan Cooper tells me that the bark of this tree has been in use in England since even before the Pilgrim Fathers landed in America."

The old man would break a piece of bark and ask any who were in doubt to take a smell. Somehow he had acquired a few big words, such as "invigorating," "exhilarating," and "aromatic fragrance." These he used to help his sales.

Most of the people in the valley knew sassafras flowers bloomed in May and were of a greenish yellow, that the bloom had no petals, and that the pollen came from one tree and the seed from another. The fruit ripens in August; hangs in clusters on long, red stems; and serves as food for squirrels. Some found it hard to identify sassafras bushes by their leaves, for they sometimes have one, two, and even three lobes. Occasionally all three kinds of leaves are on the same branch.

It was not necessary to ask Bob to stay overnight, for he usually decided that question himself. A modest man, he never embarrassed the housewife by offering to stay in the house, for he preferred the haymow. The hired man would usually shake the hay next morning where Bob slept. A good airing would help the hay even if it were to be used only for bedding the shoat. Bob would linger around until after breakfast, when he was sure to get a handout. If breakfast were a little late in coming, he might hurry on to the next farm to favor them with his company.

Bob had been making the trip north for a good many years, and he rarely returned until Dog Days. Bob could tell tall stories of events happening in the north. He had come to the community shortly after the first settlement was made. He had never been specific as to his birthplace, but he knew all about boats and caves and catfish. Some of the boys classed him as a river rat.

After coming up to Canaan, he had seemed to like the atmosphere and had decided to remain. Nobody asked him to stay. For that matter, no one asked him to move on. He just liked it and found a place to squat. He built himself a sort of a cabin in the side of a hill, threw dirt and straw over it, and made himself comfortable. If the winter were cold, he built a fire in the doorway and allowed some of the smoke to escape through a stack chimney built just back and to one side of his front door. The accumulation of smoke and ashes in his poorly ventilated room did not help old Bob's appearance.

Bob came to town occasionally, bought some salt and coffee and fat meat at the general store, and hurried back to his quarters. He had a few friends in the valley to whom he would pay his respects sincerely, and, of course, they supplied him with a handout. Bob did some "trappin'" and some "fishin'" during the winter, but his supply of furs in the spring never brought him much money. Bob had no gun, but if he accompanied his neighbors on a hunt, they would give him a wild turkey or some part of a wild hog they had killed. He was friendly with his neighbors' coon dogs but was never known to have a dog of his own. He said that his duties required him to be away from home for such long periods that he wouldn't want to starve a dog to death.

When the bright yellow buttercups began to peep over the rocks and Johnny jump-ups to turn purple and the spring beauties began to show, Bob knew that it was time for him to move. He would take his old broken-handled pick and begin to work on sassafras roots. The bushes grew so luxuriantly and in such profusion that it did not take him long to fill his burlap sack. Tying both ends together, he would throw this sack over his shoulder. He was ready for his spring pilgrimage. Bob came in from his hill camp early in the morning, made the rounds of his friends, bade them good-bye, accepted a supply of provisions, and was away upon his trip north. Jimmy Cooper and his friends would watch him moving away. He was friendly to them, and they liked him. They wondered what lay beyond and thought how lucky Sassafras Bob was that he got to see all the things lying north. When he had turned the bend in the road and was lost to sight, each youngster would try to outdo the others in telling some great tale of adventure.

Sassafras Bob was a good salesman, but he could see no good reason why he should untie his sack unless you intended to buy. He never expected any family to buy too much, for, in fact, his supply had to go far. If he sold out before he had made a complete route, he would have to disappoint some. A few cents purchased enough sassafras to make tea for some time, for you were supposed to boil it over and over again. One trip each year was just right, and Bob was welcome the one time.

Bob collected some money—no one knew how much—but it was certain that he spent very little. He bought those few staple supplies. Aside from that, no one knew where his money went. True, he had earned the faith of the community, and they were free with handouts. The merchant usually had some spilled coffee and a small flour sack in which a mouse had made a hole. He was glad to give this to the scavenger. At the general store the loafers often wondered where Bob kept his cash, but no one ever ventured upon Bob's premises when he was away. Several times a group of youngbloods had bantered one another to visit Bob's dugout when he was away and find where he kept his money, but after a little thought they would be ashamed of themselves and would give up the trip. Whenever Bob was questioned about his business affairs, he gave poor answers. When asked about his parents or relatives, he merely replied that he sprang from the grass roots. Nobody in Canaan knew anything about Bob's property, his antecedents, or from where he came. He was part of the settlement, and they were part of him. He asked little; he gave what he could. If he were about and someone needed assistance, he could be counted on.

One spring Bob did not appear. When the neighbors began to think about it, they had not seen Bob for a long time. The more they thought of it, the more they feared something was wrong. At the general store that evening, folks decided to go out and look after Bob. The township constable Steve Harrigan was elected chairman of the group. A large group of men, boys, and some women made the trip. The front door of Bob's dugout was partly ajar. Tracks of dogs and wild animals showed they had been going in and out. Bob was in one corner and had been dead for weeks. The front door was thrown open, and much of the roof of the shack was removed. The place was filthy. An old cupboard contained some dishes and rusty pans with lids. Some of the pans seemed heavy. The folks examined them and found they contained gold coin. The old man had hidden over three thousand dollars, nearly all in gold. The neighbors could not understand how he came by so much gold when he was always paid for his product in nickels and dimes. An administrator was appointed for Bob's estate, and the court advertised for months in the hope of finding relatives. None was ever found, and the gold escheated to the state of Indiana.

Traveling peddlers like Sassafras Bob abounded in the towns around Canaan, as they did everywhere in the country, and Tinkering Tim's annual visit was another one Joan and especially Jimmy looked forward to. Tim was from Germany, and he said he had come to America on an immigrant boat, sleeping in the dark hold of the vessel until well out to sea, when he appeared before the captain of the boat and announced he was hungry and wanted to work. The captain was peeved that he had gotten by stowaway and resolved he would pay extra in hard work. Tim could climb the ropes, was strong as an ox, and knew how to make himself useful about the boat. America was his destination; he had landed on our shores without a cent, had never been hungry, and needed very little money. Some way the land and his trade took care of him. His general appearance showed he did not spend much time improving his personal appearance. His hair was long and reddish grey; his whiskers were bushy, all mussed up. He wore a flannel shirt and old wool coat and pants, and his clothes evidently had been cut for a larger man and left for the rain and weather to help shrink them. His shoes were rough and laced with old whang leather.

Tinkering Tim entered the valley about the same time each year. As the early summer came, Jimmy Cooper and his friends at the schoolhouse would come running, shouting, "Tinkering Tim is coming! I saw him away down the road!" Tim made his headquarters some place south, for he always came in from that direction. In his broken English he told some of the men that he lived in a houseboat down on the Ohio River, but many doubted if he stayed any one place long enough to claim a residence. He carried a little bell, and it was strange how far the music of that little bell carried. By his side in a sling he carried a little two-story stove. The lower half of this metal stove was made to burn charcoal. A grate separated the two stories, and on top of that Tim inserted his soldering irons to bring them to a high heat. He fed the fire with charcoal through the door of the lower half and poked the irons through the little door of the top story. In one pocket he carried his sticks of solder, while in a sack upon his back, he carried his supply of charcoal. Charcoal, such as was needed for his little furnace, could not readily be procured en route, and so he filled his sack when he left his river home and carried a supply for his entire trip. His charcoal sack was not heavy, but it was rather unwieldy.

As soon as Tinkering Tim entered the valley, the children crowded around him, and it was not long before every housewife in Canaan began to collect her leaky pots and pans. A good many cooking utensils can get out of order in one year, so they had plenty for Tinkering Tim to do. He had no competition in his trade; it was either get your pans soldered by Tim or let them go, because the hardware merchant and the blacksmith would have nothing to do with the repairs of kettles, pots, and pans. As Tim moved from one cottage to another, the children of the community kept him company, and it must be said to his credit and good nature that he attempted to answer many of their questions. As he worked he told stories of children in other lands. Some of his stories had, no doubt, some element of truth in them, but they were usually of some weird or wild animal that inhabited the caves or trees along the Rhine. His dramatic stories of battles between wild animals were repeated time and again by the children, long after the tinkerer had gone to his winter quarters. As time went by, some of the older children could repeat some of the stories to their little ones.

The housewives usually kept Tim fed and boarded in their sheds as long as they could, for his stories were interesting to them, and they loved to observe the children's reactions. Some years Tim turned up with a new story, but he could always add a little to the old ones, and this helped to keep up the interest. Tim had a happy way of telling his stories, and he was sure to join with the children in the final gleeful laughter, part of the never-ending interest of what some in the cities might have scoffed at as dull frontier villages.

Chapter 28

The Subscription School
1840

School was first in session the autumn when Canaan was settled. At first, the term lasted for the three winter months, but it had been getting longer and longer. This year school began October first and lasted until April first. A number of teachers had given instruction through the years in the little log schoolhouse, but in the last year the community built a rather substantial school building, with double seats instead of rough-hewn benches and a big blast stove in the center of the room to keep pupils comfortable. One teacher taught all grades, thirty-one pupils. Parents paid a modest sum or could work off the obligation of having their children in school by boarding the teacher, repairing the school, or doing work on the roads in and near the town.

One of the teachers who came to Canaan in the earliest years had insisted that all pupils study hard for so many minutes and then take a rest. He could not tell if they were studying, he said, unless they read their lessons aloud. When all the pupils were reciting in unison, the noise was terrible. The "Blab School" method was used only two terms in Canaan and then was banished from the school as a mistake.

Teacher Ainsley Hunter, in his long, black beard and long, black coat, he who read several newspapers and made astronomical prognostications, was a man with an argumentative, aloof style. He had had his troubles in the recent past, and the larger pupils had run him out. He had been determined that pupils be prompt to school, maintain quiet during school hours, and speak only when spoken to. This did not set well with some of the older pupils, who believed they should have their own way. Near the close of last term, the teacher had attempted to discipline one of the pupils. It had resulted in a general fight in which the larger pupils teamed up against the teacher and succeeded in getting him down, tearing his long coat into shreds, and separating him from part of his beard.

The teacher was a small man, but he was game. In the end, he soundly trounced the three largest aggressors. Different stories had been told of the cause of the fight. As there were quite a number of pupils who had come out second best, there were some parents who planned to prevent Hunter from returning to the school. Teacher Hunter had no real desire to return and to face trouble again, so he resigned. No other teacher in the county wanted to court trouble, and the school soon had a bad reputation. The township trustee, John Stevens, that old veteran of Tippecanoe, was in distress. He could not get a teacher. Teachers in country schools were always men. Everyone knew a woman could not control the unruly big boys. For some reason or other, there were one or more big boys in each school in Indiana and beyond who took delight in causing trouble.

The trustee knew that Joan Cooper had been a teacher and was well prepared for that profession. He believed she might just be able to control the school. Her own son would be in it, but since he seemed a well-disciplined child and constantly about his books, that did not seem to be a problem. When the trustee asked Joan to teach, she refused. "Pshaw, John, you know I have a family, a home to maintain, bread and baked goods for the poor to hand out, and more to do than can be well done." The trustee, however, felt certain that Joan was afraid to take the job because of the big boys still in school, so he went to their parents and obtained their signatures to a petition addressed to Joan. No one else had come forward for the job. When it became apparent that Jimmy would have no teacher if she didn't consent, she began to consider seriously the challenge. She talked with Peter, and between them they agreed that she should teach until another teacher could be obtained.

The Presbyterian minister on circuit and visiting in the Cooper home told Joan of a new set of readers written by a professor, actually the president of Cincinnati University, who was now being sent to pioneer school districts by the Presbyterian Missionary Society. He kept one of the readers in his saddlebags and showed it to Joan. It was called *The Fourth Peerless Pioneer Reader*. Joan read it carefully. She notified Trustee Stevens that if the school would use the readers written by William Holmes McGuffey, she would fill the position. Those who were able to purchase their own readers might do so, and those unable were to be supplied by the missionary society.

Joan was interested to find a short biography of the author of these readers on a separate sheet in his own reader. McGuffey had taught philosophy at Miami University at Oxford, Ohio, and he had studied the child's mind. He believed that while the pupil was learning to pronounce words and read sentences, a story could be told which would influence that child's character and future. "Thus the teacher and society can strike twice with one blow," he wrote. He would lead the child into reading and at the same time teach "truth, honesty, fair dealing, initiative, invention, self-reliance, history, nature, and the wonders of this world."

When he himself taught, he thought it best to arrange his pupils so he could talk to them, possibly in a circle. His instruction was illustrated with simple examples. "I believe in a world of human friendships and joyous living," he wrote. Joan looked at the picture of this author riding horseback to the college wearing a stovepipe hat on his red head and a long, black coat. As she read how he worked for his room and board by cleaning and walked miles to borrow books, she realized that he had known the true value of education. His years of teaching had convinced him that a good basic school reader could make a difference in an entire growing nation, and he dedicated himself to creating and forwarding such a children's reader.

In order to make his "readers" practical and helpful, he trained himself to speak the language of children. He tested his moral stories by seeing how they affected little ones. He would call his pupils to him by whistling as the birds, for he could imitate most birds. He had learned from his father many Indian calls and would use them to instruct and to entertain his pupils. His father had been a famous Indian fighter under St. Clair and Mad Anthony Wayne.

Joan read and reread the reader. By the time the additional readers arrived, she was eager to teach, for they gripped her interest. She copied from the readers these notes she wanted to remember: "No person can be happy without friends. The heart is formed for love and cannot be happy without the opportunity of giving and receiving affection. You cannot receive affection unless you will also give it. You cannot find others to love you, unless you will also love them." How true, she thought! It sounds like the Bible.

"The habit of reading as though you are in a hurry and want to get along fast must be avoided," McGuffey said about reciting aloud in school. "This mode of reading causes the scholar to miscall many words and to pant and to take breath more frequently and with more noise than is necessary."

She noted that in speaking of Alexander the Great, who died from the effects of drinking six bottles of wine, McGuffey said, "How shocking it is to think that a man who had subdued so many nations should suffer himself to be conquered by the sin of intemperance. It is a lamentable truth that intemperance kills more than the sword."

When writing of the Bible, McGuffey said, "The inspiration of the Holy Scriptures is evident from their divine sentiments in religion; the glorious character under which they represent Almighty God; the purity and reasonableness of their morality; the majestic simplicity of their style; their wonderful efficacy on the minds of believers; the faithfulness and disinterestedness of the writer; the miracles by which they confirmed their doctrines; the astonishing preservation of the several books to our times; and the fulfillment of their numerous and various prophecies."

Speaking of the clothing of animals and birds, he said in his Third Reader, "Nature carries her foresight still further. The same animal acquires a different fur in different climates. The northern frosts impart to the goat, rabbit, cat and sheep, a thick and furry vestment. The same animals are almost deprived of hair in the burning regions of Senegal and Guinea; while in Syria, according to the expression of a naturalist, they are covered with a long, light and silky vestment, like the robe of the Orientals."

Joan enjoyed this quotation in his recording of the beauty of the rainbow: "If we consider the rainbow merely as a phenomenon of nature, it is one of the finest sights imaginable. It is the most beautiful colored picture which the Creator has placed before our eyes. But, when we recollect that God has made it a sign of his mercy, and of the covenant which he has condescended to enter into with man, then we shall find matter in it for the most edifying reflection."

While studying the various readers, Joan found many statements that she thought she might emphasize if she were to teach. Sitting by the fire in her beautiful parlor, used by her son and his friends for their play, as she and Peter had planned, she copied some of them. McGuffey in his Third Reader when writing of bears said, "The grizzly bear, like the American black bear inhabits the northern part of America, but unlike him he is perhaps the most formidable of all bears in magnitude and ferocity. He averages twice the bulk of the black bear, to which however, he has some resemblance. His teeth are of great size and power. His feet are enormously large. The talons sometimes measure more than six inches."

On reading further Joan found that McGuffey in his Third Reader described the Icelander's home, Pompey's Pillar, birds and trees, Bonaparte crossing the Alps, and a tiny coral insect of islands in the Pacific Ocean. In this same reader he spoke of the value of knowledge, the character of Martin Luther, and a Russian peasant's generosity. Reading some of this about animals to her husband and son, she found they had real interest. The other children would also like these subjects.

The horse and the dog, two companions of man, were used to convey lessons in industry and faithfulness. The eagle and the owl were made to teach children useful lessons in courage and wisdom. The transition from one reader to the next could hardly be noticed, for all of his readers were to teach the child how to read and the philosophies of life. The idle boy came to grief, while honesty and industry were rewarded. The swan, the fawn, the elephant, and the giraffe were described in their natural habitat and made to teach a lesson in proper human conduct.

After reading the schoolbooks, Joan believed she might be the very person to teach in the school. Surely after the pupils had mastered these books, they would not only know how to read, but also would learn lessons which would go with them throughout life. Beyond that, they were interesting and full of good stories. Using these books, she would undertake the job and school would be ready on time.

Shortly before the start of the fall session, Joan wandered down the street to the schoolhouse. She went in and went to the teacher's desk at the front. Looking out at the double desks, she thought of the faces of the children in town. They had already been signed up. She knew all of them, though more, some new, were still coming every month. Those older boys would be no trouble; she already was familiar, and friends, with Johnny Cowan, who sometimes fished with Jimmy and was part of the gang at the schoolhouse. Anyway, she had some projects in mind for them. She raised the lid of the dark, scarred teacher's desk. Inside were some sheets of paper, a quill pen without any ink, and a rod. "Get ink," she told herself. Taking the wooden whipping rod out of the desk, she went to the front door and threw it out into the weeds by the path.

Chapter 29

Squeezee
1840

"Mammee! I saw the funniest looking man back in the gully!" Jimmy was out of breath and could hardly talk as he ran up to his mother. "Do you know he had no hat and no clothes except an old skin around him?"

Jimmy and three other boys had halted at the Cooper home, but they were so scared and had been running so long that they were out of wind and couldn't talk even in their excitement. Joan saw the four boys had something they wanted to tell in the shortest possible time. "He had no boots and no pants, Mammee. He looked like an Indian 'cept he had a long white beard and his hair was long," continued the boy.

"Where were you boys? What happened to you?" asked Joan, watching the boys get their breath back.

"He was all covered with hair and his eyes were as big as dollars," stammered Jimmy as he quieted down a little. "Mammee, he was not an Indian, for an Indian doesn't look like that old man. I'm sure it was Old Squeezee," said the boy after he had begun to breathe normally. "When he saw us he broke and ran back into the bushes, and heigh ho, didn't we run! You see, we got a few blackberries. We didn't lose them, either. We found a place in the shade where berries were big, black, and juicy. We were filling our buckets when we heard a noise just ahead of us. We saw him. He must have seen us at the same time, because he ran for the gully, and say, boys, didn't we break for home!" continued Jimmy.

Jimmy was the youngest of four boys who liked to pick berries near the stream, where they would wade in summertime. Johnny Cowan was older but palled with the younger boys. Boys often wandered up the stream, although every mother warned her boy of bears and bobcats and Old Squeezee.

The hillbillies didn't even like to talk about him, for he lived up their way. Their fear of him was almost pathetic. Some of them had said they wouldn't shoot the old fellow because that would be murder, but they couldn't understand why he lived just like a wild animal. The children and womenfolk up the hollow were openly afraid of the old man. Menfolk pretended not to bother about Old Squeezee, but no one seemed anxious to meet the old man. Most of the billies stayed close to their cabins.

Search parties had been formed in times past to find out more about the old creature, but even the hillbillies could not tell much. On one occasion the old man was seen. The "hollow men" attempted to surround him, but either Squeezee could run mighty fast or else the chasers were not anxious to get close enough to catch the old fellow. It was believed to be bad luck to see the old critter, let alone actually touch him.

After they had left Jimmy's mother, Johnny Cowan said to the others that because they had seen Old Squeezee, they must use some charm to throw off bad luck. "Each of us must carry a rabbit's left hind foot in our pockets for at least two weeks. It would be awful if Old Squeezee would cast a spell over us," he said.

Old Squeezee never came into the village or went to any farmer's home. Still, womenfolk were afraid of the curious creature even though he bothered no one. No one knew what he ate or how he prepared his food. He had been seen picking berries and cramming them into his mouth, but surely he ate things besides fruit. Probably he lived off fish and trapped rabbits. The billies said that children had become sick after seeing him and that brave-talking men had become timid under his spell.

On several occasions tracks of bare feet had been found in the snow. It seemed inhumane not to provide the stranger with warm footgear, but boots had been left one time far up the hollow only to be found later badly chewed by some coon dog. It was thought Old Squeezee wore a buffalo robe over his shoulders in winter, but no one had been close enough to tell whether it was his own hair or the hair of the robe. The last time the billies had followed the old fellow, he had taken them for a long walk up the hollow. When they had come to the gulch, no one wanted to go farther.

It was agreed that Old Squeezee had lived up in the gulch for a number of years. All resolutions to hunt him down or even to find out more about the old man were abandoned. Blabbering Minnie could give lots of information about the old man, but most people believed the stories she told were mere fabrications. Every time Minnie came out of the hills, she had a new story to tell about the old man. She must have had the critter on her mind much of the time, for she wore all kinds of good luck charms to keep his spell from affecting her. It was hard to tell if what she was saying was truth or her imagination.

Although Squeezee never came down to the village, he had been seen several times on the country roads. Small boys could be kept at home more easily if occasionally the story of the old hermit was repeated at home. Mothers didn't like Squeezee stories because some of the youngsters had been known to make a great noise in their sleep when they had eaten too much mince pie. When these boys were awakened, it was some time before they could be made to understand they had not seen the old man. This story of the wild-looking man was more potent at night than was any story of hobgoblins, ghosts, or spooks. Mothers had suggested that the old man be driven from his hiding place, but they wanted the men in other families to do the job.

Through the years the loafers at the general store had told all kinds of stories of the hideaway place of Old Squeezee. When the relator of the story was closely quizzed, however, he would credit the story to a "feller" in another township who had told a close friend of his in strictest confidence, and he had promised not to disclose the name of his informant.

Trowbridge, the store's owner, had often told his visitors he was tired of so much talk and so little action. He said he had no faith in the story that Squeezee and a bear occupied the same den. Why didn't some of the storytellers go up the gulch and see? He finally offered a reward to the man or group of men who would capture the old hermit and bring him to the store. There was no question that the old man was still there, for too many persons whose veracity could not be questioned had told the story. Now, to boot, the four boys out blackberrying had seen him. Noah Eldridge, son of the doctor, was one of the boys. He had been too scared to run or scream and got a good look at him for a few moments and was able to give a fair description.

Peter called Jimmy to him and had him relate carefully all the events leading up to seeing the man. It was evident he would not hurt anyone, for he had run from these boys. Jimmy told the story and declared that his eyes were big like an owl's and his hair was straggly, long, and gray. The old man had no bucket and no gun, not even a stick, and he was gone in a flash.

The next day at the mill Peter suggested it was time to find out more about the old fellow. Peter thought it would be a good plan if a large group of men would follow the millstream to the gulch and see how the old fellow lived. The hideout couldn't be many miles away, because it was known that the millstream originated in the hills. It was not many miles through the entire range. Talk at the mill and at the store continued until Peter offered to head a delegation to make the manhunt. Rules of the hunt provided that no man carry a gun and that all dogs must be on leash. The day was fixed. On the morning of that day approximately one hundred men assembled at the spot where the millstream flowed out of the hollow. The men and boys carried axes, scythes, grub hoes, and hickory clubs. The hillbillies joined the hunt as the party moved by their different cabins. The four boys who saw Old Squeezee picking berries were allowed to go with the men. Blabbering Minnie wanted to go up, too, but one of her brothers boxed her ears and told her to stay home.

The committee in charge had tried to get advance information. They sent for old Granny Whitehouse as the most reliable source. She said that the old man had been seen for five or six years, and that he must have come to the hollow about 1834. The old man had a curse on him and cursed all who saw him, according to Granny. No one in the hills had wanted to take the chance of his dog dying just because the owner had trailed Old Squeezee. It was known that the old man had no gun, no dog, and no means of protection except a staff that they took for granted was made of stout hickory. Those deep saucer-like eyes were his protection. They could carry a spell as far as they could see, she told them.

After hearing these details, the company, young and old, followed the road along the millstream's right bank. This road had been kept in passable order by the constant use of ox carts, bobsleds, riding horses, and foot passengers because it led out from the hills. As the group traveled this road, they passed the huts of many billies who were known in the Canaan community. The farther the company walked, the less worn the road became, until it faded into a mere footpath. At a point about five miles up the millstream, the worn path came to a sudden end. A few paths led on in different directions, but the dwellers farther on must supply themselves with what they could carry upon their backs. It was the consensus, supported by the billies, that the path leading to the left went toward the gulch.

The men who were mounted tied their horses to saplings and prepared to walk the remainder of the hunt. All paths soon ended where the hills on both sides crowded in close to the stream and formed a high bluff on either side. The watercourse was narrow. The stream, which was now very small, became a mere rivulet falling over the boulders and peering out between big rocks. It was difficult to follow this tortuous rill, but it could still be seen. After climbing high banks, the company came to a widening of the bluffs. Nestled between these high, rocky hills was a wide and apparently deep pool. Pursuing their way around the pool, they found a gulch lined with stunted trees from the water leading off. Both sides of the gulch were steep. In the side of a small hill, partially hidden with undergrowth, could be seen the opening to a cave. Ashes were in small piles, and feathers of wild game and fish bones were scattered about the ground.

As they approached the cave, the group saw a big boulder shelf projecting out over the entrance. Under this shelf the ground was bare and packed hard. Final directions for surrounding the cave were signaled. The dogs were held ready, for if a bear should rush out, all clubs, dogs, and men would be needed. The signal to close in was given. Some noise was made by the dogs on tight leash, and a strange-looking object appeared in the mouth of the cave. The hunters could not hide, and the dogs were frantic. Whatever it was disappeared into the cave, and the hunters rushed forward. A moment later the old man stood in plain view. He could not run, for he was surrounded. However, he started up over the hill, only to be met by others coming. He darted first one way and then another, but he was cornered. Strong arms seized him and brought him to his knees. To all questions he gave a blank stare.

A conference was called as to what to do with this pitiful creature. He wore nothing except a loincloth made from part of a deerskin. He could not, or would not, say a word. Bill Savage had brought some rope; he and Old Mike Bigger held and tied Squeezee up.

Jimmy Cooper stood wide-eyed as he stared at Squeezee. He had no fear now. Instead, he felt sorry for the old man. Jimmy's mother had not wanted the boy to take the trip, but Peter felt this would be an experience which a ten-year-old boy would never forget, and of course, there could be no danger where they were fifty to one. Jimmy had ridden behind his father until they tied the horses. He had been beside his father when the rush was made. Now the old man saw the little boy and watched him intently.

Finally Old Squeezee motioned for the boy to come forward. He paid no attention to anyone but Jimmy. Peter took his son by the hand and led him forward. He knew he could easily protect the boy from all harm. Squeezee placed his hand upon the boy's head and mumbled something which could not be understood.

Some of the hunters entered his den. In it they found on the ground an old fur that was used as a bed. They also found a few pots and pans. He evidently cooked in front of his den. He had lately eaten fish. Bones and scales were still in a pan. The searchers in the cave found a little old chest. In it they found a Bible recording births, marriages, and deaths. Between two pages of the Bible they found a silhouette of a little boy who looked to be nine or ten years old. A newspaper clipping also dropped from the Bible. The article was clipped from a Cincinnati newspaper. The men read it and murmured among themselves.

Peter, Mike Bigger, and Bill Savage brought old Squeezee into town. He would have to be taken by stage to the Indiana Hospital for the Insane, which had opened recently in Indianapolis. Peter sadly read the newspaper article to Joan: "Cincinnati, Ohio, December 25, 1829: The home of Nehemiah Schmidt on Vine Street was completely destroyed by fire last night. The fire sprang from a Christmas tree the father, who was of German descent, had arranged for his little son. The wife and son were burned to death. The father sits with his head in his hands and refuses to move or to speak. It is feared the tragedy has demented the father. Neighbors are doing all in their power, but the father will not be comforted."

"How little we know about our neighbors," Joan murmured compassionately and hugged Jimmy to her tightly.

Chapter 30

Johnny Appleseed
1842

"Mother," said Jimmy Cooper, "did you see that strange-looking man at the party last night? While everybody was dancing and having a good time, he came into the barn. He wore only a sack over his body. He had no pant legs and no sleeves. It looked as if he had cut a hole in each of the four corners of the sack, and his legs and arms stuck out."

"Oh, son," said Joan, "I have seen him many times." She and Blabbering Minnie were hanging out wash; it was Monday, wash day. Minnie had clothespins in her teeth. "Our friend is always welcome in the valley. I can remember when he was a much younger man. I advise you to look on his heart instead of at his oddness."

Jimmy continued, "Well, he had a bag full of apple seed to plant trees, he said, and he was very careful of it. He wouldn't let people have seed unless he obtained a promise that they would prepare the ground for the young apple trees. Some of the people invited him to their homes and asked him to help them plant the seed. He said he would visit the school today and give a few seeds to each child. I'll bet he'll want to see the seed planted." Trousers and two handkerchiefs from the line fell onto the grass. Jimmy picked them up and handed them to his mother, looking at her expectantly. She smiled knowingly.

"That man, Jimmy, is Johnny Appleseed. He came to our house some years before you can remember it. Each apple tree in our orchard was planted by him. I guess he'll come around, because Johnny and your father are great friends. When he comes to school, get him to tell about the wild animals, the birds, and even the bugs in the forest. He has never killed any living object, not even a mosquito. He can tell you many wonderful stories." Joan was no longer teaching; her one year had gone well, but another teacher, a wife without children in the town, had taken the job up.

"How does he make a living?"

"People take care of him and give him some coin from time to time. They do this because they love him. He talks to the animals in the woods.

He sings with the birds, and he tries to hum as do the insects. Each fall he visits the cider presses of western Pennsylvania and sorts the seed from the pomace at the cider mills. How many apple seeds do you suppose that old bag of his holds? He has made his seed bag from the skin of a deer, but he will tell you the deer died a natural death. He would not put his precious seeds in any skins from an animal killed by man. He will not eat meat, and he objects to robbing the bees of their honey. He says the Lord made vegetables and fruit for man to eat. He believes all men would be better off if they ate the things God prepared for them and did not take the lives of innocent animals and game birds. Johnny gathers his seed until the fall breezes start. Then he hides away in some old house or cave until spring comes. When the wildflowers bloom, it's time for Johnny to start west. He is a jolly old fellow and has many friends. The young folks and children mock him and laugh at him, but the older people who know of his true worth are always glad to see him. He likes to sleep in the hay mow."

"When he comes to your school," Joan continued, "see if he does not carry a little old Bible which he will read to you. It is called a Swedenborgian Bible. He will read the part which condemns the sinful and offers the hope of eternal life to those who follow in the footsteps of the Savior. He'll come here. He came years ago. I'm sorry you don't remember him. We have always had cookies for him, and he will not forget. Especially because he planted our orchard, he will want to examine each tree." Minnie was wandering away, singing to herself as she danced around with the laundry basket. "Be sure to listen to him today when he comes to your school. Then tell me all when you come home."

"Mother, some of the boys say he is touched in the head and that he is cuckoo, whatever that means. Mr. Smithers said a horse kicked him on the head when he was a boy and that he has never recovered," continued the son.

"Well, he may be a little odd, but he has a good heart and teaches all who meet him to love God and all of God's creatures. Someone has said his real name is Chapman and that he came from Massachusetts. I don't know if that is true, as he doesn't talk about his origins. The Indians always received him with pleasure when he came among them and furnished him with food. Even when some of the tribes were hostile to any white person, they would protect Johnny Appleseed. When Indians were on the warpath, he warned the white settlers and saved many lives. It is said that one time he ran thirty miles through the forest to warn the whites of Indian threats. But he did more and appreciated the Indians as God's children. He condemned the whites for taking all of the land and streams from the red man. Some of the old soldiers say that Johnny saw the Battle of Tippecanoe at four in the morning from a hollow log, but this is probably not true."

"The Battle of Tippecanoe! Grandpa Simpson was there." He looked curiously at his mother. "And so were you. . . Koo-wa." She smiled and reached to ruffle his hair.

"Johnny was a little like your grandfather Simpson. He didn't care to kill people. He never wanted to be around a gun, and he disapproved of soldiers. Your Simpson grandparents say they saw him on the Ohio River while they were on their wedding trip down the Ohio. They say he was paddling along all alone in a small canoe. His sack of seed was in the front of the boat. When he first came this way, he was leading a packhorse with the sack thrown over the pommel of the saddle in front of him, but the Indians stole his horse. Now he goes by foot."

They walked toward the house. Behind them the sheets and shirts flapped in the wind. Minnie was following them, picking up clothespins she had dropped. "What sort of apples does he favor?" Jimmy wanted to know.

His mother answered, "In his bag he has a pouch for pippin apples, one for russets, and one for harvest apples. How he could dig the seed from the piles of cider pomace and keep the seeds separated is beyond me. Our orchard is beginning to bear now, too, and the trees are mixed."

Every pupil was in place in school the next day, for word had spread that Johnny Appleseed would talk to the students. Before he began his talk, he asked permission to plant a few seeds. The children helped him prepare the ground. They watched him make a small hole in the earth with his finger, at the same time taking one of the slender black seeds from the bag. As he planted, Johnny told the children that some of the trees would no doubt be gnawed and killed by rabbits, but he said the rabbits were God's creatures, and he would not complain at anything which God had done. When the seed was planted, he stroked the ground until it was smooth, all the time mumbling some words that the children could not understand, but which were supposed to come from the strange Bible.

He said the students must share their lunch with the birds and wild animals, especially in the winter when they were hungry. He told the students to talk to the birds and they would not be afraid. He related how deer sometimes followed him through the forest. He told that he did not even build a fire. He said, "God forbid that I should be the means of killing one of God's creatures merely to keep me warm or cook me some food." He felt the best place to sleep was in a hollow log—"It is a good shelter from wind and rain and will keep you warm." He told of his experience one night when he went to his log and found it occupied by a bear and her cub. He was obliged to sleep beside the log. Everybody laughed. Johnny Cowan, who was about to graduate from school, winked and nudged Jimmy.

The visitor explained that in the spring of the year the beautiful black, almost purple, blackbirds came from the south and built their nests high in the big tree, and that their cheery call or song told that frosts were gone. Farmers must get ready to plant corn. He told the children to watch for the meadowlark, how it hunted the tall grass in the low grounds, and how the springy call brought back the sunshiny days. If they found four speckled eggs hidden in the grass, they must not touch either the eggs or nest, so the lark would return and claim her nest.

He spoke of the friendly robin, brown thrushes in the bushes, and the sweet little song that the wood thrush would sing for anyone who would listen. He instructed the pupils to place bird boxes to attract the blue martin and the swift and to watch for the mud nests of the swallows in the chimneys and the barns. He asked them to feed the redbirds so they would stay all winter and to listen to the hammer of the flickers and woodpeckers during cold winter days. He told the children that God was sending all of these beautiful birds for their pleasure and that they should be kind to all wildlife.

Johnny Appleseed tore leaves from his Swedenborgian Bible, gave them to the pupils, and asked the children to take the lessons home to their parents.

The traveler told the students that most ailments could be cured with herbs. He brought some dog fennel seed to plant in the farmers' barnyards. He spoke of the great value of horehound and catnip and said he had brought some seed with him, so the plants could be used to help cure colds.

He also knew how to foretell the weather. "Animals know when it will be cold and that the crows always keep ahead of the bad weather. And mebbe you know that if the groundhog sees his shadder on the second day of February, he will go into his hole prepared to stay six weeks, because take it from me there will be that much more cold weather. If March comes in as a lamb, it will go out as a lion." If a rooster crowed before midnight, he said, there would be rain before morning. The first thunder in the spring would awaken the snakes. Snow in the winter meant a good wheat crop. If your corns hurt, there will be rain. If it rains on Easter Sunday, it will rain for seven Sundays. Where turtledoves, rain crows some call them, coo, there will be rain. Lightning in the north means dry weather. If it rains while the sun is shining, it will rain the next day. If the new moon lies on its back, it means dry weather. If the corn shucks are tight, it means a cold winter. So he said. He did not smell good, Johnny Cowan said, but he thought school had never before been so interesting.

Johnny Appleseed appeared at the Cooper home that evening and before dark had examined every apple tree he had planted there. Joan knew that Johnny had traveled in other states. She asked him if he had ever heard of a little girl stolen by the Indians of the north. Johnny remembered a little girl who was stolen from Pennsylvania and was adopted by the Miami. She married a chief and refused to return to her people. Johnny believed her name was Frances Slocum. He said he had visited the Miami near Peru and had talked to the white woman who preferred to live the life of an Indian.

When Johnny had come into Canaan, he had no shoes, for he had given them away. Joan supplied him with shoes from Trowbridge's store and a coat, but he told her that any other garments would be in his way. His feet were calloused and gnarled. His toes were almost shapeless. "If," he said, "my feet get bruised or my toes broken or infected, I borry a hot iron and burn the wound. Then it gives me no more pain and will be well in a few days." Johnny insisted upon wearing a saucepan for a hat because that was the easiest way to carry it. The pan served a dual purpose when he had something to cook. His burlap suit of clothes had no pockets. In a big rag that he carried on the end of a stick over his shoulder were his most precious belongings, which included a few small coins. These coins he never needed to spend, because people humored him and fed him what he wanted.

Johnny stayed only a few days in the Canaan community; then went to plant other orchards. He loved the Ohio River country; some said he moved on toward the south. He took with him the good wishes of the entire community who loved his simplicity, faith, and joy in God's earthly kingdom.

Chapter 31

Murder in the Promised Land
1842

Peter often said to Joan that although they lived in Canaan, the promised land, it could not be perfect. As in the Garden of Eden, the snake of evil could, and sometimes did, appear. For some years the people in the valley had known and trusted each other, hill people, farmers, and townsfolk. If there was trouble among neighbors, they talked it out. The sheriff hardly ever had more than a few Saturday night drunks in the small jail, which was part of the town hall. Nowadays, though, strangers were in town more often. Sales drummers came and stayed at the hotel, along with repairmen for the mill machinery, farriers who maintained the livery stable, carpenters for the new homes being raised, men selling land further west, or Bibles or insurance. Peter was aware the Presbyterians from the Society of Poor and Distressed Widows had ridden into town and were signing people up. Peter had also noticed swarthy-looking men walking about who did not seem to have business. Now something truly violent had happened. It seemed as if it might have had a cause very close to home.

The men about the mill were talking in subdued tones when Peter came in to work that October day. The men told him that Missus Barr and her spinster daughter Eliza had been killed in their own kitchen the night before. An ax still fresh with blood told the tale: the women had been brutally murdered and their skulls crushed. One of the mill men, the closest neighbor, had been called to the home, and he had found blood all over the floor; the kitchen was in confusion, with chairs turned over, and it was evident there had been a struggle. The bloody ax had been thrown into one corner of the room. The poll of the ax appeared to have done the damage. The women had been dead only a few minutes, and the victims were fully dressed; in fact, their full milk pails told that they had just come in from milking. Jake, the son, had given the alarm but could offer no details. He seemed to be in shock.

Old lady Barr, her son, and her daughter had moved into the community about three years ago. The old lady was said to be something more than sixty-five, but her rough brown skin, which had evidently seen lots of weather exposure, had made her appear much older. Her daughter, Eliza, was a plain-looking woman about forty, while Jake was no doubt somewhere between forty-five and fifty. The Barrs had stopped by the store, found out the Tevis farm was for sale, and bought it.

From the day they moved in until the day of the tragedy, they had attended strictly to their own business. It was a custom when newcomers moved into the Canaan community for neighbors to make friendly calls, inviting the newcomers to their homes, to church, and to any special meeting that might be called for in the near future at the town hall. The callers, when they visited the Barrs, had been treated civilly and asked to sit down, but had been obliged to do all of the talking. After a few of the women had made first friendly calls and been treated coolly, they began to compare notes and had come to the conclusion that the Barrs wanted to be left alone.

Nobody knew what went on within the confines of the home. The two women seemed to help Jake with his crops, and he used outside assistance very little. Jake was willing to trade help at harvest time, but at all other times he worked the farm alone. The womenfolk took no interest in community affairs and did not go to church. The Presbyterian minister Hezekiah Beecher had called but was politely turned away. Jake sometimes went to the store but did not stop at the loafers' bench outside, where community decisions were made and unmade. Instead he hurried home after making his purchases.

The whole family sometimes loaded themselves into the big wagon and drove to the county seat. The women proceeded to trade their butter and eggs for staples for the family while Jake generally pulled a two-gallon jug from the back end of the wagon and made for the saloon. He did not stop in the saloon to drink, but with his jug full came back to deposit it under the hay in the big wagon. He then took his place upon the wagon seat and waited for his sister and mother to return. If he met any of his neighbors in town, he nodded as they passed by. The people of the Canaan community and a number of people in town recognized the Barr family without knowing them as neighbors.

Their standoffishness was the talk of the town, but they did make contacts sometimes, when the road needed stone or gravel work or harvest time had come. As he worked, Jake had told some of his neighbors that for many years they had lived not far from the Ohio, but when their father died they had sold the farm and moved farther north in search of more fertile soil. Jake was a good hand with Irish potatoes. The neighbors took his extra supply to use for seed, and they paid him a little more than the prevailing market price for potatoes. None of the family ever spoke of the father or, for that matter, of any of their ancestors. If it had been left to the inhabitants of Canaan to tell something of this family, they could have said no more than that they worked hard, attended to their own business, and added nothing to the community life.

The family took no newspapers, read no books, and appeared to care nothing about what happened to their neighbors. Jake occasionally took corn and wheat to the mill, waited his turn, and returned home without saying much to the millers. There had been several funerals in the neighborhood since they came, and one was for a man who had sometimes helped Jake, but none of the family attended the funeral. The neighbors wondered if the Barr family knew of the death. The minister noticed and mentioned it as the congregation left, seeking information, but there was none to give. Sunup to sundown, they were a mystery.

On the morning of the murders, the neighbors had rushed to the Barr home in droves. The sheriff and Doc Eldridge, who served as coroner, had taken charge and began to question everyone. The son could give little information, stating that he had heard his mother and sister when they left the house to milk and he had then dropped off to sleep; he had again heard scraping of chairs and some movement in the kitchen, at which time he supposed they had returned from milking. He heard no unusual noise and nothing that aroused his suspicion, but then his bedroom was at the end of the hall upstairs. He had taken his time about dressing and knew nothing of the murders until he walked into the kitchen and found his mother and sister lying in their own blood. He had then run to the nearest neighbor and called for help. The neighbors had come, first singly, and then in numbers. A boy had been placed upon a horse to rush to town to notify the authorities. The neighbors had called Doc Eldridge, who had given the scene one glance and taken charge. The bodies had not been moved until the coroner came, and it had seemed ages before he could make the drive from town.

Everything about the place had been examined. The ax handle was covered with blood. The family had no enemies, and the son could give no reason why his mother and sister had been killed. There was some money about the premises, but this had not been taken, and it appeared there had been no search for money. The guilty culprit or culprits had not gone into other rooms so far as could be detected. The murderer had evidently waited in the kitchen until the two women returned and then used the ax first upon one and then the other.

No one had visited in the home, so no neighbor could give any clue. Someone had remembered that Blabbering Minnie had said she had been in the home a few days before, and the sheriff sent for her. When this helpless girl saw the gruesome sight, the men at the mill said, she began to scream and then to blabber. It had been impossible to get any coherent statements from her. Finally she settled down and spoke.

Minnie had not waited for an invitation to call or to work for the family. As usual, she just went. This family had had so few visitors that it was a challenge for Minnie, and she had noticed that after her short stays at the Barr home, she was the center of much attention. The neighbors had wanted to know what went on in the home, and they hadn't the courage to call without an invitation. Minnie told of hard work, poor food, and little pay. They finally had found out from Minnie that the family went to bed at dark and got up at dawn. Minnie had wanted to talk a little after the supper dishes were washed, but in this home she had been left to talk to herself.

When the time for the funeral came, services were held in the largest church, and Hezekiah Beecher had the opportunity of his lifetime to deliver a funeral sermon to a great gathering of people. The local choir sang several doleful hymns in strained voices, and Reverend Beecher restrained himself by preaching not much over one hour. The preacher had not been able to tell the place of birth of the mother, and Jake had had to rack his brain to tell the age of his sister. Beecher seemed to feel regret and sadness for the two so brutally taken from the earth. He asked for God's justice for whoever had done this despicable crime. It was the shortest tribute speech ever read to an audience in the Canaan community.

Of course suspicion fell from the beginning on the son. The citizens of the community couldn't understand how a strong, able-bodied man could sleep through the whole affair and be so noncommittal afterward. At the funeral service Jake had appeared alone, and no one had offered to comfort him. It had looked for a time as if he would have to walk to the cemetery. Hezekiah Beecher had finally picked him up in his own wagon.

That evening Jake went home, milked the cows, and did the chores, with no one offering to help him. The people of the Canaan neighborhood were kindhearted, and some felt ashamed of themselves, but many were afraid. Jake had not been taken into custody, and there was angry, fearful sentiment building in the town towards him. "That son should be in jail," was the talk on the street. The sheriff tried to explain. The grand jury could not indict, for not a single bit of evidence against anyone was available. Bloodhounds had tried to find a trail the day of the murder, but they would not leave the house and looked lazy, sleepy, and hungry. The sheriff asked the neighbors to keep a close watch for unusual activity, and the coroner reported homicide in his verdict, but added that the murderer was unknown.

The murders had occurred in late October when the days were getting colder, with the farmers busy all day and too sleepy to talk of the murders at night. Still, as days passed, the farmers gathered outside the general store, and each gave his own favorite theory. The county seat newspapers printed wordy, emotional articles and featured drawings of Jake the brother. The Vincennes and Indianapolis papers even carried long articles describing the mysterious murder in Canaan. Talk and speculation continued, growing in intensity.

Peter noticed that the newcomers in the town, who had little stock in the matter, had plenty to say themselves. One of the men with big city clothes and smallpox scars on his cheeks, some sort of salesman, was accustomed to sitting himself down and offering up an opinion on any subject in any way his empty mind would lead him. On one evening he began by saying, "Look here, fellers, there's nothing strange about this murder. Why was the son so long in notifying the neighbors? The doctor was not called until the bodies were cold. Why didn't the son ring the bell, or shout and cry for help? He didn't look a bit sorry at the loss of his old mom or his bossy old sister; why didn't he talk? Why didn't he tell all so the town could work fast? Nobody saw any strangers on the roads. I tell you it's an odd piece of business. You all got vigilante justice around about these parts? I say it might be time to take a step or two in that direction."

"Well," said Rastus Coffin, "you could be right, sir. The old woman was mighty stingy and wouldn't let Jake have a dime, and the sister was as cross as an old setting hen. It seems to me that somebody might have wanted to get rid of somebody. I hain't mentioning any names, but who in the world could have wanted to kill the women unless he wanted to improve his situation? Rid himself of unpleasant company. Who knows what went on in that house, like a gol-durned house full of ha'nts." He drew himself closer to the benches. "An' here—listen to this. It seems strange we have no peace officers active against criminals in this county. I suppose they have gone back into their shell and only come out on payday. Here, we pay good money to keep those lazy galoots, and never an arrest do they make. Nary a one."

There was grumbling affirmation. The sky was getting darker; an October thunderstorm was heading in. The men headed inside the store. "I'm for takin' the law in our own hands and trying our arms on pullin' a rope," Rastus said quietly as he held the door. First there was mild shock, then nods.

Trowbridge was out back; they were free to talk in muted tones. About this time one of the younger loafers said he knew where he could find rope, and he knew the rope was just itching to string some fellow to a limb. After a while the loafers stole out of the store. Some went to their homes, but a number of youngbloods went down to the schoolhouse, where the discussion continued. The rain and thunder came in, then the storm passed.

The group of about twenty young men was soon ready, and, strange to say, there were some older ones among them. As they approached the Barr home, dusk had come and dark was upon them. They knew Jake had no dog and no gun, and they had nothing to fear. They rapped on the door, and when Jake appeared, they grabbed him. They soon had around his neck a noose, which those in front kept tight while those in the rear pushed and shoved him forward. They brought him to a large walnut tree growing in the schoolhouse yard. The rope was thrown over the lower limb; Jake's hands were tied behind him; the rope was tightened; and he was ordered to talk. The spokesman said to Jake, "If you tell the truth, we will only turn you over to the sheriff, and we will recommend leniency, but if you don't tell us who killed your mother and sister—and dad burned quick—you will find yourself in the morning hanging by your neck to this limb. We know you know, so now it's tell all or hang."

Jake blubbered something, but finally they could understand that he was trying to say he had told all he knew.

"The heck you have told all! Speak now, quickly, or you are gone!" yelled the ringleader.

Jake fought and sputtered, but it was evident he was not going to tell what they wanted.

"He's mean as hell and he won't tell, so string him up and let's be on our way."

The rope tightened and Jake struggled. He was on his way to eternity.

A gun cracked! In a moment a man with a beard and black hat came into the circle of men.

"Drop that rope!" shouted Hezekiah Beecher. "I am a man of God and would not shoot any man, but the first man who pulls that rope is a dead man. Do you hear me? No man here knows Jake is guilty, and no man dares take the law in his own hands. I know every one of you. Untie that man or I shoot."

The mob knew by his tone of voice that old Hezekiah meant business. The rope was released, and Jake stood still. "I will go with you to your home, Jake, and these men had better go to theirs," Hezekiah told him.

Not much was said of the vigilante group around Canaan. Hezekiah was not given to talk. Old Jake never did talk, and the youngbloods were afraid to talk for fear of being arrested.

November passed without any more information about the murders. Jake came into town. Going through his mother's scant supply of papers, he had found something. Finally he began to talk, and he did his talking to the judge, who had come over from the county seat. He had long suspected his sister had a secret lover. She sometimes sneaked into town at night, and he had accosted her over it when he found her outside the house one evening with one of the salesmen who were coming and going.

The judge, then the sheriff, looked at the document Jake produced. It was a "graveyard" insurance policy—made to benefit who? The very man, the one with the smallpox scars, who had suggested the hanging first in the general store, so it had been told of him. But now he was gone.

The townspeople notified the Society for Poor and Distressed Widows. They were told that a claim for the insurance had to be made sixty days after a death. The murders had occurred on the twenty-sixth day of October, and it so happened that sixty days would expire on Christmas Eve. No proof had been made to the insurance society of the deaths, and the insurance company was waiting to see who would claim the insurance. Into town rode the smirky salesman, saying he wished to spend Christmas in his favorite village. He had the policy in his pocket, ready to make a claim. The sheriff was ready, the would-be beneficiary was arrested, and because of his plea of guilty, eventually he was saved from the gallows but was sentenced to the penitentiary in Jeffersonville for the remainder of his life.

Jake was a witness at the trial and earned praise from the folks in Canaan. After this the townspeople took pains to notice him, standoffishness or not. The stranger had come to this town and courted and deceived a lonely and isolated young woman, then waited one year after the insurance was written before he had committed the act of murder, brutally killing an innocent mother and daughter. Now he would pay the price, and the town had learned that just as it takes all types of vegetables to make up a pot of old-fashioned burgoo, it takes all types of people to make up a community.

Chapter 32

The Huckster Wagon
1843

Trowbridge was an enterprising merchant who prided himself on keeping abreast of the times. He received catalogues and issues of *Godey's Lady's Book* and made himself aware of what the gentlewoman was wearing in the big cities. He was able to advise his lady customers as to the latest style of poke bonnet, dress, or gloves. The call for fashionable patterns for women's dresses was loud and insistent since Queen Victoria had married her great love and consort, Prince Albert. On walks to the schoolhouse, church, and the ladies' club social, the women of Canaan village wished to wear (even if only in muslin) frocks with pointed waists, sloping shoulders, and bell-shaped skirts. Men in the woods might be aware of waistcoats with pointed waistlines and full shoulders, dipping to the hips. A few might look forward to a tailor's visit or go themselves to Louisville or Cincinnati to get fitted, but for the most it was still shirts of cotton and homespun with pants of coarse materials and heavy woolen coats to protect from the bitter winter weather.

It was, of course, the general merchandise that he had to sell daily, weekly, and in large quantities that could make him a prosperous merchant. Trowbridge had recently added shoes in several sizes, mostly wide. His shelves were always adding new items: pianoforte music sheets, lace and all sorts of sewing items, broad-brimmed straw hats which looked like those African traders wore, chocolates, and china dolls with little beds. Out back were the usual coops of poultry and live piglets in season. Jimmy Cooper was constantly asking to go to the store for rock candy. Joan relied on her friend Trowbridge to get her pictures and doo-dads for the walls of the Cooper home, most recently a Currier and Ives print of a group of ruffed grouse looking into a thicket. She also shopped daily at the general store for the necessities of everyday life.

Trowbridge was not satisfied unless he was looking for more trade. He had been told that he could sell more goods if he started a huckster route, so the salesman from a wagon factory did not have much trouble in selling the storekeeper one of the latest huckster wagons. The huckster wagon system had been used in the East for a long time, but the roads in the Canaan community had not been improved to such an extent that the huckster could maintain a regular schedule. Trowbridge, however, was determined to give the delivery system a trial, and he thought Jason Oberly, a recent German immigrant who lived in the valley, would be just the man to operate this traveling general store. Jason spoke English with such an accent that it was difficult to understand him, but he certainly knew how to barter and sell.

The big wagon finally came, painted to catch the eye: the bed was green and the running gears red. The white canvas top gave the wagon the proper flair. The ingenious wagon maker had equipped the wagon so it would hold an unusual amount of dry goods and groceries. Swung under the rear of the wagon was a large chicken coop, fastened on behind was a compartment for ducks and geese, and on either side of the wagon bed, safely under the canvas top, were firkins for butter and eggs. While the wagon had springs, still there was plenty of jolt, and it was hard to understand why more eggs were not broken during German Jason's four-day trips over the big bumps.

The whole inside of the wagon was stocked with groceries and dry goods. As the huckster learned the wishes of his customers, he catered to their desires, and at different seasons of the year he carried different kinds of merchandise. The groceries had been weighed and packaged before leaving the store, but the butter and poultry were weighed by the roadside. Butter was piled into the wooden firkins until they could hold no more, and when the wagon reached the store, white and yellow butter would be found in the same tub, except during hot summer weather when the butter mixed well together. Rarely was any money passed, for the farmer's wife was sure to find enough articles in the wagon to equal the produce which she wished him to pick up, and it was not uncommon to send one of the children for an old hen to make up the difference due the huckster.

The huckster was due in one nearby community on Monday, in another on Tuesday, and so on until the circuit had been made, but the driver must be at the store all day Friday. Farmers were arriving with produce on Friday, and Saturday morning found the huckster with his week's "freshest goods direct from the farm" at the county seat, where he supplied the local grocers and shipped to the big cities.

The huckster was supposed to be ready to start for Canaan Saturday noon, but Jason was a friendly fellow; he had worked hard all week, and he owed it to himself to spend a spell at the corner saloon. A few drinks of cold ale revived his spirits considerably, and to these he sometimes added a few small glasses of straight whiskey. He procured a gallon jug of whiskey that he hid in the bowels of his big wagon, and this stimulus was to see him through the next week.

Jason started home before dark, but he had a good long drive, and his team was not accustomed to moving fast. As he proceeded over the road, his head became lighter and his care freer until, by the time he passed Boxley's Corner, it made no difference to him which direction he was going. The faithful team had been over the road so often that it needed no driver. The horses were sure to pull up at the well at Boxley's for their accustomed drink. The boys of this little burg well knew the customs of German Jason, and they were ready for a swig from the man's jug.

Jason often found his jug severely depleted when it reached home, and he resolved something must be done to relieve the situation. He was not given to taking others into his confidence, so he worked out a plan that was all his own. The next Saturday evening when he arrived at Boxley's Corner, the weather was extremely cold, but the boys who felt they needed a good stiff bracer were waiting for German Jason. Each fellow took a little longer pull at the jug than usual, and the German could see he would be lonesome all of next week without his friend the jug. He thought he could afford to be imposed upon this one time if it might put an end to the self-appropriation.

After the last young man had taken his snort, Jason said in a calm tone of broken English, "I regret to report Doctor Eldridge has told me I have heart ailment. In this whiskey is a large quantity of strychnine as medicine for me. I hope boys you have not taken enough to kill you dead." Almost immediately the young men began to feel pains in their stomachs, and one fellow was sure he going to expire on the spot. The group hurried over to Dr. Eldridge's office and told the medical man that they had taken strychnine by mistake and something must be done. The old doctor "smelled a mouse" and suggested they wait a few minutes, and if they didn't get better, he would pump their stomachs. For fear old Jason had really put strychnine in his whiskey, the doctor gave each a dose of ipecac and they were soon really sick and emptying their own stomachs. The next time German Jason passed Boxley's Corner, there was not a single call for "Saturday night treats."

Chapter 33

The Pioneer Doctor
1844

Doc Eldridge had been up the hollow all night and was trying to get home before sunup. Elijah Caudle's daughter, Nora, had been ill with consumption for a long time, and she was suffering the pain that precedes death as the lungs waste away and fill with fluid. The January weather was biting cold, hugging zero, and Doc was glad to see a light in the mill. He directed his horse to the hitch rack down in the shelter of the mill, saw to it that Molly's blankets were well adjusted, and hurried up the steps. Peter Cooper met him at the door, threw it open, and almost pulled the doctor toward the fire. Doc was blowing his hot breath between his stiffened fingers to help in the warming process and soon had his cold feet cocked up before the fire. Peter had hurried over to the mill this morning to build a fire so that the mill hands would work in an atmosphere that was warm.

"Have you been out all night, Doc?" inquired Peter. "It seems to me that pain and suffering come at bad times. I wonder why those people up the hollow don't try to provide for themselves better. It's a wonder to me they don't freeze to death in those shacks with the thin walls. A dugout might not be bad in summer, but during these cold days they have such a poor method of keeping warm."

"Waal," drawled the doctor, "it has been a puzzle to me for years how the hollow people live. 'lijah's little girl has never been strong. It seems she was never meant for this world. They can't keep her warm, and she coughs most of the time. I hated to leave her alone, for I am sure she will be gone before long."

"Doc, there is one thing that can be said to your credit. You go when you're called," said Peter, "and your fees may never come. I'll venture there are very few fees paid to you by those living up the hollow. Maybe someday St. Peter will pay you, and perhaps he'll say, 'Here comes good old Doc Eldridge! While he lived on earth he did much good; possibly he can be of service to us here in heaven.'"

"Well, Peter," rejoined the old doctor, "the people of this community have been mighty good to me, and I feel under obligation to every man, woman, and child in this valley. When I came to this neighborhood about twenty years ago as a young medical graduate, I had never compounded a prescription or given a dose of medicine, but somehow the people took me into their homes, got by with my medicines, and now I feel under obligation to them."

Doctor William B. Eldridge had come to Canaan after graduating from the Louisville Medical Institute. He had carried all his worldly possessions in his saddlebags, and even though they were stuffed full, it was a queer kind of load: a change of clothing, a few medical books, some medicines, and some other goods enough to last him a few days. He had built a cabin across from the store, hung out his shingle, and started his practice. The land had not been drained, and there was much fever, chills, and dysentery, as there was everywhere in this region. The general store sold only a few apothecary remedies. Doc's work was ahead of him.

Doc raised many of his own herbs from which he made drugs, and he was rather independent. The books he had brought with him recommended remedies which were hard to obtain, but he had generally been able to give a substitute drug when needed. He bought large quantities of quinine, rhubarb, and whiskey, but this last named medicine he gave in limited quantities and used principally to preserve other medicines. Doc was a teetotaler and always said whiskey did more harm than good. "Those who keep whiskey for the chills, or in case of snakebite, are fooling no one except themselves," he often repeated.

Doc Eldridge spent much time in his garden, and he took pride in explaining to Joan Cooper the nature of each herb, its botanical name, and its curative powers. The doc grew sage for a tea to be administered in case of colds. This tea would sometimes allay sweats; catnip was used by the doctor as a stimulant and tonic; boneset he used as a light emetic; horseweed roots he used for dropsy. Most of these herbs were cut and dried by the doctor. He kept them in sealed jars, carefully labeled. Doc grew horehound to be used for catarrh troubles; mullein he used in a salve for hemorrhoids; jimson weed he cut and dried with care and then made a compound for neuralgia or rheumatism. One corner of the garden was devoted to the growing of pennyroyal, which the doctor used to suppress colic in children and, incidentally, he sometimes remarked, it would drive away fleas and mosquitoes.

One day when Doc Eldridge conducted Joan through his "yarb garden," it was apparent that he took unusual pride in growing the different plants. She herself had become something of a dispenser of simple herbs, but this man knew, and grew, far more than she. She wanted to learn. While some of the shrubs were strange-looking objects and seldom seen in the Canaan neighborhood, many of them were common in the woods and pastures, and some were known as plain noxious weeds. It was strange that the good old Doc could take these hateful intruders in other people's gardens and really make something worthwhile from them. As he kept naming the different occupants of the garden, he also told of their worth in his pharmacopoeia. The doctor would touch these ugly weeds tenderly as if they were most precious.

Joan had often heard that extract from peppermint would relieve nausea and pains in the bowels, and that dogwood bark bitters was a good tonic. She had read that anise was used in making cough syrup and no doubt knew that lobelia was used as a potent emetic and was good in cases of whooping cough, but she could go little further. The doctor explained to her that white walnut bark was an excellent purgative, and he told her of a balm that he could make from the same bark that could be used in cases of fever, asthma, and headache.

Joan recognized the hateful dog's fennel, which grew so profusely in the barnyards. She had been told that it could be used as a mild stimulant when properly treated. She remembered that Johnny Appleseed was reported to have brought a start of the stinking weed into the community and that he sang many praises of its medicinal qualities. Doc showed Joan other familiar weeds, which in other gardens took time and energy to keep from choking out the vegetables. It seemed that these weeds grew fastest in hot weather when it was a real task to hoe or pull them from among vegetables.

About midway in the garden, Doc pointed to some apparently stunted shrubs that were struggling for their existence. "Have you ever seen witch hazel?" Doc asked. "Well, those bushes over there by the fence seemed determined to perish. You know that shrub likes the low meadowland, and because I have brought them to this garden, I have had to give them more than their share of attention. Witch hazel is a good remedy for bruises and burns, and it is hard for me to keep in a supply. I take the bark, pound it into a powder, and then try to extract the oil, which I use as a base for the liniment which I administer almost daily."

He continued, "The life story of the witch hazel is most interesting. It differs from other plants in that it doesn't bloom until late in November. When the branches of all other shrubs are bare and the leaves have gone for the year, this strange bush will send forth its bright yellow flowers that stand out in the loneliness. The cold frosts and early freezes of November only make this little flower stand out brighter. The petals are like little yellow ribbons that curl at the end. Another strange thing about this plant is that its fruit, which is a little oval nut, matures only at the same time the shrub is blooming, late in the fall. We have the nuts and the blossoms coming together. The plant of a brisk wintery morning has a habit of shooting the little nuts at anyone disturbing the limb. The passerby often wonders who is shooting at him with a blowgun as he wanders down in the marshes. The firing of the witch-hazel seed is the final reminder of last summer."

Near the garden gate grew elderberry plants, and Doc explained that he took the blossom and made a tea to prevent heart attacks. The wild cherry tree growing back of the woodhouse he stripped of its bark, steeped it in whiskey, and gave it for ague. Some of Doc's patients were accused of having more than their fair share of ague, in order to get a goodly supply of the tonic. Doc explained to Joan that snakeroot would stimulate the heart action; tansy, which grew along the walk, was good for malaria; and mayapple root helped cure dysentery.

As they were finishing their walk through the "yarb garden," the doc concluded his lecture by remarking with a laugh that while everyone hated pokeberries, he had to keep some in the garden for the teetotalers of the community. He explained that he soaked the berries in whiskey until the liquid had a beautiful amber color, and then it was proper to give the fluid to old men for rheumatism. Joan was as much confused at the end of the journey through the garden as one could be who knew so little of medicine.

Doc then took his visitor to his cellar, where he showed her earthen jars containing powders and liquids. Most of these jars or crocks were well covered and some sealed. Every article in Doc's pharmacopoeia was carefully labeled and enabled the doctor to be independent of medicine shops. It was a long way to a medicine shop or apothecary, and anyway these shops were often filled with pharmaceutical remedies, some of them dangerous. Doc was wary of the shops. The recently formed Pharmaceutical Society of America was acting on some of the worst of these chemical "remedies," the use of arsenic, strychnine, mercury, and especially opium. Doc had little use for chemical cures. The doctor sent to Cincinnati for his quinine and such other drugs as he was unable to find in his garden or the woods or fields.

Doc was much opposed to tent-sale medicines, for, as he often said, "If the patent medicine is harmless and has no effect on the human system, it is an imposition on ignorant people, and if it has effect it might be dangerous to take." He repeated many times that "the promises made upon the wrappers were nearly always false." There were some liniments and salves which could be used without harmful effects, but he stated that common axle grease was more potent than any of them.

When babies were due, the parents usually sent for Doctor Eldridge. It had been traditionally believed to be cowardly to need a doctor at childbirth, but in spite of that, the women wanted the doctor there increasingly instead of the old-fashioned midwife. The good doctor, as many called him, could use forceps, high and low, in the case of dangerously delayed births. He kept a list of the youngsters he had attended at birth, and it was a rather formidable list. He sometimes administered laudanum for pain but was wary of it because it could become a crutch in life all too easily.

Doc went into the homes of the poor with the same grace and dignity that he would enter the home of the biggest landowner, and he had the respect and esteem of all. When death was near, this old doctor was a great comfort. Even if he could not check the hand of the Grim Reaper, still he could hold the hand of the sick one and quiet him or her in this last hour. Doc Eldridge never left the dying until the eyes were finally closed.

He kept his own counsel, gave good advice, and never peddled gossip. He knew to be untrue many a wild story which was given him in confidence as the "gospel truth." If these stories were harmful, he would do his best to shame the speaker so the tales could travel no further. He did what he could to correct injustice and settled many disputes by inducing the parties to talk sense. He was always willing to listen to good reports but was impatient with slander.

Doc and his good wife enjoyed a meal at the Cooper home, for in this home the good in neighbors was reported and the bad was forgotten. Doc was faithful at church, always took his seat near the front, and made no demonstration, but encouraged his neighbors in rightful living. He was a deacon, assisting the pastor Hezekiah Beecher, and could be counted on to assist in every movement helpful in the community. He was chairman of the committee to build, and then improve, conditions at the county poorhouse at the county seat. He noticed that when the old and helpless were carried to the poorhouse, it was meant as the last helpful act of their neighbors toward them. The old were soon forgotten, and no one cared how they were treated. Few visited them, and they received inferior food, little clothing, scant heat, and meager attention. Ungrateful children forgot their parents, and if the children had procured a deed to the old home, these old people were of no further use. Doc and his committee advocated a law that would require children to support their parents, and sometimes they asked the county attorney to bring a suit to set aside a deed made by parents to worthless children. Doc urged good people to visit the poor unfortunates and help in seeing that they were properly fed, clothed, and housed. He urged the fortunate to spend a little of their time and go to the county home to visit the elderly, whose greatest happiness could be to be noticed and appreciated. "I believe missionary work ought to be done right near home instead of always in darkest Africa or with the heathen Chinese, as they say. Let's treat these people in the county home like the friends that they are."

Not long after Eldridge had come to the valley, he had fallen in love with one of the daughters of Rube Stockbridge, the blacksmith. They had been married. Their first humble cabin had given way to a more spacious cottage as years went by. The wife, besides being a good housekeeper, helped her husband as a nurse. Matilda had made many trips up the hollow to care for the sick. After her own family had begun to occupy her attention, she had been unable to help her husband as a nurse, but in extreme cases and where the sick were unable to procure care, she had gone with her husband to do her part. Matilda was loved and respected in the valley, and now as they both were growing older, the doctor and his good wife had a spot at any table in the town had they wished it. Their two sons were friends of Jimmy's.

Doc was a good homemade politician. He had his own ideas in politics, and while he did not run for office, he did not shirk the expression of his convictions. He was not an admirer of Martin Van Buren, who was always running for the presidency even after he had served as president of the United States, for Doc felt that Little Van's ideas of economy were only meant to deny public improvements in the West. Doc was a Whig, through and through. He could tell with great glee the story of Van and the stage driver and of how the ex-president had landed in the mud: Van Buren had decided he would take a trip west by stage as far as St. Louis, then take the steamboat to New Orleans, and finally go back to his own New York City. The people of the Middle West had been clamoring for road improvements, but Van couldn't see money wasted upon cuts and fills and grades through forests or over prairies. In order to have firsthand information for his colleagues in the East, he planned to make a field inspection and report real facts. His defeat in the presidential election of 1840 (much to the disgust of Pappy and Rastus Coffin, those inveterate Democrats up at Trowbridge's store,) had not changed his plans for the inspection trip, which he thought would serve his political purposes well. The ex-president followed the National Road west by slow stage. He was entertained in Indianapolis, and the boys there decided to have some fun. They knew that the stage driver going west from Indianapolis could be depended upon, and they remembered that mud holes were numerous and it was slow driving. There was one exceptionally deep hole just west of the village of Plainfield. The community around that village was inhabited by Quakers, and, of course, they would not be a party to any shameful act. The stage driver, however, was not a Quaker, and the boys downstate were no Democrats, so a deal was made to show the need of good roads. The events followed their plan, and the stagecoach struck the south rim of this mud hole. The north wheel of the stage disappeared toward China, and the coach with its dignified, silk-stockinged occupant landed in the deepest part of the mud. When the "Little Magician" pulled himself out of the mire, he used a language not commonly heard among Quakers. Whenever Doc told this story, his sides shook and his laugh could be heard for half a mile. He never forgot to tell that the driver was afterwards presented with a fine silk plug hat, and that he, Doc, had had an opportunity to contribute his mite for it.

In 1833 when cholera raged in all parts of the Middle West, Doctor William B. Eldridge quarantined himself from his family and devoted himself to caring for those stricken with this horrid disease. He never failed to go when called, and many afterwards owed their lives to the attention given them by this pioneer country doctor. It was no wonder the people of Canaan loved and respected him.

Chapter 34

The Blacksmith Shop
1846

The summer rain beat a steady downpour upon the clapboard roof of the blacksmith shop. Black was an appropriate term for Rube Stockbridge's shop, for everything around the shop was grimy. The dirt floor was black; the walls, the rafters, the roof, and every tool was ebony, coal-colored, nightshade. The smith's face and hands were smeared with soot and coal dust, his leather apron was greasy grime, and even the youngster who pumped the bellows had dirty charcoal face, hands, and feet.

As this was a rainy day, the farmers couldn't work in their crops. They could, however, get the horses shod. The animals were tied to the hitch rack in the side yard, each awaiting a turn. It made little difference how wet the horses were, and when the waiting owner's turn came, he rushed out into the rain, untied his nag, and hurried it inside the shop. While rainy days were busy days for the blacksmith, they were also a good time for the owner of a horse to swap news and argue politics as he switched flies off his horse.

Stockbridge had been the smith for many years and knew personally every farmer in the valley and every horse by name: Ginger, Sligo, Gray Ghost, Inverness, and so forth. He had little time for conversation while he fitted and nailed shoes, but he missed little of what was said. This smith had, for years, made his shoes and the nails, but lately shoes were being manufactured at the iron foundry, and he had them shipped to him by the keg. Stockbridge had been one of the first country blacksmiths to use the new steel horseshoe nails, with square heads and shanks that were thin, tough, and pointed. The blacksmith was able to bend and to clinch these nails so that they held the shoe firmly. The farmers examined his first ones very carefully. "Congratulations, Reuben, my boy! You are right well up to date," they said.

When the smith fitted the hot shoes to the horse's foot, the burnt hoof filled the shop with a thick smoke of a most unpleasant odor. When the shoes were pounded to the satisfaction of the blacksmith, he then held them in the slack tub and allowed them to cool slowly and thus harden. The old half-barrel slack tub was cleaned out once each year, and not only was the water salty, but as time went on it became darker and darker until it could be mistaken for black paint.

Old Jerry Hughes was in no hurry to bring his mare into the shop, for the longer he waited, the longer he could keep from work, and by giving his place to a neighbor who was sure to be in a hurry, the more gossip he would hear and the more he could talk. "Have any of you fellers noticed the pigeons in the Dexter woods?" Jerry asked, cleaning his fingernails with a penknife. "Last night some of us went over at roosting time, and there were so many in the trees that we could hear the limbs cracking. They say they are coming from the east and traveling west. They have now been in the neighborhood for more than a week. Some of the boys are having a hard time keeping them out of their wheat fields, so we took our guns to 'em. When we made a noise they lifted, and with every fire into the flock, we brought down dozens of pigeons. They don't seem to nest in this neighborhood, but when the young are big enough to fly, they pass this way. I have been told that sometimes there are so many in a flock that they darken the sun. If the shooting keeps up they won't last many decades."

Hezekiah Beecher, the brave and forthright minister who had threatened the lynch mob, was not much of a tale-teller, and he begrudged the time he wasted waiting for his turn either at the mill or the blacksmith shop, but he had to wait today. His horse must be shod, and the weather would not let him work in the fields. Hezekiah had only half listened to the talk about the pigeons and various other subjects, but he was very interested in the news from Mexico, where some of the boys of this community were serving under the American flag. Hezekiah was against war in any form, and he was especially against this war, calling it one of aggression. There were two things in Hezekiah's life more pronounced than all others: he was "agin' war" and "agin' slavery." He condemned Polk's administration for leading Americans into the war with Mexico over a boundary dispute where there was no principle involved, and he said the land beyond the Rio Grande did not belong to the United States. It was not part of the Louisiana Purchase, and the United States was simply trying to grab the land for American cattlemen. If there was any merit to the so-called dispute, it could be settled by arbitration. We did not need to send our young men as soldiers into Mexico.

When the boys asked the old Peace Presbyterian about the justness of the cause when we declared our independence and fought off England's claim, he replied that at that time we had been merely defending ourselves, which we had a right to do. Hezekiah also thought we had been justified in preventing England from "impressing" our seamen, and the wars with the Indians had not been wars but merely a defense of our homes and families. A war to acquire more land was never justified, he thought, even if the people in the territory in question did want to live under the flag of the United States.

Governor Whitcomb had attended the mass meeting at the county seat at which the young men from Canaan had joined the colors. Johnny Cowan and some of the schoolhouse gang, now young men in their twenties, had joined, but Hezekiah had not approved of the action taken. Hezekiah reported to the men waiting in the blacksmith shop that he had heard the governor say "We must carry the war into the enemy's country and plant the star-spangled banner in the city of Mexico in the halls of Montezuma." Pshaw. When the governor had called for volunteers from the state, he had at the same time pledged prompt cooperation with the federal government toward carrying the war into Mexico.

Peter Cooper had brought his riding horse over to the blacksmith shop this afternoon and was obliged to wait in line. He was twitted about waiting his turn, with some of the men insisting that they had waited twelve hours at his mill. Peter took the jokes in good turn and enjoyed the conversation, for on this occasion he was free from mill duties and could enter into the spirit of the friendly debates. Peter was a Whig in politics, a disciple of Henry Clay, and he had been opposed to the entrance into the Mexican War, but since we were in, he wanted us to make short work of it.

Peter added his bit to the conversation in saying that the state had been in poor condition to enter this war, for the militia had been disbanded and the soldiers for a long time had had no arms or equipment of war. "I am especially interested and amused at the action of young Lew Wallace and his anxiety to get into the war," he said. Lew was the son of ex-governor David Wallace, and of course the people of the state kept track of his doings. Lew was only nineteen years of age, but he was a genius in some respects. His father intended the son should be a lawyer, but the young man seemed to find other things to interfere with his study of legal subjects.

Peter continued, "This young Wallace recruited a company in about three days at Indianapolis. He wanted to kill two birds with one stone: get into the war and visit the halls of Montezuma. Lew is more of a writer than he is a lawyer, and it is to be hoped he will, for a time, at least, make a good captain of soldiers. He plays the violin, paints pictures, models in clay, writes articles, and dabbles at law. This young feller is making a study of the ancient Aztec people of Mexico. If he can get down into that country and learn something of that old civilization, you will find, I predict, when he comes home, he'll be writing a book."

Peter then went on to tell how young Wallace had rented a room in Indianapolis, hung in front of a building a flag and a sign saying, "For Mexico—Fall In," and had then hired a drummer and a fifer and started a parade. The crowd had followed the music until it stopped, and Wallace had then collected enough young men for a company—all of whom enlisted to go to Mexico, hardly knowing where it was. Peter told how the Indiana troops had been taken down the Mississippi River in steamboats to New Orleans, where they waited for arms, and how finally when some rifles came the troops had pushed across the gulf to the mouth of the Rio Grande. "These men are now deep in Mexico and reports have not yet come," Peter went on. "I think some of these officers could make a bombastic speech, but don't know a thing about military affairs. One from over at the Licks, Augustus Bowles, can't even ride a horse well. He will probably gallop in the wrong direction. He's the man who has started the hotel over there, the spa. I think he should be over there taking the waters and stay away from war."

At this point old Hezekiah broke in to ask Peter what he thought of that new congressman from Springfield, Illinois, who was opposed to the war. This lawyer was also trying to find solutions to the problem of slavery, which he didn't seem to like. "Peter," Hezekiah told him, "you know I am opposed to war, but if ever a war comes to suppress slavery, I will enlist as a private soldier."

Peter had been reading about Abraham Lincoln in the county seat paper and answered, "A friend of ours in Vincennes, name of Marie Thoreau, wrote long ago about meeting Lincoln, I recall, when he was young and crossing with his party into Illinois. She was impressed with his determination and intelligence. Perhaps because of her interest, I have followed him as a new congressman. He has a slow drawl in his voice, they say, and he can tell more stories to illustrate his point and knows how to drive home his arguments. They say over Illinois way that he has a way of keeping Stephen A. Douglas hopping. The Democrats, you know, raised a hickory pole a few days ago. What do you say to raising an ash pole in front of this blacksmith shop and inviting the new congressman over to the valley?"

"Wasn't he raised down in Spencer County?" asked a young man new to the community.

"Yes, and he can talk our language," Peter answered. As the smith continued his work, the men began to cautiously talk about articles in the paper discussing issues of slavery. Most in the shop were ready to defend the southern states' rights to have their own economic institutions and states' rights. Hezekiah Beecher raised his fist and declared, "In the face of all here, I am not afraid to announce that I am an abolitionist. I think owning human beings is wrong. Slavery is a hateful institution." A discussion followed that was as heated as the fire and smoke in the blacksmith's shop. Finally Stockbridge began clanging on the anvil. "Enough talk about it. Let the Congress continue to compromise as it did for Missouri, or we may face a situation we can't get out of! States have rights! Our young men shouldn't have to take up guns and kill or be killed."

All was silent for a while. Peter Cooper said, in a conciliatory voice, "I've got an idea. Let's have a brass band and a barbecue and invite the whole county. We'll invite this Abraham Lincoln to come over and address us. He's a man who is trying to tiptoe between two courses and avoid trouble over the question of slavery. He can give us some middle ground to hope for. And we can get two for one: he can speak against intemperance." Some of the other men in the smithy weren't sure of that last suggestion. As the discussion continued, however, they selected a committee to get the speaker and make arrangements.

They soon heard that Lincoln couldn't come, but that didn't dampen their enthusiasm for a flag raisin' party complete with speeches and the local band from the seminary in the county seat playing "My Country Tis of Thee."

Chapter 35

The Fox Chase
1850

Jimmy Cooper was now twenty years old, a young man. He was seeking out young men's pursuits. "Mother," he said one day in early fall, "there is to be a fox chase next Saturday, and I want to be part of it. Boys and men are to come from every direction."

Joan Cooper put down the newspaper and her reading glasses on a small table by her settee. "Jimmy, fox hunts are old-fashioned customs. They belong to the past, when there were many more foxes than there are today and they harmed crops. We used to call them fox chases or roundups in those days, and we could use the same encircling methods for squirrels. Fox hunt, pshaw! I keep thinking of what Johnny Appleseed would say about these men galloping over hill and dale in pursuit of an animal about a foot long."

"Well, but it is a social thing, well organized. There will be four captains, one from each direction. All my friends will be there, and I want to go."

Jimmy's father had his own opinion. "The judge says that though he used to be avid for chasing a few foxes in the hollow, in 1850, the way people now view it, it is a play party, a feigned British import. Aristocratic nonsense." Jimmy frowned.

"And how exactly is it well organized? " Joan asked, looking seriously at her son.

"Each man or boy is to take his own dinner. Lines are to start promptly at ten o'clock in the morning. These are to be six miles long on each side at the start. Then we are to crowd in together until the lines will be only a quarter of a mile long when we reach Boxley Corner Meadow. One line is coming over the McCurdy hill, and one will come through the hollow. The boys from Coon Hollow are rarin'. They say they will bring out plenty of foxes. I bet there are lots of red foxes still hidden along Sycamore Creek."

She stood up. "Your father has taken part in several of those chases, and he says he will never go on another. The last time he was so tired and sore, we had to bathe his ankles in liniment. I suppose a young man your age could stand the long grind, though." After all, he was now a man and should be able to find his own social experiences.

"Look here, son, if you go," she said wagging a finger, "you must take care not to trip or fall. Those hills and rills are rough indeed. You could break a leg running like thunder and not looking. But I'll prepare you a bag of grub, because you won't want to carry a basket home."

Rules of the chase were printed and posted at every crossroad corner for miles around. The roundup was to be in Boxley Corner meadow, only a short distance out of Canaan, where there was plenty of room. Several hundred men and boys were expected to take part in the chase. Usual rules: each of four sides of six miles long would stretch out in a straight line at the start. As the four lines coming from the four directions neared the center point, the ends of the lines were to close in so that a circle would be formed. The old cannon was pulled from the courthouse yard at the county seat and placed in the center of the meadow. Exactly at ten o'clock in the morning, the cannon was to be fired as a starting signal. At half-hour intervals rifles were to be fired by the captains to notify those in opposite directions of the position of the advancing lines.

Three hours were to be used in reaching the meadow. Each man and boy was to carry a noise-making instrument, such as a horn, drum, horse fiddle, or rattle box. Old pans were to be beaten with clubs. Any other noise-making contraption would be welcome. No dogs except those on strong leashes were allowed in the chase. The thirty-six square miles to be covered were to include some of the woods and hollows in which foxes were known to hide. The captains were to be on horseback, but all others were to plod along afoot. The noon meal was to be eaten on the march, from bags carried in the hunters' pockets. There must be no stops or breaking of the lines.

The noise was supposed to frighten every rabbit, possum, coon, fox, and deer from his lair. Of course, the wildlife would run ahead of the noise makers. As the hunters would draw near Boxley Meadow, and as the lines would close in, the animals would always run first in one direction and then in another. Rabbits, coons, and possums were to be allowed to escape. A fox aroused from his den would leap leisurely ahead of the chasers until he heard the noises coming toward him in the opposite direction. When he would become confused, he would run in circles, only to be headed off whichever way he turned. The lines would grow shorter and more crowded, and a big circle would be formed at the roundup.

Jimmy told his parents that there would be a party before the fox hunt day. According to a long-established custom, a jamboree was held in Canaan the night before the chase. Before sundown, a large pile of wood was stacked in a field a short distance from the village. Even before dark, farmers and their families came to the village. Some families drove for miles and came in their farm wagons. Others came on horseback. Many farm hands just broke through the fields.

And so it was young Jim was allowed to go. He watched as evening shadows settled and the bonfire was started. As its lurid light lit up the sky, it was not hard to tell that the festivities were on. Jim and his friend Johnny Cowan, back from the Mexican War, older and wiser, along with the school hoopla crowd, the village elders, Steve Harrigan, Bill Savage, and even ancient Pappy Thorne joined with men from the hills, many of them now with productive farms. Mike Bigger and Minnie's brothers were around the fire, while women and children could be seen dimly in the background shadows. Feats of strength were performed, such as wrestling and foot races. Potatoes were baked in the hot coals. Even steaks sizzled upon long sticks held before the fire, as in the olden days. "That strikes a memory in me," Joan said to Peter. "I believe I have eaten steak on a stick that way."

"I know I have," her husband answered. "But I would rather eat it in our dining room un-charred and in comfort." Men dropped eggs into boiling water in a big kettle placed on a spider over the hot coals.

As men and sometimes the women gathered around the bonfire to eat, they formed a big circle. Trowbridge, the master of ceremonies, then called on the old and veteran fox hunters to tell of their experiences of years ago. These fox stories never lost anything in the telling. In a slow, droll Hoosier dialect, Rube Stockbridge the blacksmith related how a sly old fox was outwitted. This long-winded storyteller threw in adventures with a wildcat or other wild animal. He began telling jokes, starting with himself and then about others whose faces were lit with bonfire light. Young people snorted, not appreciating the jokes. Soon fiddles were brought forth not so much for their music as to lead in the old songs which followed. Joan nudged Peter. "I'm glad Jimmy went. He should experience this, as these events are getting to be a thing of the past. I don't think chasing foxes along the tracks of the new railroad we are due to get soon sounds like a good idea."

"I know. And look around you in the shadows. What are you seeing in those woods? Second-growth trees. Where are the giants, the sycamores and poplars it took five men to circle holding hands? We entered the Canaan Valley, we marveled at the magnificent forests, and. . . .." He was silent, staring into the fire.

"And we all cut them down. That is what we did," Joan said. "We cut them all down." She smiled a little sadly and listened to the festivities.

No bonfire jamboree would be a success unless old Bob Riddeley was present and sang. He was at his best when he sang the songs of hunting like "Bo-Reynard." Many of these men and boys could not carry a tune. It was doubtful if they ever tried to sing upon any other occasion during the year. As Bob sang the first verse of his favorite song, one that must have been a couple of hundred years old, the crowd joined lustily and off-key in the chorus, which went:

Come all ye jolly sportsmen
Who live to hunt the fox;
Who love to hunt Bo-Reynard
Among the hills and rocks.
With a hip, hip, hip of the hollowing
Along the merrily stream.
With a ran tan tan
And a tippy, tippy tan.
Away with the howling bow-wow dogs
And a Yankee-fi-diddle, diddle, di-de-do,
As through the fields we run, brave boys
As through the fields we run.

Since the chase was well advertised, and most men loved this sort of sport, many boys and men were on hand promptly the next day. It was sometimes hard to induce the sly old fox to leave his den under the roots of trees or under big rocks. Some foxes were bypassed, but still the chasers should be able to count on a good turnout. Jimmy explained to Cowan and the boys why all game wasn't corralled. Rabbits were allowed to escape at this season of the year. The pelts of possum and raccoon were no good in sum-

mer, so they were often left alone. It was thought unfair to take advantage of
deer in this manner, but some of them were always saved for the roundup,
even if allowed to escape later. And anyway, by the 1850s in southern Indiana, these animals were getting to be few and far between, even foxes. It was
reported the last "panther," wildcat, had been seen in Knox County a few
years before, and no more had ever been seen there. This chase was to catch
the sly old fox who never respected the rights of the farmers' chicken roosts.
They were pests, but at this time of more intense settlement, how many
could they nab? Whatever amount it was, it would be fine sport.

They knew the red or grey fox would steal from his hole, look carefully
around, and then leisurely lope ahead of the noise. The dogs on leash would
be helpful in locating fox burrows. They would be allowed to start Mr. Bo
Reynard upon his last run. Whenever a fox or deer attempted to break past
the lines, the noise from that section would usually cause the animal to
change his mind and break for the opposite direction.

As the lines reached the big meadow and began to close in, hundreds
of men and boys could be seen coming from every direction. All noise ma-
chines were now used, while those carrying guns fired their blanks as often
as possible. The tall grass was moving in every direction. Wildlife was thoroughly frightened. Some animals tried hiding, but most kept on the run.
Finally the lines closed, and the men crowding in closer formed a single file
around the entire circle. The noise was deafening. The animals were completely bewildered. Rabbits and even foxes sometimes jumped into the arms
of the men. When the circle was considered small enough, little boys were
provided with hickory clubs and placed in the pen to complete the final act.
Farmers had no pity for a fox, which never showed any pity for his prey and
each year caused the farmer great damage among his poultry.

The few dead foxes they had brought to the center were clubbed and
put in a small pile. Hunters knew that even at this season of the year, fur
buyers would attempt to cure those pelts. Only a couple of deer were killed.
These usually went to those who lived up the hollow. The hunters looked at
each other. No more deer? Had the time come when deer would actually be
gone from Indiana?

None of the sportsmen knew how tired they were until they started
home. Then sore feet began to announce their presence. It took no coaxing
that evening to persuade a fox hunter to hunt his bed. The judge walked

alongside Jimmy as they left the event. "I know what we should say about this," he said, looking back at the scene. Jimmy turned to him expectantly. "We'll remember this as the last fox hunt in Indiana. That's memorable, isn't it?" They both laughed.

"Well, how did you like it?" Peter asked his son when the young man dragged into the house, red-faced and breathing hard. The brisk October weather had caused Peter to make a fire in the huge fireplace, no longer used for cooking, and he was stoking it.

"I liked it very well, Father," Jimmy said, collapsing in an armchair. "But I shan't do it again, I think. I think we did nab every fox in the county. And if we didn't get 'em, I say let them go. There's far more of us than of them. Fair game now; let them go."

The Civil War, Summer of 1863

Jimmy and his cohorts in the Ninetieth Indiana were part of a force which defeated Morgan the Raider on July 19, 1863. Morgan's troops, which had been attempting to cross the Ohio and return into Kentucky, were scattered in that encounter, and a week later a part of the raiders fought the skirmish shown above, at Washington, Ohio. Morgan was soon captured, and Jimmy's regiment moved on to Tennessee, some of them to eventual capture and incarceration at Andersonville.

Etching from *Harper's Weekly* August, 1863

Chapter 36

Captain Jimmy in Camp and in the Field
1862–1865

Civil War had come for Canaan and the rest of the northern states. And in the South, mothers and fathers were saying goodbye to their own sons, just as was happening in Indiana. Grim fighting was going on in Virginia and along the Mississippi. But Indiana would not be invaded directly—would it? Joan and Peter Cooper wondered nightly about this as they watched their son reading newspapers and eager to join the army. "I need you at the mill," his father said. "We are furnishing grain for these troops, and I cannot do this alone for the war effort."

It was true that the Cooper mill was grinding corn and wheat for the Union army. The entire output had been commandeered by Governor Oliver Perry Morton, with instructions to keep the mill going night and day. Big wagonloads of meal and flour were going south to the troops. Jimmy Cooper was now thirty years old, sound in body, unmarried, and able to do more than a man's share of work. When Governor Morton had recently told Jimmy that he could do the cause more good by staying at the mill, he had replied, "My friends are coming home wounded and in their faded suits of blue, and some in wooden coffins, after fighting in Kentucky and at Antietam, and I say I am grinding corn for the war. No, sir, now that there are new companies forming, I will muster a company and be on the firing lines as soon as I can get to the war."

When Jimmy announced his intention of going into the cavalry in 1862 and was mustered into a newly organized company the next year, many of his friends went with him. Johnny Cowan had been wounded in the Mexican War and sadly wished the contingent from the county off. Others from other counties would join this cavalry unit. "Father," Jimmy had said, "I'll take old Strideout. Together we can outrun any rebel horse. The recruiting office has sent instructions that a man may bring his own horse. The government will make allowances for it. Strideout and I, together with about fifty other stalwarts from this county, have decided to start for Camp

Carrington tomorrow morning."

A company headed by Jimmy, who had been elected temporary captain, started north with their own horses for the Indianapolis recruiting and training camp. Jimmy was formally elected captain, but he was not long in training. The demand for soldiers was so great down south that no time could be lost. Captain James Cooper was off to war.

Peter and Joan soon received a letter telling them the new company of cavalry would be shipped south within a few days. The parents drove to the nearest railroad station on the Jeffersonville and Indianapolis railroad and took the train for the capital. Camp Carrington was a military camp and training ground immediately west of the statehouse. The surrounding community was a sea of tents with young soldiers marching and loitering around them. Cavalry horses were staked at the extreme west side near White River. For good reason Peter and Joan made for the horse stockade. The neigh of old Strideout was the first sign of recognition they received. The horse knew them and wanted to be noticed and petted.

The Coopers had made the trip to Indianapolis often in recent years, and they felt at home at the Bates House. In fact, when Abraham Lincoln had been on his way to Washington to assume the presidency, he had spoken from the balcony of the Bates House. There Peter and Joan, finally able to see the man whom Miss Thoreau had so admired, had listened to his sad but wise words. This lively lady had lived to see the young man she had spoken to elevated to the office of president. She had earlier come to visit her Joan and Peter several times on the stage, getting to know Jimmy and telling her old stories of the coming, and growing up, of Koo-wa in Vincennes. Joan missed her and wished for her infrequent visits. That Miss Thoreau was still among them, a surprisingly spry old lady, as they said in Canaan, was even more important to Joan because her own parents and Peter's loved mother and father could come no more.

When Joan saw Captain Jimmy in his new uniform, her eyes shone. He wore a wide-brimmed blue-black hat with a double gold cord, shoulders covered with broad yellow epaulets. The front of his coat, the cuffs, and the collar were trimmed with yellow braid, and a broad band came up the outside seam of his trouser legs. He wore riding boots and spurs and carried a sword in a scabbard at his side. In his belt was a complement of cartridges that would fit the revolver carried in a holster.

Joan could not help but think of that long ago time when as a suffering outcast of a child, her father had often told her, she had admired the uniforms of the Corydon Guards, stroking the buttons, warmed by the coat of a military unit. She could actually remember some of that time, though everything before it was gone. Strideout had on the same bridle and saddle he had carried from home, except the trimmings were now yellow in keeping with the cavalry colors. The parents stayed for dress parade. Jimmy handled his men in formation like a veteran. Joan had made arrangements with the official photographers to take a picture, which was mailed to Canaan. Though long in coming, it was framed and hung in the living room, where it remained during the long war. Of course they were only one of thousands of Hoosier families, and these were not the earliest days of the war, but any leave-taking to the dangerous fields of battle was trying—and called forth a mother's tears. Her son would go with his Fifth Indiana Cavalry to Tennessee for a year.

During the summer of 1863, rumor was rampant that General John Morgan, the rebel raider, was training and recruiting his troops in Kentucky, preparing to make a raid into Indiana. Every home, village, and town south of Indianapolis was alive with apprehension. People in Canaan, not far from the Kentucky border, discussed ways and means of protecting themselves. The entire state seemed to have risen in alarm. Home guards, which had formed into the Indiana Legion, prepared to defend the state. Older men could be seen marching and drilling with arms in almost every schoolyard. Every old gun was pressed into service. Since every farmer owned a deer or squirrel rifle, neighborhoods were not without arms.

Governor Morton responded to the challenge by sending military supplies into the communities of southern Indiana as fast as he could. Word went through the Canaan community, hill and valley, that Morgan had promised to do damage in a short time by burning towns, confiscating horses, and frightening people out of their wits. Morgan's supporters in the South hoped for an uprising from southern sympathizers, the Copperheads, who had plotted opposition to the war with direct encouragement from that disastrous officer of the Mexican War, Augustus Bowles of the Licks. They encouraged themselves with the prospect of an armed uprising to end the war in the state of Indiana. It was not to be. Most southern sympathizers who lived in Indiana could not face the idea of rebellion.

The Fifth Indiana Cavalry confronted Morgan at the Ohio River and prevented him from crossing the river into Kentucky. After one last foray to Washington, Ohio, and other towns, he was captured. Jimmy's cavalry unit operated attached to the Ninetieth Indiana Volunteers throughout Kentucky for some months and then went on into Tennessee. The next reports said that the cavalry had gone over the Cumberland Mountains. Later they were entering Knoxville as part of Burnside's army. They then moved over the Smokies, and a hot fight was registered at Blountsville. Newspapers coming to Canaan reported that for seven Sundays the Ninetieth fought at Rheatown, then into Georgia. Word seldom came from the men who had gone out from Canaan. In December meager reports were received of harassing Longstreet and of the battles of Dandridge and Strawberry Plains. Sherman was marching to the sea, and Jimmy and his comrades in arms were doing their part, moving to support him.

The folks at home heard that General George Stoneman had then taken command, and the orders were to support the march to Atlanta, to move forward. For a long time Wheeler's Cavalry fought Stoneman's advance in bloody conflicts, quick-moving hit-and-run raids.

A few weeks later Joan and Peter received this letter:

July 12, 1864
On horseback near Atlanta, Ga.
Dear Mother and Father:
It is just breaking dawn. We have been on our horses all night. Of course, we have not slept a wink. I can see a little of the sun through the burnt trees. Strideout is wide awake and ready to go. This letter will be hard to read, for I can hardly see to write. We have been detailed to bring on the fight and will ride out in front of the rebel fortifications as soon as it is light. The general wants to locate their main body. We are not anxious to become targets, but maybe they will not be straight shooters. Several companies volunteered, but we got the job. Sherman is driving hard. As I finish, it is light. We have already eaten a bit, and the bugle is sounding. Don't worry. Strideout will take me through. He can't stand still; we're off! Hurrah!

With love from Jimmy

At Macon, Georgia, a short time later, Jimmy's company was ordered to hold the line so that Stoneman's army could escape from a trap during a raid that was doomed from the start. The escape maneuver failed, General Joe Wheeler closed in, and many in the Fifth Cavalry were captured. Captain Jimmy's men were sent to Andersonville, while he as an officer was sent to Libby Prison. His parents frantically mourned and prayed and finally received word that he had been released. He was still alive and to serve again with his unit.

A year later in Canaan, Pete Moran, an undertaker from Canaan and his wife, Molly, drove to the county seat on Saturday afternoon to buy provisions. Pete intended to take a little "sniff" with his friends. The liquor flowed a little too freely for Pete, and Molly was eager to get him started toward home. He usually took home a jug which was supposed to last several weeks, but this time Pete wasn't able to wait.

Pete and Molly were still in town after dark when the Evening Special arrived from the south. They saw a tall, straight, haggard, and extremely thin cavalry captain, dressed in a new uniform, step from the train and look up and down the tracks as if expecting to meet a friend. Then slowly, it seemed painfully, he helped himself into his navy blue overcoat, to which was attached a large cape. The captain was admired by the crowd, but no one seemed to know him. Finally he came over toward Pete and Molly and said, "Pete, what would be the chance of a ride out to Canaan?"

Molly recognized him, and throwing both arms around him, yelled, "Jimmy! It's Jimmy Cooper! They have let you go!" The liquor left old Pete's brain that moment. Soon he was also embracing the boy. The local man's Irish brogue almost brought tears to Jimmy's eyes as he heard, "We never expected to see you again! Does your mither know you're comin'? Jump in, me boy, jump in! Get up on this seat or pile into the hay." In a few minutes the exhausted captain was asleep in the hay. No noises, no bumps, no rough roads counted, for Jimmy was very tired. It had been a long, long trip, physically and emotionally, from Libby Prison, and he had never recovered in the duty he'd served afterwards. Although Pete used the whip, it took a long time to drive the distance.

As the party came near Canaan, Jimmy awakened and saw the lights twinkling at the village center. Pete poured on the speed, and the old horses responded, for they seemed to know there was something special in the off-ing. As the wagon rounded the corner with the horses in a gallop, the loafers at the store realized something was astir. They rushed to the front door. Everybody in the town ran out to the street where the wagon was bumping, old Pete was shouting, and Molly was waving her arms. The whole party followed up the rise to the Cooper home. There with a "whoa" that could be heard for a mile, the wagon came to a stop.

Captain Jimmy sprang from the wagon and was clasped in the arms of his mother and then his father. He was home. The war would soon be over, and peace could settle like a mantle over the pioneering village of Canaan, the home and safe haven of his family in the deep woods of Indiana.

Epilogue

Miss Marie Thoreau, a maiden lady now somewhat advanced in age but of good health and erect carriage, still lived in the old home in Vincennes. She had always intended to make a visit to Quebec and also to her beloved France, but lately some information had come to her that made her want to hasten her visit to France. She had given up her classes some time ago. Lately she had devoted herself to a study of the closing years of the eighteenth century and the early days of the nineteenth century in the homeland of her ancestors.

Since roads had improved in central Indiana after the stagecoach had come into common use, she had made several trips during the summers to Canaan to visit her favorite pupil. The stagecoach trip was so long that the visit had to be taken in a vacation period, but now the railroad provided easy and quick travel between the two homes. Miss Thoreau liked to make her visits at times when Joan did not have other company; she wanted to be helpful in the home. Because young Jimmy belonged to Joan, he was dear to the heart of the little white-haired lady. Joan had tried to persuade the old teacher to come and live with her, but Miss Thoreau was as independent as in the days when she had conducted her school on lines she herself had originated. And of course in the last years of the visits, Jimmy was grown up, then gone.

She had lived in her large family home alone since the death of her father. It was built in the old ways and was large and hard to keep and improve with the passing of time. Merchants were offering to buy the site so that it might be used for business. The old teacher did some of her own housework but kept an old creole woman as housekeeper. Miss Thoreau felt free to come and go, and with the information she had lately gained, she was determined to go to France. The Civil War was over. Jimmy had come home. The old teacher wanted to visit Joan to explain to her the cause of this trip abroad. She told Joan she expected to stay in Europe a year or two to study the old records of some of the churches. She had been collecting history of the old abbeys and cathedrals in Normandy and had found this study very interesting. Some of the churches had been centuries in the building, and the architecture was of surpassing beauty. She had never had time in her brief student year in France to travel and appreciate the countryside. In the libraries of these churches, she knew, had been written the life story of the men and women who had been connected with them. Those who had made the fight for church and state would be most interesting to her.

Marie Thoreau knew that her ancestors had lived deep in France near the German border, but she was not going to France primarily to seek her own genealogical history. She did not tell Joan that she wanted to go to France to solve in her own mind a problem in which she had been interested since the day the little Indian girl who wasn't an Indian came into the home of James Simpson.

Sea traffic was again normal, and Miss Thoreau landed at LeHavre in June, 1866, after having sailed on the *Goodwill*. She went at once to the old haunts of her schooldays in Paris. The great French capital had changed, of course, and the friends she had known as a girl were all gone. The French she spoke seemed strange even to her own ears. It was only with difficulty that she could make herself understood, and this was disappointing. After spending a few days visiting old places and meeting new faces, she settled to the work she had in mind.

The former schoolteacher had learned that in the eighteenth and the opening years of the nineteenth century, many prominent men engaged in the fur trade and went in ships to America to obtain fine furs for the whole of Europe. The men of Normandy were known then as seafaring men, hardy individuals who lived in towns dotting the coast and were always seeking profitable trade. They usually accompanied their ships.

In the big library where she had decided to study first, she was deluged with books on many subjects about the colonies in North America, but these books did not give names of those men who had crossed the sea more than a half century ago. Most of the books in this library were based on original church records, which were only to be found in the archives of the old Catholic churches. Reference was made in some of them to the fact that many prominent men went to Canada, sending at a fine profit their valuable furs to the coast towns of Normandy.

"The sea begins at Rouen" is a common expression in Normandy. While it may be considered an inland city, Rouen is also a seaport, for the tide in the Seine extends that far inland. This capital city of the province of Normandy is only eighty-seven miles from Paris. At the time of Marie Thoreau's visit, it was a large commercial city. The fur-trading industry, however, had naturally declined with the passing of time and the elimination of most of the beaver and other fur-bearing animals. She found that the most beautiful cathedral was the old church of Notre Dame, which had required centuries to build. One of the old writers in a travel book she bought described it by saying, "It has seen many vicissitudes, but its imposing façade surmounted by lofty towers, its richly decorated walls, its exquisite wood carvings, fine sculpture, and beautiful rose window render Notre Dame one of the most remarkable and artistic of Christian temples."

She was interested to read that Rouen had become the capital of Normandy in 912. Since that time, it had been entirely French in character. It had been the principal residence of the dukes. William the Conqueror, wounded at Nantes, had died at Rouen. The church of Saint Ouen was begun in the twelfth century but had not been completed until the sixteenth century. In 1431 Joan of Arc had been tried in this city and later burned at the stake. Since that time she had been considered by all Frenchmen a martyr and a saint. Her dear Joan was named after the sainted heroine, and that connection, in this very town, thrilled Miss Thoreau.

Miss Thoreau found the old cathedral of Rouen filled with works of art, including painting, sculpture, and tapestry. This old church was in the center of the city and was built on the site of an earlier cathedral. The three centuries necessary to build the church had ushered in many changes in architecture, with the western façade, for instance, belonging to the flamboyant style. The north tower, her book told her, was from the twelfth century; the southern tower, on the other hand, was of a style altogether Norman, consisting of a square tower pierced by high windows and surmounted by a balustrade and pinnacles. The western façade was still under construction when Miss Thoreau visited the church, and the stained glass windows of the edifice showed evidence of each of the three centuries of constant building. How interesting, she thought.

It was in this church that Miss Thoreau began studying the records of births, marriages, and deaths. Among the old records from the close of the eighteenth century and now yellowing with age, she found a record which called forth a small cry of elation from her. Eagerly she copied the following:

"Félicité Ravellettée, fille et troisième enfant du Duc de Vallez, naquit en 1785.

En 1804 elle epousa Louis Ravellettée.

De ce mariage naquit, en 1806, une fille Christine Antoine.

Parents et enfant s'embarquèrent pour Montreal (Canada) et s'engagèrent dans le commerce des fourrurres, à un poste sur la rivière Detroit.

En 1808 l'enfant fut enlevée par des Indiens, et le mari tué en essayant de la sauver.

Félicité retourna alors à Rouen (France) en 1810 ou elle mourut en 1825."

She murmured the words in English:

"Félicité Ravellettée, daughter and third child of the Duke of Vallez, was born in 1785.

In 1804 she married Louis Ravellettée.

From this marriage was born, in 1806, a daughter Christine Antoine.

Parents and child embarked for Montreal (Canada) and engaged there in fur trading at a post on the Detroit River.

In 1808 the child was kidnapped by the Indians, and the husband was killed trying to save her.

Félicité returned then to Rouen (France) in 1810 where she died in 1825."

An ardent student of Indiana pioneer and Civil War history, Emsley W. Johnson, Sr. (1878-1950) was president for seven years of The Society of Indiana Pioneers. Whether on his hands and knees giving "pony rides" to children or figuratively standing tall as an attorney prosecuting powerful politicians who accepted graft from the Ku Klux Klan, Johnson was a family man and proverbial lover of "God and country." An attorney, banker, gentleman farmer, amateur astronomer, and civic leader, he and his first wife Katherine had two children. After her early death, he and his second wife Elizabeth raised the children and later enjoyed five grandchildren. Johnson blended stories from his ancestors into historical speeches and into this novel to pass on Hoosier heritage to his children and others of future generations.

The Society of Indiana Pioneers

Mission: To honor the memory and work
of the pioneers of Indiana.
Founded 1916.

Why join the Society?

- Pay tribute to your pioneer ancestors.
- Add your family to Society records, so your background is never lost.
- Perhaps learn more about your own family in Society archives of over 8,500 pioneers.
- Discover more about local history on pilgrimages to historic sites.
- Help promote education and research about Indiana history through the Society's awards to grade schools, graduate fellowships, historical markers, programs and publications.
- Enjoy friendships with others interested in preserving Hoosier history for current and future generations.

Membership: Regular membership is open to anyone showing direct descent from an ancestor in Indiana by December 31, 1840 (Howard Co., Lake Co. or Tipton Co. by 1845, Starke County by 1850 or Newton County by 1855). Associate Membership is open to anyone interested in Indiana pioneer history. Junior Membership is open to those under 18.
Applications are available online or from the office manager.

The Society of Indiana Pioneers
Indiana State Library, 140 N. Senate Ave.
Indianapolis, IN 46204
(317) 233-6588
societyofindianapioneers@yahoo.com
www.indianapioneers.org

Visit the website.